Dear Alice

Happy Birthday!

I hope, you will enjoy
'Climbing to the top!'
—
and I hope, we can stay
there for a while!

Matthias   3.11.2001

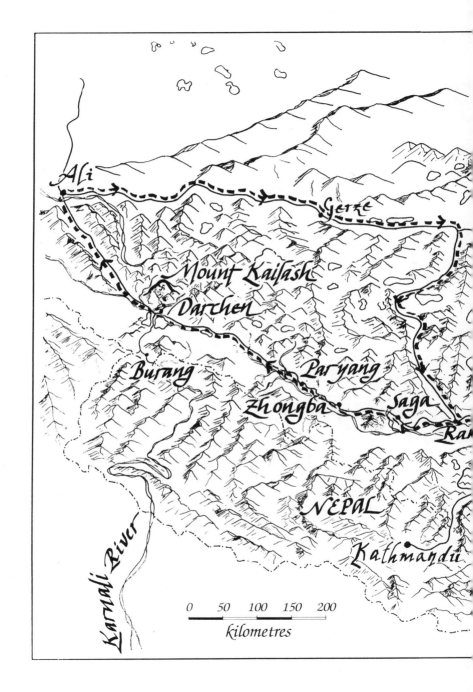

Ali

Gerze

Mount Kailash

Darchen

Burang

Paryang

Zhongba

Saga

Ra

NEPAL

Kathmandu

Karnali River

0   50   100   150   200
kilometres

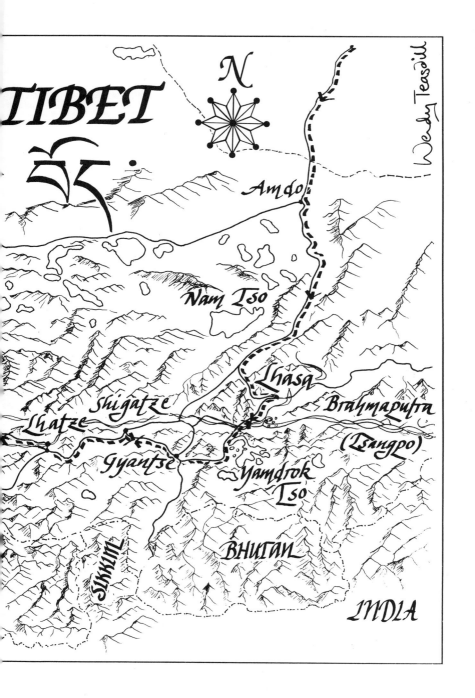

Walking to the Mountain

This is the story of a journey made on foot across Tibet to Mount Kailash. Kailash has been attracting pilgrims of all religions for thousands of years, but until recently only a handful of Westerners had ever been there.

Because of the October riots in 1987, Tibet was officially closed to individual travellers in the summer of 1988. Unless one paid thousands of dollars to the Chinese government and went in a jeep, it was completely forbidden to go to Mount Kailash.

Wendy Teasdill went, anyway. She hitch-hiked from Lhasa and walked the last four hundred miles or so, taking the southern road, prohibited to tourists both for political reasons and because the summer rains had swollen the rivers so much that vehicles could not cross them. She walked alone through the plains of the Brahmaputra, between the Himalaya and the Trans Himalaya, living on hard-tack biscuits, noodles and nettles. She survived, to tell the tale of the people, landscapes, dangers, delights and thoughts that she encountered on the way.

Walking to the Mountain

Wendy Teasdill

Asia 2000 Limited
Hong Kong

ISBN 962-7160-27-x

Published by Asia 2000 Ltd
1101 Seabird House,
22–28 Wyndham Street, Central,
Hong Kong

http://www.asia2000.com.hk

Typeset with Ventura Publisher in Adobe Garamond by Asia 2000
Maps drawn by Wendy Teasdill, lettered by Aaron Steiner
Printed in Hong Kong by Regal Printing

First printing 1996
Second printing 1998

Distributed in the United States by
University of Washington Press
PO Box 50096, Seattle, WA 98145

and in Canada by
University of British Columbia Press
6344 Memorial Road, Vancouver, BC V6T 1Z2

As the bee seeks nectar
from all kinds of flowers
seek teachings everywhere

Like a deer that finds
a quiet place to graze
seek seclusion to digest
all you have gathered

Like a madman
beyond all limits
go wherever you please
and live like a lion
completely free of all fear

Dzogchen Tantra

Foreword

Setting ourselves a clear goal and a firm determination to achieve it are two of the most powerful elements in accomplishing whatever we wish. There were many examples of this in Tibet. Great scholars often tell of their youthful ambition to study in the great monastic universities and earn their degrees, and, no matter what hardship they faced, they never gave up. Likewise, there are many tales of yogis who resolved never to leave their caves until they had gained the feats of meditation. Exceptional though these cases may be, even ordinary people are capable of freely fulfilling strenuous goals. While a pilgrimage is not a required act, many Tibetans set off on long journeys to particular places with the hope of creating virtue and gaining merit. A journey through wild, open lands can provide the inspiration and experiences that help shape the proper attitude and inner awareness to accomplish that end.

Many pilgrimage sites are associated with great spiritual practitioners. Elsewhere, it is the particular shape of a mountain or curve of a river that provides the indication of positive significance. The famed Mount Kailash, Gang Rinpoche to us Tibetans, possesses both qualities and has long been the object of pilgrims from all over Tibet.

In her book, *Walking to the Mountain*, Wendy Teasdill provides a vivid personal account of how she too was drawn to Mount Kailash. With the resolution characteristic of a pilgrim she travelled the southern road. When she had to, she walked and forded rivers, but when she could she rode in a truck. Inspired by the beauty of the landscape and her admiration for the Tibetan people she met, she reached her goal.

In my Five Point Peace Plan, I have proposed that all of Tibet become a sanctuary, a zone of peace, a place of harmony between people, animals and the environment. Visitors from all over the world could come to Tibet to experience the peace and harmony, much as this author has done. This is one of my goals, but as these aspirations and those of the entire Tibetan people can only be fulfilled with the help of others, I hope that readers of this book may be inspired to lend us their support.

THE DALAI LAMA

Contents

Part One

Part One

1 - Sources

I WAS BROUGHT UP in a cottage in the Chiltern Hills, not far from the river Thames. We had no neighbours but cows, so my brother and I played with the toys our parents made us, and our imaginations. One day I was interrupted in a visit to one of my fantasy friends, Mrs Egg, or Mrs Tooth, I forget which. 'And what do you want to be when you grow up?' asked an endearing adult friend of our parents.

'I want to travel round the world and write books,' I said.

'Oh,' said Mrs Bloggs-Smith, or whatever her name was, impressed by such decisiveness, yet wanting to be realistic. 'Don't you want to be a teacher like your Mummy and Daddy? Wouldn't you like to get married and have a little baby, like your baby sister?' Her eyes widened at the beautiful, child-like simplicity of the bourgeois dream.

'Oh, yes. I want to be a teacher too.' I was practising, giving lessons to the felt and fuzzy animals and dolls our mother had sewn, drawing figures with coloured chalks on a black-board and easel made by my father. Conditioning! I used to cry when, years later, I found myself prancing with a clutch of coloured pens between a white-board and a class of eager pupils. But if I say that, then I must also acknowledge the fact that we had a small fleet of sundry wooden boats for exploring the lagoons and backwaters of the Thames; that I had a couple of horses; that we didn't go on holiday to hotels, as normal people seemed to do, but always went camping. From a skiff or a punt up the river to the hills and cliffs of southern Ireland, we avoided the madding crowd and, with the collective ideal of getting as far away from Other People as possible, enjoyed always quiet, beautiful places. If we found litter in a good spot, we'd virtuously bury it before galloping on to another, unspoilt, Good Spot.

When we were very young, we went to church regularly — once at Easter and once at Christmas. It was fun. I cracked peanuts and my sister swung a foot-ball rattle. Our parents stopped taking us after a while, and there was, in the natural peace that surrounded our home, absolutely no reason at all not to believe in God.

As for Tibet, the only tenuous claim to childhood influence lies in the spine of *Seven Years in Tibet* by Heinrich Harrer. The dark lunar black-blues of the hard-back cover illustration suggested magic and mystery long before I read it. And as soon as I was old enough to read this magical and mysterious-looking tome, I realised that Tibet was the Ultimate

Destination. The realisation was stashed away for future reference in a safe corner of my brain for many years, and I got there by a roundabout route. Mrs Bloggs-Smith and her like beamed approvingly on as I graduated with a BA (Hons) in English from a respectable university. They supposed I'd be going on to do my PGCE, or was I thinking about publishing or management, perhaps?

I hared off overland to Afghanistan, India, Sri Lanka and Nepal. 'Well, one has to do it while one can. No chance later on. I wish I'd been able to do that' — and when I came back, they fed me cups of herbal tea and listened to tales of my adVENtures. It was a pity I'd caught hepatitis, but as the doctor said — if you go running off to these barbaric countries, you can expect to catch savage diseases. I slipped into depression, (which, the medical encyclopaedia had comfortingly informed me, is a symptom of hepatitis) and could only write about dead black cats and what's the point of it all?

Old friends found I'd turned strange. I didn't go to the pub any more. 'Don't you remember the time you drank twelve pints of Guinness after the cross country race?' they'd plead.

Er yes, I did.

And then one of the Mrs Bloggs-Smiths taught me some yoga, and I discovered that it's simply not true that 'there's no cure for hepatitis except rest and proper diet'. Yoga cured the hepatitis and I've been studying and practicing yoga ever since. Back then, I tore back to life with renewed vigour. I took a succession of jobs: life-guard attendant; cleaning up cat-shit in the mansion of some rather dodgy black magic practitioners; delivering milk around the front-doors of Brixton; spraying weeds in Wales. The trouble was — I seemed unable to hold a job down. Invariably I'd give in my notice after six weeks or so.

'But you make such a good milkwoman!' — 'But we've never had such a hard worker!' — 'But I was going to make you general manager for South Wales!' — The puzzled slave-drivers would object, but the stone angels of the cemetery whose weeds we were assassinating that May wept in vain. Finally I had enough means saved to escape their grip and finance the Preparatory Certificate for Teaching English as a Foreign Language course with International House. I packed up the floral dresses collected at jumble-sales for this very purpose, and hitch-hiked down to Hastings to do so. We practised on exiled members of the toppled Iranian government.

So then I was a teacher. But what about travelling round the world and writing about it? — After a few months of playing genial monkeyon-the stick, turning cartwheels, having nightmares — I took a cheap Laker flight to New York, and found myself making sandwiches on a mountain in Aspen with the grand-daughter of the man who discovered Machu Picchu.

'Machu Picchu? What's that?' I asked.

'It's the lost city of the Incas,' she said. So I went there, dilly-dallying on the way.

In LA a Scientologist asked me where I thought would be the ideal place in the world to be. 'A mountain among mountains,' I said. 'Somewhere high and cold and holy, and very peaceful. Very remote.'

'It sounds a stupid sort of place,' he retorted. 'What would you eat?'

He had a point. I like food. But he failed to convert me to Scientology. I made pizzas in the heart of the San Francisco gay area, taught English in Mexico City, and meandered via Mayan ruins down the Pan American highway.

Eighteen months later I was summoned back from the Bolivian shores of Lake Titicaca, to be a bridesmaid at my sister's wedding.

'It'll be your turn next!' Well-meaning guests reassured me.

I kicked at the confetti, eyed the sweet run of the Thames rolling by, cast up mine eyes to the Chiltern Hills and punched my brother. 'No, he's next.'

And they all laughed. I had had boyfriends, but I had a bad habit of leaving them to go off travelling.

Back to India, off to France, or Spain, or both in the Pyrennees — I'd dash off, then come back to my home-town and write about it. I'd meet my well-wishers in Waitrose supermarket. At first, they were very tolerant. 'Writing a book! I can't wait to read it!'

After quite a number of years, their patience began to wear thin. Their own children had company cars, mortgages, kids. I'd not published anything and was still hitch-hiking to work. Eyeing me stiffly over trolleys laden with roast beef, double chocolate walnut ice-cream and 'homemade' pasta, they'd inevitably come round to the point of it all.

'How do you supPORT yourself?'

I'd resist the temptation to tell them I dealt drugs, prostituted myself or did things with traveller's cheques.

'Well, I'm doing some gardening work. And some cleaning for Mrs Bloggs-Smith. Oh, and I'm teaching English to Germans in Oxford.'

The words 'Oxford' and 'teaching' usually had a soothing effect, but still they couldn't help asking: 'And how do you afFORD to keep on going away on holiday?'

'I live very frugally.' Indicating my own trolley, modestly heaped with lentils, flour for making my own bread, avocados and Brie cheese.

'Those aren't cheap!' Accusing fingers pointed out the offending articles.

No, but I don't subscribe to the artist's ideal of dining off interminable boiled cabbage either. I felt I didn't quite fit in anywhere in England. I began to mutter about going on a long walk, and dreamed of Japan, China, Tibet.

'If you go to Tibet,' a friend said, 'You can go to Mount Kailash.'

I'd never heard of Kailash, but even the name corresponded with an unsung tune within. 'Where's that?'

'On the western edge of Tibet, near India and Nepal. It's where Lord Shiva lives, a very high, austere place. Hard to get to. A few Westerners have been there now that Tibet's beginning to open up, but not many. It's a long pilgrimage. The pilgrimage of a life-time for many Asians....'
I recognised it as the place I'd always wanted to go to.

As for my parents — their only comment on my life-style was that I was 'beyond the pale'.

I decided to clear off.

I had an invitation to stay with a Chinese family in Hong Kong. I threw out or gave away a mountain of accumulated things, disentangled myself from some human bondage, the usual sort of moss that one gathers when one stands still, and cleared off to Hong Kong in 1986.

I loved Hong Kong from the moment I made my first improbable landing there. I had thought it was just a big noisy city, but now saw how the sky-scrapers were animated with shrines, coloured clothes and caged birdsong, how they grew next to mountains where pure springs sprout and flow. I was enchanted by the jazzy coalition between sophistication and slip-shod practicality, the conspiracy between tradition and innovation, and the immediate possibilities of either teaching in nice new clothes or dashing off to the places I'd long been dreaming about.

I began to establish the new pattern: trucked around China, taught English in Hong Kong, walked around half the eighty-eight sacred Kobo Daishi temples on Shikoku, Japan, and taught English in Tokyo. In October 1987 I flew back to Hong Kong, ready to go to Tibet — and met all the Westerners who'd just been kicked out of Tibet by the Chinese authorities.

For the first time since the Dalai Lama fled his homeland in 1959, negotiations had begun regarding his return as head of the Tibetan people.

On the twenty-first September, 1987, the Dalai Lama addressed the United States Congressional Human Rights Caucus with his Five Point

Peace Plan, of which the first was to turn Tibet into a 'zone of peace' and allowing the Chinese Communist Party control of most administrative matters within the 'Tibet Autonomous Region', TAR, including defence. The Chinese said the exile could come back as the spiritual ruler of his people, just as long as he lived in Beijing. His Holiness replied that he'd have to live in the Potala Palace in Lhasa, which was after all his home. The US Congress, the West German Bundestag and the European Parliament all adopted resolutions calling on China to accept the Dalai Lama's proposals and start negotiations with him.

Beijing was furious that the Dalai Lama hadn't given up claims for independence. In Tibet it's forbidden to as much as mention the word. The Chinese accused him of trying to split the Great Motherland, and ended negotiations.

The Tibetans in Lhasa demonstrated when they heard this. Stones were thrown, slogans shouted, and the terrified Chinese army fired into the crowd. Westerners who witnessed the carnage were hurried out of the zone. Tibet was closed again to individual travellers, just as it has been throughout most of its history. Hung with turquoise, smelling of yak butter, reminiscing happily about the time they didn't wash for three weeks, the fortunate ones told me stories about Tibet while we all waited for it to open again. I taught some more English, and began to find out more about Mount Kailash. I even met a few people who'd been there. By truck or bicycle, it was hard, they said. And of course it would be impossible to walk there.

2 - The Ice Pagoda

MOUNT KAILASH IS THE NAVEL of the world. It stands alone, separate from surrounding mountain ranges, protected by legends of inaccessibility. The icy domed mountain is distinctive, scored on the southern face by a great cross. At the foot, shaped roughly like the sun and the moon, are the two lakes of Manasarovar and Rakastal, the highest fresh water lakes in the world. From the compass points surrounding Kailash spring the four major rivers of South Asia — the Indus, the Brahmaputra, the Karnali (which feeds the Ganges) and the Sutlej — making it an immense but hidden water-source on which millions depend.

Mount Kailash has long been seen in the east as being the holiest place on earth. For the Hindus, it is the home of Lord Shiva, the ascetic god of destruction and transformation. The oldest Sanskrit scriptures talk of Mount Meru, a mythical and magical mountain which later came to be identified with Kailash. The Vedas describe the mountain and its area as being full of different herbs, vegetables, sweet flowers, waterfalls and birds, charged with opulent jewels and minerals, sanctified by Vedic hymns and mystic yoga practices.

Followers of Bon, the animistic faith which preceded Buddhism in Tibet, had always held the mountain holy. When Buddhism got big, the Bons and the Buddhists competed for dominion over the Jewel of the Snows, and the Buddhists won. The Bons were given a nearby mountain as compensation, and are still allowed to circumambulate Kailash in their own manner, widdershins.

For the Buddhists, the mountain is inhabited by a vast number of Bodhisattvas, the enlightened ones who have renounced Nirvana for themselves until they have saved all other living beings. They are, in a subtle form, always present at Kailash, radiating generous amounts of compassion to a misguided world. The Jains of India, to whom all life is sacred, hold the same view. Whatever their beliefs, Mount Kailash has been attracting pilgrims for as long as man has walked the earth.

Mount Meru, and so Kailash, is the axis about which the mandalas of meditation, whether Vedic or Buddhist, revolve. Contained in the outer petals of a mandala are universes, hells and heavens. Gates lead the concentration from the confusion of the outer planes through to the inner zones of peace, to unite the meditator at last with the divine centre. In the calm of being at one with the inner sanctum represented by Mount Meru, all mysteries are supposed to be resolved. On earth, Mount Kailash is where myth and reality unite, a keystone of creation, a symbol of an ideal state of mind, body and soul. The mountain continues to attract people of many faiths and even of no faith at all, and it is sanctified simply by being the focus of such devotion. And more. All energies are of divine origin, and there are places — I had been to a few — where the natural forces are purer and more concentrated than others. Faiths focus at these points, and hang up their dogma on the peaks.

The Hindus believe it is not up to us whether or not we get to Kailash — it is the mountain itself which gives us permission.

The Ice Pagoda of the ancient scriptures issued forth an irresistible magnetism from far west of Hong Kong. Divinely charged, it seemed to represent everything that is generous, good and positive. Now it made sense to me to walk to Kailash, alone, by the southern road. I didn't know what the mountain was thinking about this, but while I did yoga every day I began to visualise Kailash, and prayed that by the grace of God I might get there.

Part Two

Part Two

3 - Into Tibet

IT WAS THE YEAR of the dragon. March winds blew friends to the railhead at Golmud and back to Hong Kong again — Tibet was officially closed to individual travellers until a few dodgy dates had passed by.... After the October riots, the Chinese didn't want to risk tourists' holidays being spoilt by the activities of a few reactionary splittists — meaning any Tibetans who dared demonstrate against them on these dates, and who were in no way representative of the Tibetan people as a whole's gratitude towards the Motherland. What they were really worried about was March tenth, the date of the Tibetans' first uprising against the Chinese in 1959. That was the day the occupying Chinese invited the Dalai Lama to their military camp outside Lhasa to be entertained by a Chinese circus — no bodyguards, just him, they stipulated. The ordinary Tibetans suspected that an 'unaccompanied trip to a Chinese circus' was a euphemism for 'kidnap', and on that day twenty to thirty thousand of the Dalai Lama's people swarmed to the Norbulingka summer palace where he was residing, and surrounded it for a week. They would not let their Precious Conqueror go to the Chinese circus, and raised their fists as they shouted anti-Chinese slogans to make it clear. On the same day the Tibetan government renounced the Chinese 'Seventeen Point Agreement for the Peaceful Liberation of Tibet', which they had been going along with since 1951, and open hostilities began. After a week of this siege of love and hate, the Dalai Lama slipped away one night in a soldier's clothes; by the time the Chinese started shelling the palace, killing at least twelve thousand people, he was well away on a long mountainous trek into exile. Chinese troops and aircraft failed to find him, and the Chinese have been rather bitter about this ever since. The bitterness warps their judgement and confuses them. Photographs of crowds protesting about the Norbulingka that week appear in a Chinese propaganda booklet under a caption: 'Tibetan serfs rebelling against their feudal overlords'. Nowadays, of course, all Tibetans are smiling happily as they drive Chinese tractors and bring in bumper harvests. Ever cautious, however, the Chinese kept a watchful eye for spoilsports.

The dodgy dates slipped by. I washed a bald and diseased kitten I'd found on the streets of Wanchai with medicated soap and listened to the half-stifled rumours of demonstrations in Lhasa that wafted back to Hong Kong. Then there was silence. People began setting off for Lhasa and not coming back. More silence. I zipped back to England for my brother's prophesied wedding, and when I returned the merry month of May was pouring a balmy onslaught of humidity over Hong Kong. Tropical foliage grew visibly, material luxuries and distractions slumped sweltering in the sun, and people seemed to talk too much. Hopes and fears concerning Kailash were squashed by the frenzied preoccupations of the Fragrant Harbour: I was hoping to find in Tibet no more than a minute or two to myself in a climate cool enough to think in.

Frogs, morning glories, bats and people had moved in with the spring, and very soon I was fleeing the tropical clutches. I went for a last swim and staggered off the island under a sweat-pressing burden of books, tent, several kilos of muesli, dehydrated soup, sleeping bag and umbrella. On top of it all perched a handsome young glossy-haired black and white cat on the end of her leash, staring pop-eyed at the waves of the sea and purring with the excitement. The medicated shampoo had worked — hurrah for civilisation. The taxi driver threw malevolent glances at her while gorm-lessly watching me fill his back seat with the ungainly load, swept us off in a puff of air conditioning to the home of a Japanese family. We daintily consumed ice coffee and cream cakes while the cat scoffed down her first plateful of what was to be her diet for the next eight months — smoked salmon from the delicatessen section of Daimaru, the Japanese depart-ment store next door. She was totally indifferent to my departure.

I took the train to Canton, and began a ten-day rail journey in 'hard-seat' compartments across China. Westwards to Xian and Xining, round Koko Nor to Golmud reached the tracks. Every so often there'd be a dormitory stop, and I'd stretch out on hotel roofs — I find dormitories claustrophobic — grading the drop in temperature and the quickening of my splattered senses.

The thing to do at Xian is to see the terracotta soldiers, so I saw them: they stand ranked in a cool hall in the middle of a hot brittle plain, listening to Chinese classical music. The red dust of the individual faces is faded to rosy pink, their expressions as exquisitely impassive as ever. One is naturally reminded of China's glorious artistic heritage, of her supremacy, of the force of silent and obedient numbers.

By Xining the temperature had dropped, and already the very earth that threw up uncultivated waves of brown into the pale blue air about the Chinese town was that of Tibet proper, before the Chinese pared down her borders. The thing to do at Xining is to go to the Tibetan monastery Kumbum. Here the great reformer Tsong K'apa, founder of the Gelugpa, or 'Yellow Sect', was born; *'Kumbum'* means 'a hundred thousand images', and the name stems from the magical tree that grew, according to legend, from the blood of his birth. Later in life, when Tsong K'apa was involved in reformation work in Central Tibet, his mother sent word that she'd like him to come home for a while. Tsong K'apa, however, was too busy reforming to comply — he had a big job on his hands, and realised through a vision that a home-visit would benefit nobody. He sent a letter saying so, and along with it two pictures: one of Manjusri, sword-wielding Bodhisattva of learning, and another of Demchog, the terrible tantric transformation of Shiva who is recognised in Tibet as the protective deity of Kailash. At the moment the letter and pictures were handed to his mother, Tsong K'apa exercised his magic so that the hundred thousand leaves of the tree were miraculously stamped with exact replicas of these two images, and the tree gave off a perfume that could be smelt for five miles.

It was not far from the green tiled roofs of this monastery that the present Dalai Lama was discovered, and his brother was the abbot of Kumbum until compelled by circumstances to renounce his vows and flee to the USA. The Chinese closed this one down for quite a while, but it is now apparently in full working order. In rooms supported by bright flower-painted posts, tourists can stay and drink beer; here in the pre-dawn dark the priests rumble and lurk with *mantras* until daybreak, when they all assemble and fly like a flock of protected birds into the *sutra* chanting-hall.

Around the great salt lake of Koko Nor went the train. Koko Nor! The words shot, on the strength of their exclamation mark, from the pages of one of the books that had provoked in me these savage yearnings for solitude in remote places: Ella Maillart's *Forbidden Journey*. Over fifty years ago, she and an English journalist, Peter Fleming, had set off with horses (which later died) from four days east of here. They travelled right through 'the heart of Asia' on a forbidden journey to the west: by closed desert basins encrusted with salt lakes, through Kashgar and into India. Koko Nor had been the first sighting of a faraway place with a faraway name, the place where leaden skies had transformed to an immense stretch of whiteness — for it was frozen when they saw it. Now, brilliant white dunes of salt frilled the sidelines of a wide blue sheet of undrinkable water; but I knew I couldn't see from the train window quite as clearly as they'd seen. A sight must be hungered and ravened for to be really appreciated. At small stations, people who saw the lake every day of their lives leapt on the train with strings of ripe fish. Their odour mixed with the sharp draughts. I would save my appetite, and take the road to Tibet down which Ella Maillart had cast a longing glance as she rode past. There were still a few wide open spaces left.

My own entry into Tibet was a very prosaic and regular affair. Individual tourists were not allowed in, but groups were, and the Chinese were happy to supply — in time and for a price — Japanese buses for hire by any such groups as might happen to appear. So individuals came seeping out of caves in Turkestan, from the bright paintwork of Kumbum, and accumulated at Golmud.

Golmud is not an exciting place — a spacious concrete model town in the middle of a desert, on whose wide pavements traders sell day-glo crimplene wear and sinister dark dust goggles. The thing to do in Golmud was to play snooker on bald and undulating tables until the daily confrontation with the CITS woman. Elaborations on what CITS might stand for grew in graffiti down the wall — Comrade Isolate the Stranger, Complete Incompetence and Total Stupidity, and so on — but actually it's China International Travel Service, which implies a happy state of co-operation between the Chinese and the tourist. It's an enigmatic phenomenon, represented here by the staunch English-speaking comrade who wore her hair in little pigtails to convince us of her sweetness. What with the contradictory demands of Beijing and Lhasa, which of course is autonomous and has a mind of its own, and the caprices of the bus station (as she patiently and repeatedly pointed out to us), the poor thing ran in circles trying to please this daily roomful of irate and ignorant tourists.

The apparent adversity welded twenty individual travellers into a bona fide group. Long unhurried days were passed playing snooker on the roof of the department store. Faces became names, names acquired characters. There was Joan, a gentle giantess of a seawoman. She carried an amethyst crystal with her wherever she went, and a rapt smile illuminated her delicate rose-petal skin as she talked on fey topics. Then there was her doting seaman husband, Kim, and Tom Tom the farmer's son, delineating in his terribly proper English accent how to wangle a ride in a lorry from Dover to Calais for the price of a few Mars Bars — the only way to go, he enthusiastically implied. There was American Larry, bursting with eccentricities suppressed during a two-year teaching stint in Korea, squatting at salient points and opening his mouth wide to supply the snooker table with the pockets in which it was deficient. Day after day we shot balls into Larry's mouth, and there was nothing but barren horizons to trouble the tranquillity and general bonhomie of simply hanging out. In our strange touristic spacewarp, everything was a joke, and the Chinese were the butt of every wit.

But eventually a bus did appear, and with alacrity and amazingly little fuss the accumulated band of crack-shot snooker-players boarded the bus at six AM one June morning, and by daybreak we were bowling up the long slight incline of the road to Lhasa. Very simple.

Yellow and purple, tiny resilient flowers crawled over the ground, and a ring of immense white peaks horned the sky. A pile of stones and a tangle of coloured prayer flags marks the pass which is now the official entry into Tibet, and here I threw a firecracker out of the back window. A Tibetan would shout: *'Tsho tsho tsho!'* — but I didn't know how to pronounce things like that then, nor was I acquainted with the exact tone of exultancy with which they shout it — and the Chinese believe that firecrackers dispel evil spirits. Whatever — I was in Tibet. Hooray hooray!

The first night we stopped at a truck stop in Amdo. An altitude headache split my head as wide apart as the fantastic skies, where gold and pink and purple blue clouds overlapped one another with huge scales of singular transparency. All I wanted to do was sleep, but was prevailed upon to go for a walk. On a bank of earth where soft-nosed yaks grazed, tourists and Tibetans confronted one another. There was unrelenting curiosity on either side; they were probably exclaiming in scandalised horror at our long noses and peculiar blue eyes, while I was impressed by the long flop of gold brocade sleeve that hung unused from the rich sky-coloured coat of one of the men, and by the lively expressions playing across the face of a baby, tied by a scrappy rag to its older sister's shoulders. It looked so alert and knowing, as if it really were born with memories of previous incarnations intact. I dizzily followed Joan's lead, and tried out my first *'Tashi Dillee'*. It means 'good luck', and is the Tibetan way of saying 'Hello'. After some giggling and delay, which might have gone on forever were it not for Joan's obvious and ardent expectation of a reply, they returned the greeting. Tashi dillee!

Blue and gold swirled and revolved into the sunset in ever widening circles. Tibet has a reputation for magic and mystery, and though it was ridiculous to expect it right away, served up by the side of the road like a hamburger in a Denny's Diner, and though my headache doubtless accounted for the rose-coloured aura which always surrounds this first memory of Tibet — certainly it was a visually impressive beginning.

The following afternoon the bus entered the outskirts of what, at first glance, resembled any other grey Chinese town of gridded concrete. But there, up on a hill, was the Potala itself, cinching the millions of pictures and photographs of it which circulate around the world. So much had I read and heard about it, that it was not with astonishment but with simple relief that I regarded this immense and wonderful structure flying high above and transcending the Chinese invasion.

The golden roofs were dull under heavy skies. For myself, I was preoccupied with reaching the air beyond the buildings of man. So far I'd not done much but buy tickets and sit cross-legged for long dreamy stretches of time; there were a few small things to sort out before the journey began.

4 - Lhasa

WE WERE IN Lhasa, whose very name means 'soil of the gods'. The bus turned sharp left and drew into the Yak Hotel. I hadn't meant to stay here, but just got driven in with the herd. The hotel is a Tibetan building — frills coloured in the five holy colours hung above the windows in white walls, and there was a sheaf of Tibetan incense in the cupboard. The long brown sticks had a heavy, earthy feel and smell. The smoke from fires lit early for our hot showers mixed that afternoon with the rain of a heavy thunderstorm, and I wondered about how I was going to haul myself from all this luxury to the greater luxury of putting up my tent in the midst of the void. There were many things to do — and I still knew but two words of Tibetan.

I quickly learnt a third. The clocks in Tibet run on Beijing time, which means that it doesn't get really dark till not far off midnight. Early evening felt like mid-afternoon when I went to do my first *kora* round the Jokhang. A 'kora' is a circumambulation of an object, building or place of veneration, and the traditional clockwise kora about the temple was more fascinating than my wildest dreams had anticipated. People wearing regional costumes from all over Tibet, pilgrims who might have travelled for months to get here, rubbed shoulders with people who may have been

born in Lhasa and never missed a kora in their life — except of course
for the years in the sixties and seventies, when the Cultural Revolution
policy was to forbid such superstitious practices. Stalls of things for sale
cluttered the track: Tibetans sold everything, from the head-piece of a
suit of armour to defunct kerosene stoves; some stalls consisted of metal
tables with plastic sacking roofs, others were impromptu lay-outs, poignant stocks of travel-worn personal possessions which must be sold to
finance the journey back home. If they had nothing left to sell, they
simply sat and chanted mantras of benediction for the benefit of all
passers-by; often whole families or groups of monks sat in a line, chanting
for the fare home. Not that pilgrims necessarily arrive in Lhasa by public
transport — it is not unusual for a pilgrim, high on the energy of religious
fervour, to spend months on the road from their home town, prostrating
their body's length on the ground with every step that they take.
Self-sealed by their concentration, they swooped up and down through
the lumbering clockwise throng, through the shrieks of laughter, through
the intonations and the swinging prayer wheels, oblivious to everything
going on around them, intent only on humbling themselves every inch
of the way. Strangely, Chinese vendors in peaked green Mao caps sold
prayer flags and the white scarves of salutation and blessing, *kathas,* to
the Tibetan crowd. Here were the tall Khampas from the region of Kham:
red and black tassels lengthened the plaits twisted about their heads, and
short knives poked out of their belted robes to remind the rest of the
world of their glorious warrior heritage. The hair of the Khampa women,
who assailed the tourists to change money and buy their gew-gaws and
heirlooms, was laced with turquoise.

'Changee money? FEC?' — the business proposition fell enticingly from
laughing lips.

In those days one wasn't usually enticed to change money in China,
one was compelled. When Ted Tourist took his US dollar traveller's
cheques to the Chinese bank, he didn't receive money in return, but
Foreign Exchange Certificates — FECs. These were pieces of fine quality
paper, stamped with scenarios of Chinese tourist spots, which could be
exchanged for the necessities of Western life in tourist hotels and the
government-run Friendship Stores. They were not at all the same as the
renminbi, People's Money, the common currency of China — usually
called *kwai,* the Chinese word for 'sheet'. The thing is — Ted Tourist was
sometimes jaded by Western necessities, or perhaps he just didn't want
to pay the official rates; and the Chinese people were beginning to crave
the luxury items that could only be bought in the Friendship Stores —

American shampoo and Shanghai bicycles, for example. And so, that Ted might enjoy a simple pot of tea for a fraction of a kwai in a genuine ethnic setting, and that the Chinese People might taste forbidden bourgeois decadence, it was to mutual advantage for them to change money with one another. The black market was thriving at that time, and one could get anything up to 200 renminbi for every 100 FEC. All over China, tourists slipped up back alleys with hissing strangers to watch that they didn't get ripped off by any one of the number of tricks they'd been warned about.

I changed money with a Khampa woman, and it was endearing how she could bring me into the nearest shop run by a Tibetan — which happened to be a shop selling the women's floor-length pinafores, drab outside but gorgeously lined — and there, in happy contrast to the sleight-of-hand paranoia attached to such transactions in the rest of China, conduct a deal that was open and straightforward. The shop owner smiled and grinned and provided change from behind the counter, and the woman clapped me on the shoulder. All honest complicity, she intimated. Probably they were just delighted to have found a tourist who neither knew nor cared too much what the going rate was.

Hand-painted notices were up, prohibiting just about everything that was going on, and incense wound unperturbed from big clay censers in front of the temple. Here dozens of Tibetans, their bodies sheathed in sturdy folds of cloth, suede, leather and cardboard, tied with string and straggling strands of matted plaits and yak-hair — prostrated themselves over and over before the doors with a deep whooshing sound.

One of the more enthusiastic measures by which the Chinese Communist government had hoped to cure the Tibetan people of their superstitious and credulous nature was to turn the Jokhang into a cinema hall for several years. Now it's back in full working order as a temple. Rich tourists sopped up the scenes of worship through their camera lenses. There was a sensation of intensity with a precarious foot-hold — this place is also the political hub. The Jokhang was originally built in the seventh century AD, to house two golden statues of Sakyamuni. These statues mark the arrival of Buddhism in Tibet; one of them came, ironically, with a Chinese princess who had been forced to marry the Tibetan king of that time, Songsten Gampo, because he had defeated her father in war. The other came with the king's other wife, a practising Buddhist princess from Nepal. Songsten Gampo was converted to Buddhism, and his kingdom along with him. The temple is therefore the root of Tibetan Buddhism, and it is here that the Tibetans today from time to time voice their desire for independence, and it is here that the Chinese remind them who's in control.

An exiled Tibetan has commented: 'A holiday in Tibet is subsidising the eventual extinction of the Tibetan race.' The company was all good. But there was something disturbing in the drunken laughter and elated companionship of the tourists. As we decided how many *mao* (tenths of kwai) to give the beggars, what piece of turquoise would look prettiest on a sister-in-law's throat at Christmas, and discussed how jolly and frank the Tibetan race were, how vastly superior to the Chinese — the dead thousands were still dead, and thousands more still imprisoned. Their crime was that they were born in Tibet and our innocence was our money. Religious tolerance in Tibet extends as far as the tourist's eyes can see.

To my joy, I ran into a friend from Hong Kong: Britta, who had been here during the October riots of the year before. She related blood-curdling stories of Chinese treatment of dissidents. Here under the golden wheel of the Dharma, monks had been battered to death by Chinese rifle butts. And there was a new police station in place of the old which had been burnt down, and here were the houses of the hated collaborators … and the gulf between Tibetans and tourists had widened; the family she had stayed with last year now didn't dare to offer her a cup of tea when she went to visit them.

I did yoga in the ladies' showers every night, just visualising the mountain; I felt smothered with good company and the trappings of civilisation and longed to swim in the Lhasa river, to re-establish my link with nature. My breath was still short with the altitude; it's supposed to take three weeks to get acclimatised, and meanwhile there was plenty to do. For my breath, I danced, in the yard of the Yak, and round about the Jokhang at full moon, with my room-mate and a string of beautifully screeching little Tibetan girls. I hung out with Tibetans in the fields, battered my teeth on chunks of hard cheese, and learnt the Tibetan words for every part of the body. They yelped with ribald laughter as I mastered the more private areas, and incited me to repeat them over and over. It felt like being back at school and lying on the playing fields with a group of chums at lunch-time.

There was little occasion to go anywhere alone; we cycled out to monasteries where pop-eyed gods and fearsome protectors leapt out of buttery dark recesses, where centuries of devotion retained their ring. Heavy-pillared sutra chanting-halls reverberated with the vibration of mantra, with the triumph of faith over oppression. Even the kitchens were alive with the hum of *'Om mani padme hum'*.

There are many mantras in Tibet, but the one which is on everyone's lips, the one inscribed on the outside of every prayer wheel, the one written thousands of times over on paper inside every prayer wheel, the one inscribed on a million stones throughout Tibet — is 'Om mani padme hum'. A literal translation could be: 'All glories to the jewel in the heart of the lotus', which does no justice at all to the real meaning. *Om* is the seed of all sound and of all creation; in it are contained the three modes of nature — action, balance and torpor. The vibration of the three concepts, pronounced in one sacred syllable, releases a fourth, transcendental state, in which the universality of all things is realised; *mani,* the jewel, is the diamond of complete knowledge latent in the mind of every man, and in its brilliance lie the transformative powers capable of cutting away the bondage of passion and ignorance; *padme,* the lotus, fed by and yet detached from the air, mud and water that nourish it, is the symbol always for spiritual unfolding; and *hum* is the seal of integration, the syllable that says: 'Right, just because you've realised the unity of all things, you have no right to space out in bliss and neglect the responsibilities you hold here on earth for your finite body. You've experienced the relative values of the eternal and the imminent, that they're both part of the same whole; now get on with your life, and use this realisation to better your actions for the sake of your own salvation and that of all living beings.'

Monks were friendly and approachable, offered us rivers of butter tea poured from battered pewter pots. They tried to feed us from their supply of meaty dishes, and, when we declined, sloshed in the tea all the more vigorously. Due to a certain xenophobia on the part of the Tibetans, only a few foreigners ever made it into Tibet before the mid-1980s. Some Tibetans say that because of this grasping for isolation it was their karma that they should be taken over by the Chinese, that green canvas army boots should stamp and scatter them all over the world they had sought to keep out. Though it was simply hunger for revenue that prompted the Chinese to introduce tourism into Tibet, the situation was more stable and conditions for the survivors more liberal than at any time since the 'peaceful liberation of Tibet' in 1951. All the same, however comparatively kind the Motherland these days, the Tibetans want the Chinese to quit Tibet and the Dalai Lama back, simple as that. Tibetans seem glad to see foreigners, and have a touching faith that we are all capable of relaying their burning cause back to the United Nations.

But they did not bind themselves with anxiety: instead, they laughed and joked with a natural and spontaneous grace. In a soft amalgam of mantra and high spirits they repeated, with a gleeful tone: 'Chinese no good.' Nothing can quench the Tibetan sense of humour.

The river flowed past unswum as I spent days beetling up and down the road past the Potala on a bicycle, getting dustier and dustier under the sun between the Yak and the Lhasa Hotel, obtaining a Nepalese visa I knew would probably have expired by the time I needed it, piecing together embassy and photo-copier opening hours and using the one photocopier in Lhasa to copy a borrowed map of Tibet. The map was just a section of a large one of China, but in any case it was the best (and only) one I could find. As to whether it was possible to go to Kailash or not — well, the CITS would get you there quite legally in a Landcruiser for 6,000 US dollars. Otherwise, it was completely out of bounds. Well, never mind. I studied my photocopied map. It seemed sensible, considering the weight of my supplies, to take the bus as far as it went, which was Shigatze, and then just to see what happened. The ideal plan seemed to be to buy a horse, but when and where and how seemed more appropriately considered when the time came.

I did get to swim in the river before leaving Lhasa. The first time I went with a party of easy companionship. Under a moody evening sun we straggled across a murky channel over slimy stones, across a bridge hung with so many prayer flags that they matted, in the holy colours of white, blue, red, green and yellow, a shaggy corridor of cloth either side of the swinging planks. The other side was sleazy with broken green beer bottles and a few flat cakes of dung, human and animal, but we came to where it was clean and unpopulated, with the swift pale green river flowing round white pebbles. I say the river was green, but it flickered with violet shadows, which in turn seemed to contain all the colours of the rainbow. I dived in, somersaulted, swam on the spot against the current, watched the skies that had been brooding rain all afternoon and had turned especially grim since I'd suggested a swim. They dropped onto the mountains, shed shadows onto their naked earth colours, slanted rain in shafts of dark release upon various spots.

Swimming up a small backwater, currents collected in an interesting way under the lively surface stretched before me. Above rose the Potala. The golden roofs hid in shades of burnt Sienna, and the wistful stare of the many windows high up, and the blank silence of the lower walls of the torture chambers, were intensified by the dull-bright vibrancy of the air and the bullets of lightning that cracked out in the hills.

I found the Potala a haunting edifice. Wherever you go in Lhasa, even if you can see neither stick nor stone of the rest of Lhasa — you can see

the Potala. Under the circumstances, I never felt like repeating the first
visit I made there. The atmosphere of the place is dominated by a marked
absence; reminders are tended in flames and dusters; the few monks there
are divested of their robes and dressed in Chinese navy cotton coats
instead, presumably to rob them of identity — but their devotion is
intact. Pilgrims circumambulate the dark rooms, and tip or spoon a
dollop of rancid yak's butter into each goblet of bronze, silver and gold;
and thus their silent, stealthy, continuous support ensures that the flames
never die out. These hot rich flames are beacons across the realm of
possibility towards the hope that.... There are photos of the Dalai Lama
everywhere, pinned to the shadows. Before them, and before the Buddha
Matreiya, and before all the golden statues of lamas and Dalai Lamas
throughout the ages, are strung on lines all the simple offerings left
behind by the pilgrims. As well as the white kathas strewn like cobwebs
everywhere, the sweet glooms of devotion are spangled with bangles and
rings, sweets and safety pins — by which the offerers hope to sharpen
their mental powers — crumpled paper kwai and, occasionally, large
fresh dollar bills.

It is the pathos of this that looks out of the windows at you everywhere
around Lhasa. But the mountains, skies and even the water here were as
beautiful as they always have been, and the faith of the Tibetans grows
stronger under oppression.

The last time we went to swim we went upriver to a wide stretch of
undivided torrent. Here were strange whirlpools — you could be carried
for quite a way upstream under the blue and white sky. But when I tried
to swim down-river, and swam in anticipation of fun towards an eddy
— I found I could not float on my back, that my legs got snatched under,
that the water stole all my expectations. After that the game was dodging
the whirlpools, which, as they dodged about themselves with an amazing
agility, was a bit hair-raising. But at least I was contacting the elements again.

One who not only contacted but also controlled the elements was the
great tantric wizard Padmasambhava. Although not originally from
Tibet, he is as greatly revered today as he was in the eighth century, for
his actions and words were not just for that time but for the whole history
of the Tibetan people. There is one of his prophecies which unfortunately
is coming all too true right now; it goes: 'When the iron bird flies and
horses run on wheels, the Tibetan people will be scattered like ants across
the world and the Dharma will come to the land of the Red Man.' For
us Red Men and Women it is not such a bad thing that the mysteries of

Tibetan Buddhism have been made available to us; but the sacrifice the Tibetans have made is a tragedy.

In the middle of my last night in Lhasa, during a violent thunderstorm, I did a kora of the Jokhang. Yearning music came from snug windows canopied with blue and white. Britta had just shown me the bullet holes in the walls of the temple, fired during the October riots of the year before; and something seemed very sad. I wondered about my own position — was I not a hated collaborator too, meekly staying in the hotel decreed by the Chinese, paying in FECs, grateful (albeit guiltily) to them for allowing me to come here? I thought of the prediction that the present Dalai Lama will be the last one, and that the Tibetan people are already scattered like ants across the surface of the earth. And I thought how negative it all was, and wasn't there a way to sublimate it all? I touched my forehead to a cornerstone, in the greasy yellow spots where so many pilgrims have done so before me, and envisaged a lotus. Of all plants it grows from the foulest mire. Dim deities flew out of the peripheral thoughts to which they'd been exiled, and in a surge of glory settled on the petals. Om mani padme hum — in the lotus is a jewel. At the closed doors I offered a katha, wishing for a silent benediction. Two men lurking under the huge brass prayer wheel leapt out with a dynamic cry of 'Tashi dillee!' and kept the spin of the wheel going till I was out of sight.

5 - Shigatze

AN HOUR LATER I was woken up by Joan to go and take an early morning bus from outside the Potala — to Shigatze, or Gyantse, or somewhere. A small group of us plodded down, but it was several hours and buses later before we actually drove out of Lhasa. Wiped out, I curled into a small ball on my seat, dimly reflecting that the only way I'd got out of Lhasa was by having people to buy my ticket and wake me up for the event. Scarcely the staunch lone explorer starting off into the wide wilds — but someone had drawn my name in a heart on the grubby bus window beside me, and as rain poured down outside I felt warm and protected for the moment, knowing that I would be detaching from such securities soon enough. We skirted the loopy edge of the turquoise scorpion lake and tumbled down a steep valley. At stops I made sure to wallow hands and splash face in the waters of lake and stream, to keep in touch with the elements. Naturally.

Shigatze is the second major town of Tibet after Lhasa, built up around the Tashilumpo monastery, seat of the Panchen Lama. The Panchen Lama is the reincarnation of the tutor to the original Dalai Lama, whose name was Chenresig. Once a misunderstanding with a snake upon a path caused the serpent to put a curse of perpetual rift between Chenresig and his tutor. This rift has always existed, but whether it is the result of anticipation or the fulfilment of a prophecy is neither here nor there to the faithful Tibetan. Though the Panchen Lama, now deceased, but then alive and well in Beijing, was a Chinese choice, and though he appeared, having been brought up under strong Chinese influence, to be a handy bridge over which government propaganda troops could be driven — the Tibetans pay unreserved homage such as is due to their very precious God-king's teacher. The Panchen Lama himself once surprised everyone by giving a pro-Tibetan speech — after which he disappeared for a number of years. After emerging a reformed man, he was kept under cautious lock and key in Beijing. Meanwhile, his monastery in Shigatze is in full swing again. With gorgeous and costly renovation work, the mistakes of the Cultural Revolution are still being righted. This is the showpiece monastery. Down a square mile of hillside pour a profusion of buildings — from the top golden-roofed halls scatter sturdy cubes of stone and mud to the outer ruins, and around the whole complex runs a mud-daubed wall. Outside the wall live the reincarnated souls of the monks who didn't quite make it, they say, now in the scabby bodies of dogs who live peacefully off the offerings of the passers-by.

Inside a tall hall the great Buddha Matreiya looked placidly down from an altitude of gold with blue and slender tilted eyes. The lotus he sits on is of beaten brass. This is the main tourist attraction, and who could not be attracted by such a monument? There are many pictures of the Panchen Lama propped and pinned about the place, and with unquestioning adoration the pilgrims pushed aside the tourists to pay their obeisances to his expansive smiling image.

It was raining lightly outside, and damp pilgrims slid out, up the steep wooden steps whose banisters are tamped in silver and overlaid with a soft shiny cushion of pure black dirt. Round the buttery suffocation of dark corridors and temples they went, scuffling, dolloping the molten rancid butter from plastic bags and thermoses into the lamps there, knocking their heads against a certain silk in the sutra hall, and all the mothers following their own knock with a sideways duck to ensure the blessings of the faith and dirt-impregnated silk upon the brows of their attached infants.

One altar-tending monk made an aeroplane out of a wad of *tsampa* dough — the mainstay of the Tibetan diet made from barley — and flew it around to show me how I must have got here, and young monks made a scrum about my Mickey Mouse watch. No urgent political messages here. Outside the sutra chanting hall about a hundred monks young and old gathered. Thick pleated capes of homespun jutted off their shoulders, and the yellow hats of their sect — Gelugpa — sprouted off their heads at erratic angles. A few uncloaked ones ran around, enormous copper kettles perched upon their shoulders, cooped with brass and full of steaming yak-butter tea. All were barefoot, and their coloured felt footwear piled up in a heap. Then they set up a sort of howling and scuffling, and all pressed into the hall. We were allowed to press in after them, and stood simply listening to their chanting. It was very sweet and liquid — and all these monks on Beijing's pay-roll, according to the Lonely Planet guide-book. Demons danced in new paint along the walls and depicted disturbing states of the human mind.

There was a strange overlay of mask, apparency, and fact. Doubtless they all co-ordinated somewhere in the depths of the general air of conspiracy, and maybe one day I would have sufficient time and peace in which to contemplate the ganglion of causes and effects enacted here, and thereby arrive at some approximation of the truth. But meanwhile I never feel so near to any kind of truth as when out under the boundless sky, devoid of allegiance to anything but the hierarchy of nature. Clockwise in a kora about the walls of Tashilumpo perpetually walk the pilgrims, treading thick cotton-soled felt boots or Chinese army sneakers into the mud. This walking worship I understood. Trailing strings of prayer beads which bounced behind their homespun backs, twirling the prayer wheels set into walls at intervals, the Tibetans showed me which stones to touch, which ones to walk around, where stones were to be thrown up onto the mani walls, which niches not to be forgotten; from this I understood that surrender to the serenity of absolute faith is vital, and that these people had more freedom and peace than most in the cities of the democratic and liberated countries of the world.

At the highest point of the kora I detached, and climbed up the mountainside to a point where I could look out over three valleys. Along the western one ran a thread of pale mud. This was the road that led to Kailash — why not just walk down the hill, turn right, and go?

A certain degree of caution was called for. The road I was looking at continues to the town of Lhatze, where it divides; one road going down to the border with Nepal, and this is also the way one takes to go to Everest Base Camp. As long as they are equipped with Alien Travel Permits for the area, tourists are at perfect liberty to go by jeep, truck, horse, yak or foot to Everest, and stay at the monastery there; and though this was the only official trek open in Tibet, there are few who would not be satisfied by the beauty and excitement the trail through Tibetan villages offers. But the other road goes west, in the direction of Kailash. First one must cross over the Brahmaputra river, known in Tibet as the Tsang Po (meaning simply 'river'), by ferry. The road continues west for some time until it divides again, at a place marked on the map as Saga. One route cuts right up through the middle of Tibet, turns sharp left and proceeds to Ali; along this long austere road go many trucks from Lhasa, to Kashgar in Turkestan, and back again. From Ali another road drops south to Kailash, linking up with the southern route direct from Saga. All these roads and the areas which they traverse were completely out of bounds for tourists — unless of course safely encapsuled in expensive Landcruisers. It seemed sensible to obtain permits for as far as they were available and, when the time came, to just nip off.

It was the southern route, the one that carries on in a straight line from Saga to Kailash, that I was interested in. It is the most direct route from where I was, and also the one I had long set my heart on. The fact that at the moment it was closed, and would remain so until at least September, only added to its desirability in my eyes. No traffic was going that way because no traffic could. The road lies along the floor of the Brahmaputra valley, between the Himalaya and the Trans Himalaya; India at the moment was having mega-monsoons, the heaviest for four years, and the Tibetan plateau was catching some overspill. The streams, flowing out of the parallel mountain ranges to join the Tsang Po, were swollen, cutting the road at several points and rendering it totally impassable. If no-one was going that way there'd be no-one to see and stop me, and as for the rivers — I'd cross them when I came to them.

6 - By horse?

WHITE SQUARES OF paper, printed with wind horses and Tibetan prayers, littered the hillside. Prayer flags released their messages on the wind. There was such an impossible weight stashed under my bed at the hotel that I'd never carried it all myself at once. It was the joke of the kind American journalist, who had gallantly carried my surplus between hotels and buses so far, to threaten me with the RSPCA should I think of inflicting the burden on an animal. I however had more faith in the beast's strength, and watched the many heavily laden horses coming sturdily into Shigatze. A yak or donkey would be cheaper, but I had experience of neither. I am perfectly at home with horses, however, and so I coerced the hotel boss to take me to the livestock market one morning. There were plenty of yaks and donkeys, young and old, and a few horses. They were ponies by European standards, and all of them a bit bony and sore-ridden to even contemplate taking along.

The next day I went shopping for a horse again, this time in the company of two lively young English children. The elder one collected yaks' bones, with special attention to their jaw bones and teeth, and the younger one introduced me on the way to the delights of 761 biscuits. These biscuits are compact hard-tack bricks of calories, and at first taste quite pleasant, like shortbread. We studied the livestock for sale that day, the Tibetans studied us, and I found the ideal animal — a young and gentle-tempered grey mare with a big heart, wide knees, sound hooves, a healthy covering of fat, no sores and young teeth. Negotiations between myself and the Khampa vendor underwent all the stages — I had a ride, the children had a ride — and, though she wasn't as responsive as my ponies in England had been, she seemed schooled well enough for the purpose of heading in a straight line to Kailash. Then a Tibetan man from the crowd leapt on her back, to show us how to do it — with lots of noise, wind-mill action and a stick. He got her to do no more than I did, but everybody enjoyed the spectacle. Finally with an unreliable ink pen and the back of a cigarette packet, the Khampa and I got down to business. We had just reached the stage where I was writing 750 and he was writing 850 — meaning that in a few minutes she would have been mine for 800 kwai — when a Public Security Bureau official (the police branch who keep an eye on tourists) broke through the thick crowd.

People stopped plucking at my Mickey Mouse watch, at my hair, at
the children's hair — to watch the PSB man yell. His blast was directed at
the Khampa man mostly, saying I know not what; to me he insisted, in
English, that I could go nowhere but Lhasa, and there I must go by bus.
I nodded in comprehension, an ignorant tourist being enlightened. Ah
well....

Tom had told me that the PSB in Shigatze were 'perfect poppets', that
there was no problem getting Alien Travel Permits from them, as long as
one wanted to go to Everest Base Camp. I asked Tom, who did, to ask
about the road to Kailash. He reported back to me that the road on the
other side of the ferry crossing at Lhatze was, according to the perfect
poppets, broken and impassable. I chose to disbelieve it, and went to see
them to obtain all permits available.

The man who had intercepted yesterday's deal was there. Out of
uniform, relaxed and chatty, the perfect poppets gave me tea, and explained that in 1986 an Australian had bought a horse and rode off to
Mount Kailash — and died on the way. And so foreigners are not allowed
to buy horses. I changed the subject, and established once and for all that
to say 'up' and 'down' in Tibetan is *yucky* and *mucky* respectively. I left with
a fan of ATPs of which only the Lhatze one was ever likely to be useful.

Somehow or another I wandered into the Tibetan hospital, and began
a daily exchange of English for Tibetan with a doctor there. He was not
a very busy doctor. Before him his appointment diary stood open on his
desk. It was of Chinese make. A quarter of the page was taken up with
the date and a small calendar showing where in the month the day stood;
half was taken up with a printed picture, different every day — of a
temple or a willow tree or a bonsai in a pot — something like that. And
the remaining quarter, held back with a rather ornate and tasteful tie-pin,
was completely innocent of any appointment. Sometimes a patient
would come in and politely wait until I suggested that he saw to them,
and then he'd reluctantly feel the pulse for a minute, write a prescription
and return with undisguised relief to the glossary of the Tibetan grammar
book. As he read, his long slim grimy fingers pressed the half-mooned
nails of dirt into the page; he wore a floppy cotton hat and a crumpled
white coat over his nylon blue-grey suit, and his shoes had a 'T' strap
across the front and heels such as were fashionable amongst the girls when
I was in the sixth form at school. From a European viewpoint, a most
incongruous figure of a doctor. But placed in his environment — one
where traditional dress has been invaded by the cheap factory products
of the Stepmotherland, one in which only a certain meek conformity

could have allowed him into the position of Tibetan doctor in Tibet in 1988 — he was absolutely natural for the post. As he came to the English phrase for 'to give an injection', he reached for his pen and carefully copied it out, letter by letter, onto the back of a prescription pad. His eyes and half open mouth had the eagerness of a child. As for me, I learnt how to say a few useful things, such as 'the cup is on the table', and 'how much is that horse?' Subject, object, preposition and verb seemed to square-dance round one another as the chunky syllables grated clumsily off my foreign tongue.

Ah well — perhaps I could after all buy a horse from the people I presumed I'd meet when I'd gone as far as I could by truck. It would not be such a subtle thing to do, to ride a horse out of Shigatze, and the rations I had now would be sufficient for about two months, plenty to get me from Saga to Kailash. Just to be sure, I bought twenty-six packets of 761 biscuits outside the gates of Tashilumpo. My purchase was eyed through the discreet dark glasses of one of the plainclothes tourist watchers who hung about the town at certain spots. I took them back to the hotel and added them to the stockpile under my bed.

My bed was on the wide balcony that formed an inner circuit in the centre of the hotel. Symbols of Tibetan Buddhism were painted about the sea-green walls, and by my bed were two goldfish in a circle, symbolising spiritual liberation. A white canopy, appliquéed with the knot of eternity, formed a high tent above the bed, and it sluiced the heavy rain down in nightly waterfalls to form ankle-deep floods on the solid earth floors. Occasionally, when it wasn't raining, I could see the stars from there.

It was easy to remember the Tibetan word for 'below' — below it was indeed mucky. Into the central courtyard was thrown all the dirty water and rubbish from upstairs; yak carcases hung from posts, and by day they teemed with the many flies attracted to their rich odour. I burned Tibetan incense constantly, and put the sticks into the bolt of the open window from the adjoining room, where the Tibetan staff and family of the hotel slept. There was a little boy among their ranks, who every morning would walk about the balcony with a ladle full of burning juniper leaves, chanting in a high voice. He was very young, but extremely self-assured, and the prayers came out of him like leaves unfolding from buds along a branch, as if they were an inherent part of his make-up. One night as I put some incense in the door bolt, the little boy popped his head out, seized the incense, and sang what was apparently a prayer in his clear and lovely voice. He played like a child and worked and laughed with the confidence of an adult; there was nothing fantastic in assuming that he'd accustomed his voice over a number of incarnations to the rhythms of the mantras. It turned out that he was indeed recognised as a *thulku*, or reincarnation of a previously high lama. It was easy to believe, for he was obviously happy to have, for now, the freedom of a young boy's soprano with which to express the joy of life.

Above was the flat walkway of the roof, with a few more rooms perched up there. From my bed I could see everything going on in the hotel at all three levels. The bed became a hub where people conglomerated and socialised. The table by my head was the breakfast table, and I'd wake up to hear the stories of hardship and adventures from the latest arrivals back from Everest Base Camp. I'd go back to sleep and be woken up again by Joan and Tom and so on coming to relate to me their latest travel plans or wanting to borrow something or to tell me that I was a lazy slob. Only when someone brought me my breakfast did I really open more than one eye. There were a couple of days when I never got up at all beyond (rather frequent) trips to the stinking pit of a toilet, when I was overtaken by a strange feverless malady; I'd sleep, and dream of Kailash arising from behind the skylines of the cities of the world, and I'd wake up, and see old women across the balcony dipping long strands of sheep's wool into great vats of dye. They had fires going, and smoke and steam streamed about the bushy hanks of wool already dyed in ghastly colours that hung from lines. Only the red and the green rang true, but rainbows caught in the water drops. And beyond that sat a man and a woman who occupied their whole days knotting carpets with rapid nimble fingers; I could sleep for hours, wake up to the same scene and notice no difference save in the casting of the shadows.

Up, well and out, I'd return at night to find my bed transformed into scenes of decadence. Beer bottles and cigarette ends flooded from the people gathered there, giving one another massages and telling stories of inaccessible regions they'd been to. The bunch was assorted — from the pathology professor from Hong Kong University who was able to advise me on the walking power contained in my provisions, through euphoric Tibetan-speaking Americans, to people of all nationalities with different focuses and each with interesting stories to tell. On no two nights was the exact same group assembled.

To all but a few close friends I had been keeping quiet about where precisely I was headed. I'd answer questions with 'Um, somewhere in western Tibet, maybe,' and imply that I didn't really know where I was going, afraid that by naming Kailash I might jinx the trip. One night in conversation in the Happy Small restaurant, the matter did come up. Britta and I were dining in the company of an English-Australian couple. He proffered many valid reasons for not attempting to go, and seemed disappointed that I didn't take him up on them; and she, a very down-to-earth and capable midwife from Yorkshire, who was a surprising mine of information on dodging visa restrictions in Taiwan, said she couldn't see the point of going to Kailash unless you were a Buddhist. I said nothing, but Britta spoke up.

'People get drawn to the mountain from all over the world,' she said, 'whether they are Buddhist or not; though they don't know why they must go, they must; and when they have been there — I haven't, but I know people who have been there, and I feel it — they have it with them for the rest of their lives.'

Our dinner companions were speechless, and it was the voice of a hitherto unseen middle-aged French hippy, dining alone at the next table, that broke the silence that followed. 'I 'ave wanted to go to Kailash for twenty years,' he announced. 'And I 'ave not get there yet.' It turned out he had just returned from an unsuccessful attempt at hitching to Mount Kailash. 'The only way to go to Kailash is by car,' he went on, scraping severely at his gravy with his chopsticks. 'I come back next year with my lama in a jeep. It is the only way.'

Our whole table drifted over to his, to pore over the map and see where he'd been, where he'd waited for three days, where the map was 'false' and where there was 'nozzing'. The Yorkshire-Australian duet, with whom we'd been getting along very chattily before, slid off without saying good-bye.

Back at the hotel the Frenchman showed me his file on Kailash which constituted a large part of his luggage. He had sheets and sheets of information and maps, each sheet encased in protective plastic. He had marked out every detail of Kailash on the maps — where to find fossils in a particular stream, where to pick up a particular sand to take back as *prashadan* (gift from God), where borax and gold can be found. When people tried to mine the gold many years ago, the whole party died of smallpox. Mining of any sort is traditionally unacceptable in Tibet, for it is seen as robbing the earth of what is rightfully hers. Mining was discontinued, though nowadays the Chinese are planning mine-shafts for every rich mineral seam they can find. Then there are the different koras one can do — even down to the tiny little ones of two lakes that could be no more than puddles. 'This one is black, that one is white,' said the Frenchman of the puddles. And waving an authoritative hand over the gompas marked around the mountain and lakes — 'This one is gone, that one is gone.'

Though he knew everything about Kailash, he seemed rather vague about how he was going to get there. But, he announced, carefully packing up the map I'd sellotaped up for him — meeting me had given him courage. He'd been ready to give up hope, but he had a very efficient water filter and we had to think about it like an expedition —

'We?' — I know what it's like. After a few days, let alone weeks or months, in the company of someone who 'just happened to be going that way too — why don't we?' — I invariably want to knock their brains out. Whether that's my fault or theirs — I suspect the former — is immaterial. I wanted to go alone, and explained this as tactfully as I was able. He saw my point, and continued to talk about 'we'.

One day an Italian girl, Franca, also appeared, looking for me. She was going to Kailash too, had been trying to get there for months from Kathmandu; it was impossible, so she'd flown to Hong Kong and was trying again. She spent her days flying energetically about Shigatze, tracing rumours of pilgrim trucks with her Chinese and Tibetan phrase books, and in the evening she would come sighing back to me and report what she hadn't found. She'd heard, she said hopefully, that it would be impossible to cross the rivers that cut up the southern road without ropes. As we were going the same way, it made sense that we should stick together, didn't it? Again I explained, again it seemed to have little impact. But by dogmatically asserting that I was going to walk by the southern road, with a horse if possible, without if not, rivers or no rivers — the craziness of the plan put her off wanting to go with me. But at least we could hitch together to the point where our roads divided, couldn't we? I supposed so.

The revellers would leave my bed, I'd tidy the chaos and sweep up the debris and make hot chocolate for us three who dreamed of Kailash. The Frenchman gracefully decided to leave the mountain for now, and go back to cultivate his garden; with affable equanimity he traded large parts of his survival kit with Franca for an emerald ear-ring — he was coming back next year with his lama in a jeep, after all. Sometimes we'd talk about Kailash, other times anything but.

When they left, I would take a clandestine wash in a dark corner somewhere, and regain sovereignty over my small kingdom under the fish on the dark sea wall. Alone at last, it seemed always to be the middle of the night, with the sound of thousands of dogs barking up from the dark streets of the town beyond the safe hotel walls, and rain falling as

often as not from the knot of eternity on the canopy above my head. This
was the real time of preparation, in which I'd write, do yoga, and continue
to visualise the mountain somewhere over there, in western Tibet.

The fuel-bags under my bed were more than cruel, though filled with
kindness; they sopped up the left-over tsampa and noodles of various
Everest Base Camp expeditions, a bottle of vitamin pills and vanilla sugar
from Britta, Arpège perfume and pictures and maps of Kailash from the
Frenchman. They were full enough; I'd been in Tibet two and a half
weeks and could breathe fine. It was time to go.

7 - Truck to Raka

WALKING THROUGH Shigatze to the truck stop with Franca, it felt as if
a house had fallen down on top of me. But perhaps the load just
felt heavier than it really was because I'd been up all night reading *Seven
Years in Tibet* again. I'd borrowed it to see if there was any mention of the
rivers: Heinrich Harrer and Peter Aufschnaiter had entered Tibet through
northern India, and had crossed western Tibet at this time of year. Walking
right past Kailash and the shores of Manasarovar, they had covered the
route I planned to take in reverse, following the Brahmaputra valley
down in the direction of Lhasa. They had donkeys and companions, and
their main concern had been avoiding the local chiefs. Rain fell in
torrents as I read, sluiced off the appliquéed canopies over my head and
flooded the earthen floor.

An Austrian girl who knew the author lurked half the night in another
recess on the balcony, and every so often would slosh ankle-deep in water
past me, hissing stirring calumnies against my childhood hero. Un-
moved, I read on. No mention was made of rivers, nor even of rain, but
it was still one of my favourite books. I returned the book at dawn, and
my body stumbling down the centre of the tree-lined road that morning

was ready to sleep. It wanted to dream dreams inspired by the book, but found itself instead on the point of acting them out.

The day before we had located a Tibetan truck driver going to Lhatze with a pile of half-cured skins, who said he'd take us. When we arrived at the truck stop however he was wisely still sleeping, and continued to do so for many hours. When we'd tired of drinking tea and refusing tsampa and he was still sleeping, we simply stepped out into the road and stopped the first truck we saw. It was a Chinese driver, going all the way to Gerze. Franca flapped with her Tibetan and Chinese phrase books, I waggled my fingers and exercised my rather limited Chinese vocabulary, he smiled widely, and we established that he wanted thirty kwai, about three pounds. We hopped in and in a minute were heading down the pale thread of westward road which I'd been gazing at so wistfully from above the Tashilumpo all week.

In a couple of hours we were at Lhatze. There was apparently a check-point here, and had we gone with a Tibetan driver we would have had to alight, as Tibetan drivers weren't allowed to carry foreigners and could incur heavy fines for doing so. As we both had permits for Lhatze it was almost disappointing that we saw nothing of the check-point; true we did stop outside a compound for thirty seconds, but not really long enough to relieve ourselves of the morning's tea before our driver shouted to us to get back in, and very soon we were established nineteenth in a line of trucks waiting to cross the Brahmaputra by ferry.

On one side of the valley it was deep blue summer. On the other it was mid-winter. Our driver gathered with others of his tribe about a gas-jet of flame which heated their noodles and tinned pork, while Franca and I picnicked in the back of the truck on large discs of Shigatze bread with garlic and cream cheese, made by hanging up yoghurt in a silk scarf. A crowd of raggedy children climbed up the bank of the road-side, brandishing at us their vicious-edged cans which served as begging bowls. I distributed bits of bread and cheese into them, and tried to be fair, but it was hard, as they would take each others', have fights, and come back for more and more. On the winter side of the valley thunder and lightning sparred with the mountains, and already it was annoying me that Franca wisely gave away nothing of her share and talked to me while I ate. 'Don't bother me!' I snapped.

It was several hours before we crossed the river, and we slept on the banks of the river half a mile apart before a downpour brought us both back together in the cab again. I read aloud the Kailash chapter of *The Way of the White Clouds* in an attempt to dissolve the petty differences between us, and the enchanted syntax indeed cast a new calm over the atmosphere. At the words: 'people are drawn to it from near and far … and they will undergo untold hardships and privations in their inexplicable urge to approach and to worship the centre of this sacred power', we both laughed. Where was the hardship in sitting in a snug warm cab while it rained and hailed outside? We talked about Kailash till it was our go to cross the river.

A dozen or so Tibetans, men and women, heaved at a huge tree-trunk which acted as a lever on a thick wire, which in turn propelled a platform across the muscular brown water. Once across, we drove briskly up the road, past a small settlement rich in rapeseed fields and contented brown cows. There were trees there too, the last I would see for months. It felt good to be moving again.

The road had a rather undulating surface anyway, but when we rounded the next bend it was to confront a rush of water which had chosen that moment to descend from the mountains and blend with the road. For a while it seemed we were swimming, but we lurched through all right. Not so successful was the truck behind us. He got completely stuck, and it was twenty-four hours before he or anything behind him moved again. As we and that truck were apparently part of the same convoy, we didn't move either beyond a few hundred yards up the road. That night our driver went to drink Chinese firewater with his mates and to sleep in their cab, while Franca slept on the seats and I coiled myself about the gear-lever, steering shaft, brake and accelerator etcetera on the floor. Puddles of water collected under my space blanket, the gear lever dug into my hips, three times I had to squirm out to see to my ailing stomach — but I slept well.

Seated on an elevation above the water, I spent the morning watching the excavation of the truck. The hills about were coloured with all my favourite memories — sludge-green runnelled with muddy brown and peppered, when you looked closely, with tiny bright flowers, lichen and pebbles, and all colours intensified by the constant rain. I was reminded of Ireland when I was a child, of the nostalgic yearning for the future, for this.

As soon as the truck was out, we were off again, plunging westwards in the dim smoke and reverie-filled capsule of the cab. Our driver was a happy enough man, and occasionally burst into conversation in Chinese, to which I nodded and made noises while Franca dozed. We stopped once in between rainfalls for the drivers to blast out the fire for their noodles; they reluctantly gave us a bit of tepid water in which our tea-leaves floated in a half-soaked mockery and I stretched my legs in a walk up to the saddle of a small pass. That night we stopped outside a compound and made the same sleeping arrangements as the night before. I awoke to Franca slapping my shoulder with a brusque 'Get up! Get up!'

No sooner had I uncurled and cleared the floor of my things, than we were driving off. We breakfasted on what we'd been eating for three days — bread, cream cheese and garlic, and suddenly the driver stopped. We had come to the place where our roads divided in a right angle. The driver kindly hurled my luggage off the back of the truck, groaning with the weight of each item, and collected his fee while Franca frantically wrote her addresses in the back of my diary. Her Italian blood rose to the occasion of a sentimental parting and she was still blowing me kisses as they drove away.

I watched the truck, behind the rest of the convoy, disappear in a puff of exhaust smoke into a wave of white-topped blue stretching as far as the eye could see. This was the Trans Himalaya. It looked beautiful and it looked easy, but I wanted to feel, smell, hear and taste the inches of the way. Now perhaps I could begin that long walk I'd been muttering about for years.

I was standing alone on the valley floor but for a blue and white signpost written in Chinese. It marked the joining of the wispy roads, looking very small and lost in such surroundings; and into the paint was scratched the Frenchman's name. It was already rusty. This must be where he had waited for three days. I did something I've never done before, and added my own name to the sign; if I never came back it would be a clue. Certainly the map was false, for there was 'nozzing' in the way of habitation to claim the name of 'Saga'. Just a pool of clear water and the start of the southern road.

I had a wash, assembled my bags into one unit and, before putting them on my back, paid my obeisances. Though I am neither Buddhist nor extremist, out of respect to those whose goal has been and was and is the same as mine, I did this — prostrated myself full length on the ground in the direction of Kailash. And it was love of the mountain too that moved me to do it, and hope for divine aid, and the belief that if I reached the mountain it was by the grace of the power beyond my control which had brought me here. I prostrated myself in the desire never to be proud of my own haphazard efforts should I make it, and in the prayer that I would make it.

An icy wind was blowing, so I put socks on my hands and shouldered the load. My head bowed down and I watched a green shoe make the first step, the other one make the second: it really was possible, then. The walking kept me warm, and when I looked up it was to see an enormous rainbow arched right over my path.

8 - Day with a lama family

T HE ROAD WAS a sort of glistening sepia brown, puddled and pebbled, but quite good, ditched at either side and marked with black and white kilometre stones which presumably announced the distance from Lhasa. I don't remember the figures, but I was able to pace my progress by them. Feeling a bit stunned, compressed by the solid weight upon my back, my vision became wedged to the mud, and all merry fantasies of skipping along sunny meadows were lost with it. But released at the frequent rest stops I took, to a view of wide green plains sweeping up to the Trans Himalaya and to the smell of freshly rained air, I felt I really had nothing to complain about. The Chang Tang is noted for its whimsical changes of weather and extreme temperatures. This is the two thirds of Tibet where no crops can grow; its barren embrace includes the whole of Central Tibet, salt lakes, Trans Himalaya and all, and sweeps right up to the high Pamirs in the northwest. It is what we call 'The Tibetan Plateau', though the height and the profusion of mountains hardly give the impression implied by the name.

It looked as if there was nothing around but air and mountains, but I was soon to learn that the appearance of void and simplicity can be beguiling. The most surprising things can leak out of the silences and the spaces — details manifest themselves from the bare earth, appearing like mirages at first; but they soon bring you back to earth, reminding you of the proportions of man for a while. Here I was, all set to continue in a straight and solitary line to Kailash, prepared to walk around the few villages marked on the map at night — yet in the first five days I met quite a few people, and of the four vehicles that came by, three gave me lifts. Along the first part of the southern road is twisted a human lifeline, loosely woven from matted plaits of hair, an occasional trail of exhaust, tangled yaks' tails and the stream of hot butter tea. When it swung near me I grasped it, grateful for the initial support.

Two black dots scudded across the valley floor. Men on horses. Rounding a bend I came upon a small complex of cubic buildings, from which people walked down to greet me: 'Cha dhoo!' — 'Drink tea!'

The hot butter tea was delicious, and there was a comforting warmth in the way the family enfolded me with their friendly curiosity. The father had two pigtails, and indicating a small room dedicated to the worship of Padmasambhava (or Guru Rinpoche as he is popularly known in Tibet) let me know he was a lama. Evidently a married lama, as there was a wife and two teenage daughters. Whereas members of the reformed sect, the Gelugpa, of whom the Dalai Lama is the head, remain celibate, it is quite common for monks of the old school to marry. Padmasambhava was a powerful tantric magician brought from the Swat Valley in Pakistan or thereabouts — accounts differ — in order to restore the knowledge lost to Tibet after a period of disintegration. He founded what is now known as 'the old school', the Nyingmapa sect. As well as being a mighty magician, Guru Rinpoche was a man of the world, and had several consorts. Here, over a thousand years later, this pigtailed lama's consort wore a traditional robe, and only stopped filling my cup with tea to fill it with yoghurt. Both the daughters wore Chinese crimplene trousers and checked shirts but had nothing more in common. One spent half an hour brushing and arranging her hair in a scaffolding of bright plastic hair ornaments before demanding that I taught her to disco dance; while the other, who had perhaps mislaid her comb several years ago, exuded a bright aura of overwhelming health, notwithstanding the cigarettes she brought out of her pocket and smoked from time to time in defiance of Tibetan convention.

With gestures, much revving of vocal chords and repetition of the word: *'mocha'* — motor truck — I thought they indicated that they were going to Saga tomorrow by truck, and that I could stay the night there and go with them. It seemed an excellent plan at that moment, so, duly grateful, I accepted, and spent the day there. I heaved yak-hair sacks of yak dung with the radiant daughter, and taught the gaudy one to disco dance. Uncertain Chinese disco music jolted out of one or another of the five radio cassette players that sat in assorted sizes — all large — along a shelf, and to the entertainment of a group that had appeared out of the void and sat sewing up the sacks of dung and grain with big-eyed needles

— I let rip and she followed suit. She was a natural, and soon was prancing to the beat with the verve of a jumping jack. I helped her do the family washing too, stamping in the stream on the strange selection of garments whose odd tasteless synthetic fibres might have come from an English jumble sale in the less wealthy part of town. Buttercups grew in the grass and the mercurial weather, so cold a couple of hours ago, was suddenly warm enough for a bath to be a pleasure. Feeling the fresh water cold and clean, and seeing the snowy blue mountains dancing, gave such delight that suddenly it was worth five years' wait, just for this moment.

But it seems human society is never without complications. As soon as one returns a greeting one becomes involved in an interchange of give and take, and then one has to be so careful not to offend the interdependence. I unwittingly gave offence when in the early evening I said I didn't want to dance again right at that moment. At this the gaudy daughter began to sulk. I said 'Let's disco dance then,' and now she didn't want to. With the long twilight a strange gloom fell over the household; I and the radiant daughter polished brass altar bowls by the stove, the lama father stuffed sheep's stomachs with lumps of cheesy butter, the dulled gaudy one cooked up a pot of sheep's legs.

A truck came, presumably the one they'd been talking about, as onto it they packed all the neatly sewn up sacks. But the drivers did not want to take me. The uneasy silence picked up again and I debated with myself which would offend them least — if I stayed or if I left. The gaudy daughter, who had already been thoroughly through my bags and lightened my load of several items, intercepted her sulks with demands for the hair slides I was wearing. As I found them rather useful for keeping the hair out of my eyes, I only gave her one. And so she fastened her attention on the other one, and I stared out of the open door at the mountains and wondered how I'd become embroiled in such trivia so soon.

In near-silence we ate — I declined their meat but accepted a bowl of sticky rice to go with a few wilting carrots I had left over from Shigatze.

And when we'd finished eating, in the last hour before nightfall, unexpected by all of us, came another truck. This time the family gave the drivers no chance to say no to me — they climbed up the wheels and over the bonnet till the impassive Tibetan men in the truck admitted that they could take me to Saga for fifteen kwai; my things were bundled in with gusto, and I gave the coveted hairslide to the demanding daughter. She accepted the black velvet and silver glitter with a renewed happiness. The whole family had burst into life and smiles at my departure. I

exchanged many thanks for their joyous Tashi Dillees and their hands
and my hair waved vigorously in my eyes as I was driven away.

They said it was forty kilometres to Saga, which I estimated to be two
days' walking. With a certain guilty pleasure at being saved the agony of
the incline I watched a small darkening pass fall easily under the wheels.
The driver and his mate didn't talk much, but when at nightfall we turned
into a small Tibetan compound and I asked, in my essential Tibetan: 'Is
this Saga?' the driver replied: 'This is not Saga.'

Where it was, I don't know, but we spent the night there in a small
dark room lit only by a small tin stove. Here I had my first real encounter
with tsampa, and was dismayed to find my mouth filled with an
even-textured lump of something that resembled nothing so much as
clay. I could distinguish no flavour and extract no pleasure from it, and
was alarmed that, at last, something was as bad as other people made it
out to be.

Other people being still the fresh veg. tourists I had left behind. Now
I was completely surrounded by Tibetans, involved in the rough spin of
their clothes, their mostly unintelligible speech, the dense dry heavy flow
of their tsampa, the orange flare of their juniper fire and the mild
suffocation of their smoke. When I'd laboriously munched through a
whole dreary terrain of tsampa and the drivers had exchanged all their
news with the men and women there, we slept. I on the earth floor by
the stove, listening in gratification to the rain that fell outside. But when
would I get to set up my tent?

In brilliant sunshine the following morning we continued, stopping
at a nomad tent where juniper roots heated bitter tea and the woman
gave us delectable yoghurt. As the truckers unloaded some sacks, I played
football with five little boys in the mud, the broken glass, the shit and
the sun. Nobody seemed too surprised that I was there, and I met only
with kindness.

The drivers deposited me by the side of the road just outside Saga. By
this, and by the walled compound of regular cement that balanced the
earthen cubes of the Tibetan dwellings, it was obvious that there were
Chinese here. And where there were Chinese, I feared a check-point.

Not really knowing what the best policy was, I simply stayed at the
bend of the road where they'd left me, drying out wet washing and writing
in the morning sunshine. After about an hour I looked up to see two
Chinese policemen walking towards me — I diverted my attention from
the loathsome uniforms to assembling my scattered things into one unit,
chanting 'Hare Krishna' under my breath most fervently.

'Ni hao!' they chorused together — the universal Chinese greeting, hoping that you are well.

'Ni hao!' I sang back. They stood, holding hands and watching me for a while, and two Tibetan women stood behind them, also watching, knitting like the women at the foot of the French guillotine. *Hare Krishna Hare Krishna, Krishna Krishna Hare Hare Hare Rama Hare Rama Rama Rama Hare Hare* — I attended competently to my stuff.

Suddenly: '— bye bye!' they all sang in unison again, and they were walking languidly down the road out of town while I shouldered my load, clamped my hat down low, and, looking neither to right nor left, walked straight up the road through the town. I only raised my eyes when a woman at the last house popped out and asked me in for tea. Ragged with sweat, I gratefully accepted three rapid cups before hurtling on, determined to put as much space between me and civilisation as possible.

9 - Truck to Zhongba and the first night out

AFTER THAT KICK-START to the day's walking, I soon began to feel quite comfortable under the load. True it was very heavy, true it dug into my back, and as long as people were giving me tsampa and yoghurt I was making no inroads upon the provisions I'd brought from Hong Kong, but it wasn't so bad until after a couple of hours I came to an incline. Then I sat down to groan at the sight of it. At which point — I couldn't believe my ears — came the sweet roar of a jeep engine. I put out a hand and it stopped.

'Where are you going?' they asked with proper civility, as if there were plenty of ways to go and plenty of lifts to choose from, and perhaps they weren't going the same way as me but if they were they'd be delighted to....

'Kang Rinpoche,' I replied. The Jewel of the Snows.

They were four Tibetan doctors trained in Western medicine, coming from Shigatze and going to Zhongba. With practised hospitality they fitted me in, plied me with cigarettes and bread, and knocked what I estimated to be about a week's walking off my journey in an afternoon. When we arrived at Zhongba they enquired if I would take a room there for the night, or would I continue? I tried to suppress my agitation as I said oh, I'd continue, and they slowly unloaded my things into the centre of the main village street before carefully helping me to assemble them, lifting them onto my back, giving me their address in Shigatze and shaking my hand with speeches of good luck. Again I scuttled off, and even caught sight of a nylon-clad foot, encased in a high heeled shoe and protruding from the olive green trouser which is the mark of the Chinese militia. Beside the knee of the trouser was a table strewn with a card game, but I was gone before I could see more of how the Chinese occupation occupied itself.

When I next raised my head I was well out of town, with a sand dune obliterating it from sight. A beautiful tall dark nomad boy walked beside me; he was carrying a bundle of silk-covered quilts on his back, and singing in a very high-pitched voice.

Then he commanded me to perform: 'Loo!' Obediently I sang. *Jerusalem* bounded out of my throat, the deep pink and gold silk became liquid in the evening sun, green and pleasant hills wafted out of the wide expanse of plain and I found myself desperate for breath. We took it in turns to sing till our ways divided; he went off to some distant black yak-hair tents, and I rounded a hillock to open up my tent for the first time.

The buying of the tent had been a brief episode in the humid Hong Kong preparations; I didn't even know if it had a fly sheet or not. Now I discovered that the sleek and flimsy blue nylon did not. Oh, no! But for now it was a clear mild evening. I pitched the tent in what seemed to be a sheltered spot and went to wash myself and my clothes in a nearby pool of water in the marsh. The water was pungent with the smell of yak, and cold. Feeling that all was quite right with the world I arranged my new home, with a rice-straw mat on the floor, covered by a pretty cotton sarong from Thailand, and lay out my sleeping bag. I propped up a small picture of Shiva against the pot of Nutella, lit a candle and incense, scraped the mould off and devoured the remains of the Shigatze maize bread with Vegemite and butter. With the flaps of the tent held back like curtains to the view of swirling pink and gold skies, I settled comfortably down to write. What more could I ask out of life?

The trouble with happiness based on material premises is that it's always rather temporary. As I wrote about the luck I'd had with the lifts and so on, night fell. Wind blew. Rain began to fall. I got out the space blanket and improvised half a fly sheet with it. I closed the tent flaps, and lightning began to crack, thunder to roll. At first I tried to pretend it wasn't happening, but after a while I couldn't help but notice the rain that was beginning to seep in at the seams of the tent. Then the candle blew out and one of the tent poles blew down, and suddenly I found myself squatting and holding the pole with one hand to keep it upright, arranging with the other hand an island of the rest of my things in the centre. Wind squeezed the tent walls together, water shot all over the place, pools formed in the corners of the fitted groundsheet. And suddenly it was very cold. For an hour or so I hunched there, holding the pole in the dark, musing upon the cheap Hong Kong tent which had been doubtless designed for cosy week-end jaunts in the mapped hills of the New Territories, in the dry season of course. I had prepared so carefully in some ways, and left great glaring deficiencies in others. It was a precarious and confined dance just to keep dry, and would I ever sleep?

When the wind had dropped I was able to go out and fix the guy ropes so that they held the poles. Then I developed the system which was to keep me dry for the next couple of months — to lay all the clothes I wasn't wearing about the edges of the tent, and to allow them to sop up the flood. A narrow strip of comparative dryness was preserved down the middle of the tent, and on this I slept long and deep. And when I finally arose the next day I just wrung the water into the sand, and lay around in the dull sunshine waiting for them to dry.

It was four o'clock by the time I put my first foot forward, but any sense of urgency was diminished by the eccentricities of the Beijing clock and absorbed by the greater scales of the distances visible about me. I wanted to be at Kailash by the twenty-seventh of August — the day after my thirty-first birthday, the night of the full moon held sacred in India to Shiva. There was an indeterminate number of hundreds of kilometres to go and six weeks to do it in; calculations with the fuzzy photocopied map seemed to make it a feasible proposition if I walked about twenty kilometres a day.

But in just the first five kilometres the elements seemed out to inform me of the protean odds I was up against. As soon as I began to walk it began to rain, and with the rain came vicious gusts of bitterly cold wind. The road by this time was less sophisticated, and I regretted my complacency regarding the alleged rivers as soon as I found myself wading knee-deep through streams that intersected the road so frequently that removing shoes and socks was a waste of time. My luggage seemed to weigh twice as much as ever before, but I plodded on. The road led across the valley floor, between water-pooled marshes, to a fine concrete suspension bridge that appeared like a mirage over a major tributary to the Brahmaputra. But it was real enough — and here another phenomenon leaked out of the dull green marshes, in the form of four men on horses, herding yaks. I loitered by the bridge in the rain, brushing my teeth in the muddy water and rearranging the space blanket as a raincoat for my luggage.

They were curious and sympathetic, but would not sell me one of their lovely horses. I gazed longingly at the sturdy muscles of the beasts, at their gentle muzzles, at the comfortable carpet-covered wooden saddles. But no — they loved and needed their horses. And I was crazy to want to go to Kang Rinpoche — didn't I know about the *'choo chembow'* — big water — that cut up the road? Better I should return with them to their tents. It was warm there, and they'd feed me, and I would no longer be alone. All this I understood by their gestures and a few stray words — so I thanked them kindly, and went on.

Half a dozen knee-deep rivers later, I was surprised to see two blue Landcruisers weaving towards me out of the drizzle. They stopped, and the Tibetan driver unwound the window to allow a great sigh of comforting warm air breathe out of the snug rugged interior. They were a party of French tourists who sat with quietly pained expressions as their guide did the talking. They had just come from Kailash — how was it? — Oh, it was superb, but if I wanted to walk there I should know that it was impossible. 'There is one big RIVer ...' they had had to go more than fifty-five kilometres out of their way, and anyway, it was very long and 'ard, such a long way, with many small rivers also, like these — she indicated the dull gleams that snaked across the vast marshes — but while they were at Kailash they had met one American girl who had hitch-hiked there by the northern road in only two weeks, so if I wanted to go back and try that way there were trucks coming behind them which would give me a lift to the fork ... the warm sigh from the interior brought with it associations of company and firesides I have known. I thanked them, and said yes, maybe. They looked comforted, and drove off.

But after the rain the sun, after the sun the rain — I wanted to walk, didn't I? Certainly I had enough food, and even if I had to walk fifty-five kilometres round the river, I'd already saved enough distance by the lifts I'd been given to do it. So I persevered on through the icy blasts of rain that swept the plain from the Himalaya, until I came with the last fibre of daylight to the foot of the hills, where the remains of a stone wall formed a wind-break to the tent. I wailed a bit to myself over a 761 biscuit topped with chocolate, but when at midnight three trucks, presumably the provision carriers for the French party, drove past, I lay still. A river rampaged loudly round the near corner but I preferred not to think about it. I fell asleep with the candle burning, and the rain heavily falling outside and seeping inside.

It seemed the worse it was for my body, the better for my dreams. Though the morning began viciously enough as I washed in a cold and muddy puddle in the road, I still moved in the sunny land of flower-sprinkled meadows of which I had been dreaming. Just as I was ready to leave, three more trucks rollicked past in the direction of Lhasa. I lurked in the enclosure of wet stones and mutely watched them cover in minutes the last painful hour of yesterday's walking. I couldn't give up now, as I'd only just begun.

10 - Company and fireside

THE RIVER SNARLED to the left of the road, which today led through a narrower valley far preferable to the plains of the last couple of days. After a while the sun shone, and bees appeared out of nowhere to potter between sweet-smelling flowers of deep violet and yellow. The velvet mountains crushed tufts of cumulus, and there was no difference between the dream and reality. If only I had breath to sing! And out of long-smothered memories of primary school assemblies leaked the music and the words of the Christian pilgrim's hymn:

> He-ee who would valiant be
> 'Gainst all disaster
> Le-et him in constancy
> Follow the master.

There's no discouragement
Will ma-ake him once relent
His first avo-owed intent
To be a pilgrim.

I wasn't sure what sort of a pilgrim I was; I chanted 'Hare Krishna' non-stop in my head all day, lit incense to Shiva every evening, read about Tibetan Buddhism, put stones on any mani walls I passed and could never drop the habit — begun in those same assemblies — of saying the Lord's prayer every night. I was an out and out heretic to all religions, moved by an unshakeable belief in God; and I was going to Kailash, the destination beyond segregation. And there I'd do yoga and align myself in the way I know best with the divinity manifest there, and perhaps be able to drop the babble that would keep leaping through my head ... for suddenly life was very simple, and required no thought. All I had to do was put one foot before the other. Yet the mind rattled on, and when suddenly it began to thunder and lightning and then to hail and my stomach simultaneously brandished knives — it was interesting to see how my mood flipped accordingly. Had I had anyone with me then, they'd doubtless be doing everything wrong in my opinion.

The valley widened out onto another plain, and my opinion seemed quite absurd on such an empty stage. The road seemed to veer north towards a cliff, coloured maroon like the Nyingmapa monks' robes — I'd have lunch there, I decided. Head down, one foot followed another. After a few hours I had divorced from the pains and took only occasional rest-stops, and those only for long enough to catch some breath. Walking was meditation. I reached the cliffs at about eleven at night.

A small gathering of cubic walls distinguished themselves out of the half-lit cliffs as I drew near, and on drawing nearer these in turn yielded quiet figures who ushered me inside.

The family behaved with uncurious attentiveness, as if it was quite expected and normal that I should be there. My cup was immediately filled with hot butter tea, my wet feet placed before a raging fire. Here was the warmth and the fireside, here was congenial company. One typically tall and handsome woman alternately churned tea and breast-fed her baby; an old couple hacked red meat off a fresh yak-haunch while a couple of younger men sawed up the rest of the carcass in the corner. The tsampa they gave me was delicious, perhaps due to it being freshly ground. The barley wouldn't be able to grow in the barren soil here and these people had probably traded wool for it. Tsampa is made by first roasting the barley grains in woks full of hot sand until the grains pop. These are then sieved and milled through stones to produce a ready-cooked flour which can be added to anything, even to cold water if there's nothing else. Straight from the millstones, the texture that night was the very same steadfast bulk of the sacks that bolstered the walls, of the homespun weave of sacks, clothes and plaits, of the mud-matted pile of the carpets covering the beds, of the strong dry planks of wood that made shelves along the walls. It tasted not of clay, but of good earth.

I gave them three Dalai Lama photos and they uncovered a carpeted bed in the next room for me to sleep on. They watched me brush my teeth, poured hot water over my hands to wash, and watched me into bed. Six children appeared from the night to watch me write, to take it in turns to examine the ridiculous Mickey Mouse watch on Hong Kong time, to replenish the candle stuck in the wall when it wilted. When they'd finished with Mickey they politely handed him back to me with an appraising: *'Yagadoo!'* — 'good' — and seized with fervour on *The Way of the White Clouds*. They perused the pictures with interest, and asked me what the captions said. When I named the statue of Tomo Geshe Rinpoche, they touched the picture to their heads in veneration. Out of the lost world streamed the lamas and anchorites described by the archaic Indian print, right to their heads in front of me, and for the first time I felt a tangible relation between what I was reading about and what I was living.

11 - Lift to Paryang

THE MUESLI I put in my morning salt and butter tea was exotic as a parrot on my tongue, but it matched the brilliance of the colours outside. I thoughtlessly gave away all my cigarette-lighters, and they helped me on with my load. One of the elder boys of the night before walked with me for the first kilometre or so, loosely leading a flock of

sheep which ambled behind him at some hundred yards distance. A few
minutes after he left me I met a group of men seated on a grassy bank by
a very crude stone building, who called and waved to me. They were
inviting me for tea. A few dry green tea-leaves floated on top of a huge
pot of cold water and there was no fire to be seen.

Still, it was yet only about mid-day — I sat down in the sun and
watched as one of them sewed up a sheepskin bag, woolly side out, open
at one end and held taut by two lashed sticks. From the other end
protruded an old exhaust pipe. When he'd finished, he passed it to the
man sitting smoking by a pile of yak dung; who, after he'd smoked his
cigarette, put the smouldering butt under the pot, surrounded it with
flakes of dried yak dung, clamped the exhaust pipe into place with stones,
and began to pump the sheepskin up and down. Now I understood —
bellows! The cigarette-end lent its spark to the yak dung, and in this
ingenious manner he had the pot boiling in not less than half an hour. I
drank two cups of tea while politely countering their investigative forays
upon my rucksack; they were particularly interested in my Peter Storm
rain jacket, and wanted to trade it for a sheepskin. But I had no room
for a sheepskin and a lot of use for the jacket. They reluctantly agreed to
the logic of this, and accepted with some puzzlement the red plastic sun
visor for which none of us had any use at all. I warded off further offers
of tea, waved goodbye to all and walked off again.

I had hardly gone a few kilometres when I heard the seductive murmur
of a mocha going my way. Deciding that it doesn't do to disdain the
offerings of fate at such moments, I flagged it down. I couldn't understand the name of where they were going to — but twenty kwai for
anywhere towards Kailash was OK. I hopped in. I spent the day ardently
appreciating this new stroke of luck. The truck followed a wandering
course across the sandy flats and the sun shone. I sat amidst homespun
sacks full of tsampa with a merry lot of fellow travellers, who came and
went at the stops we made at nomad encampments. We'd stop for an
hour at a time — to pick up new people, more sacks of tsampa and saddles
covered with bright carpets. At each stop the nomads would give us fruit
of the yak — yoghurt, or curds and whey, and then we'd each bring out
our own cup, our butter and tsampa, and feast. One of the young men
sat drawing flamey feathered birds in a red pen over every surface he could
find — beginning with a sheet of Chinese print, his artistry progressed
over every piece of flesh exposed within his reach, so that after a while
we were all tattooed somewhere between shoulder and finger-tips with
the wild red wings.

When we moved, it was through plains where great sand-dunes rose up in heaps of gold — where pools of water lay in the green grass like beads of skin-polished turquoise. In the distance rose up a dun gold mountain in an island, floating in the deep Prussian-blue sea of the Himalaya. And then there was one which flipped up a double tip, just like a fish's tail. In fact — that was just what it must be — Machupuchari, the Fishtail peak in Nepal. I wondered which were Makalu and Dhaulagiri. Of course, Heinrich Harrer, waltzing this way to Lhasa, pack-donkey in tow, had had no trouble identifying them. He was a great mountaineer, raised among mountains and familiar with their names world-over; he'd been thrilled to recognise the Himalayan peaks he could see from here, many of which he'd climbed, the textures of whose icy crevices and fissures were known by all the muscles of his body. I was thrilled to bump across his shadow, but had no such grip on their names and heights. Still, the mountains had been there before the names. In the near-distance another hill whose name I would never know surprised me with its glowing coral pink. And so I was perpetually in wonder, for when walking my eyes were on the ground, and the rest-stops afforded no such free-range visions as these.

In the bright evening we left the road and bumped into a small compound set on the side of a hill. We'd stop here tonight, and tomorrow continue to wherever-it-was.

12 - Jonja

THE TIGHT-KNIT UNITY of the travelling group instantly unravelled. Everyone leapt off with their things and were assimilated into the rows of rooms that lined the small walled community. I did what I usually do when in doubt — sat down. A couple of women who had lurked on the wings of the flurry now invited me to go and drink tea, and so I, the loose end, also trailed off into the mud and plaster of the place. Though the buildings were Chinese-style, the inhabitants were all Tibetan. The woman to whose room we went dressed in Chinese fashion — nylon trousers and shirt, and her long plaited hair was coiled about her head. Her friend, her next door neighbour, was dressed all Tibetan but for a peaked green Chinese army cap. I could never work out the status of Chinese influence in this place — whether it was superimposed or infiltrated. Certainly it was there, but my Tibetan was for survival and not for probing, and as they never mentioned any anti-Chinese sentiments I remained mystified.

My hostess's name was Norchi, and I stayed two days and nights with her and her small three year-old son in the one room. To the walls above the brightly painted cupboards were pinned large posters of Chamba (who to the Chinese is the Buddha Matreiya, the Buddha of the future) alongside Chairman Mao. She knitted at a pair of thick long-johns in between spinning wool, heaping yak dung on the stove and eternally filling my cup with more tea and sometimes yoghurt. Yet despite the serene and humble activities she seemed possessed of a certain refinement more than other Tibetan women I had met. Every hair on her head was combed into place, and she wore a straw hat to cross the yard. She seized upon the creams, ribbons and ear-cleaners I gave her, and immediately put the last to use, though her neighbours rejected them when she tried to pass them on. Why use these strange synthetic things when fingernails were right there at the fingers' tips and matchsticks were plentiful? She never gobbed or spat, she used a handkerchief, and regularly washed both herself and her son. He was brightly curious and never far from her. When he got too inquisitive about the contents of my luggage she would admonish him. She said that she was alone with the child. Did I have no man? No man. No, she had no man either. It was a fact which gave her no pleasure, but she maintained discretion and did not elaborate beyond a passing face of resignation. What was her story? Where had she learned the English Chinese and Tibetan alphabets? What was it that kept her constantly tuned into the radio? She smiled all innocence, shovelled more yak dung on the fire with her fingers, and then washed and dried them before picking up her knitting again.

She loved to get me to dance, and would heat up a whole succession of batteries on the stove to feed the radio so that it in turn would provide the music. Sometimes she'd dance too, sometimes she'd just watch. I knew better than to desist this time, and danced on to every radio station, Indian Australian and Chinese, that she could find. One night when I lay awake on a carpet on the floor, she managed to tune into Beethoven's

Fifth. The familiar notes beat my mind awake, and later, as she and her son slept on a raised earthen bed, I wandered outside and wondered about the 'choo chembow'. The moon radiated suggestive colours into the spongy rainclouds. How far was it to the 'one big RIVer', and how would I cross it?

Just outside the walls of the compound was pitched a magnificent white tent, appliquéed with flourishing blue flowers and eternal knots. The occupants were a merry band of Khampas who raucously invited me inside to sit upon a sack and eat dry yak-haired pastries in pastel colours. It was a very well-equipped tent, furnished with heavy, painted cupboards, large radios and bottles of beer. There was one woman, thousands of turquoise beads braided into her hair, and two men. Thin moustaches edged their upper lips, rich red tassels of silk dangled alluringly from the gleaming coils about their heads. One of them drank beer and the other read aloud from a loose-leafed book of sutras in the corner. A couple of dozen children from the village corked up the doorway with their curiosity. The turquoise queen ransacked the contents of my bag, and as she passed items around for general inspection, all the demons of Tibet were released, streamed across the rusty rosy faces of the children in a sea of gargoyles terrible to behold. From the corner came the chanting of sutras, the children bobbed and howled as the woman pecked at my clothes. 'Change money?' she shrieked from time to time. 'How muchee?' It seemed to be habit bred of the Jokhang and no answer could be made to the storms of laughter this drove her to.

They thought that it was a brilliant joke too that I was going to Kang Rinpoche. What about the choo chembow? Could I swim? — They all grew high on laughing at the very idea.

Though they kindly ordered me to stay and sleep there, I slipped off. Without a rucksack it was possible to bound up the hill behind the compound. At the summit were two small *chortens* hung with prayer flags, and amongst the inscribed stones of 'Om mani padme hum' shone one brightly-painted stone — a portrait of a benevolent Chairman Mao. At the foot of the hill lurked a crazy woman, who lived alone in a yak-hair tent amongst broken glass between wall and rock. She would pull me up and down by the hand, encouraging me to follow her example in paying constant obeisances in the direction of Kang Rinpoche, and I energetically joined in.

Beyond the arena of broken glass was a black yak-dotted land, bogged with pools of yellowy yak-tasting water. After wandering all Sunday under the sun there, I returned at evening to the odd retreat of the single mother and her crackly radio. To the south the blue fish tail peak flipped up into the subtle intensity of the sky, which I watched, hypnotised, from her doorstep. Whale-like thunderstorms moved through a flush of brick red to passive mauve, and the paints in my bag remained untouched. It would be indecent for a human hand to try and copy all that clarity and glory.

Norchi awoke me on Monday morning by throwing water all over the floor, pronouncing: 'Mocha! Mocha!' in urgent tones. She fed me noodles with chili as I waited on the doorstep, listening to the interesting aural collage she created from the radio. I learnt that Russian troops were withdrawing from Afghanistan and another station sang about an illegal alien in New York. A bout of Chinese altercated with Tibetan, followed by the latest musical sprig from George Harrison at which Louis Armstrong pitched in to sing about what a wonderful world it is.

The Tibetans believe that the mountains, lakes and trees speak to us in many strange ways. Now it was neither remote nor desolate — both mountain and radio seemed to agree that right here was the hub of the Universe. Or at least — getting there.

After three hours or so the truck was ready. I piled up behind the wrought red star with a set of painted cupboards, and was very quickly transported to Paryang. That was the last truck, and Paryang the last compound, the last roof. The all-Tibetan village was set in the midst of the plain, with eight prayer wheels in the centre. I turned them, and walked on — in the wrong direction. An old man and some children called me back and put me on the right path. They fingered prayer beads and mentioned that there was a 'choo chembow'. Yes, so I gathered. I thanked them, and walked off across the wide and sandy valley floor.

13 - Hermitage and first choo chembow

CASTING MY MIND back on that journey, it didn't really begin until Paryang had fallen out of sight, and with it the exhaust smoke and compounds of civilisation. Though it's against my hitch-hiking nature not to take advantage of passing vehicles, it was far preferable, now that my back had been broken in gently by their help, to have no choice but to walk. It was just a matter of heading in a long northwesterly curve to Kailash. Somewhere beyond these wide flat valley floors stood the mountain, radiating spokes of irresistible attraction, and now I was just beginning to feel my grasp on one of them. Infinite ranges of colour daubed the earth, and from my head leaked all sorts of odd memories and associations. Earth looked empty but was full of nuances. It was easy to see how the Tibetan Buddhist doctrines of the interdependence of form and void had flourished from such a nature. On the one hand, the open space and silence create an impression of void, annihilating all hitherto known forms and conceptions. On the other hand, the imagination seethes at the confrontation, expressing new forms into the nothingness. The mind fluctuates between the suggestion of cosmic emptiness and a crazy urge to populate it. Demons leap out of the clouds, sail from world to world and back again.

The path suddenly rounded a small hill that seemed to pop up from nowhere, and at the base of it flowed a thick clear stream of water between banks of vibrant green. After all the yakky pools and muddy streams, it was too good to walk any further that night. In the grass grew slim yellow trumpet flowers, and a few birds sang. I tried eating the flowers, and they tasted fresh and good, like faintly scented salad. It was mid-evening, and the whole of nature seemed to be saying: 'Stay'. The northwest sky was blue and routed with clouds of bronze; the Himalaya to the south rippled a silver spray of more clouds; while the northeast was dark with dense threads of storm that dipped in curves down to the earth, black noodles bending into a pot of boiling water. The sun shone one long shaft of brilliance into the murk and maintained two broad ends of a double rainbow there for over an hour. I stayed. While taking a bath in the stream it began to hail. The white stones plopped into the water, and it was so beautiful that I felt outrageously happy.

On top of the next small hill was perched what I romantically imagined to be a ruined hermitage. There were three rooms with smoke-blackened roofs, built of mud and stone. A yard wall ran round the outside, enclosing a litter of debris — lots of shiny black sheep droppings, heaps of dried yak dung, an old kettle, a shovel with no handle, a rain-faded portrait of Chairman Mao and a wooden pot broken into three pieces. Outside one of the rooms lay the skulls of about fifty yaks, and bones trailed up the hillside to a mani wall set on the next hilltop. A mani wall is usually about fourteen feet long and a few feet low and wide, built of flat stones all inscribed with the root mantra: 'Om mani padme hum'. It is considered auspicious to look at them in the course of a journey. Many of the yak skulls said the same thing, and the whole air was porous with left-over carnage and devotion.

I set up camp on my space blanket in the largest room, where the floor was of earth and cobbled with mani stones and sheep dung. In honour of the sanctity of the place, I opened up the one tin of tomatoes I had brought, and into the pot with it went cloves, sage, cumin seed, pepper, chili and rice vermicelli. This was my first go at a yak dung fire and I experienced no difficulty with the fire, only with the smoke. I removed the fire on the shovel to outside, and let the wind do the work. Later, clean and satiated, I lay looking at the gibbous moon through the open doorway. Here I felt a richness of life and an appreciation such as I had not experienced in a long time. And this was luxury — the same luxury as to be found in sleeping in a French barn under sacks with a black cat on a haycart or under a Japanese temple in the rain. A luxury that depends upon a cohesion between my immediate needs being met and my appreciation of them. I wallowed in the vast extravagances of the arrangement.

I tried to extend the pleasures of eating hot savoury food the next day. All day I cooked a stew of packet soup and pasta over a slow-burning, thick-smoked, fire of yak dung; but the last concoction, which I drank just before setting off, was a rather foul mixture of onion-tasting cocoa which left a disturbing impression on my tongue. It was a grey and drizzly day and I couldn't have set out much later than I did, but anyway, there was no avoiding it. Here it was, after just a few kilometres — the first choo chembow. The broad brown river surged confidently between its banks of packed shale and sand. Just before it were a couple of rows of houses with tin roofs, seemingly uninhabited; but when five dogs leapt out of their naps to chase me at full voice, an old man emerged from the room nearest the river. He wore only a congealed sheepskin about his loins, and a string of prayer beads hung on his naked torso. 'Choo chembow?' I enquired chattily of him, hoping perhaps he could offer some solution, or some encouragement, or a cup of tea perhaps — the room behind him flamed orange from a large hot fire — but he just made a deprecatory gesture and looked morosely at the ground. So I walked to the bank of the widest part of the river, hoping that that would mean it was also the shallowest.

I'd planned to sit and contemplate the river a while — but the dogs would not shut up. Because the water was opaque with sand, I couldn't see how deep it was. It was swift. I chose a part where I could see the water catching mid-stream on some boulders, took a deep breath, chanted 'Hare Krishna', and began to walk straight across. Long grasses wrapped about my ankles, then it was knee, thigh, chest-deep. Half way across I remembered a promise I'd made to my father as I said goodbye to him — not to take any risks. Yet here I was like Macbeth: having stepped across so far, to return would be as tedious as to go o'er. I carried on. Three quarters of the way across the water closed over my head. Instinctively I tried to swim; impossible with all that weight on my back. My feet gave a little jump on the sandy river bed and fortunately the place where they touched down was higher again. My nose popped out above the water, and I could breathe. Chest, waist, thigh-deep — I was on the bank, and the only things that hadn't got wet were, miraculously, the matches, incense, down sleeping bag, pyjamas and jacket. The long evening fell, and through it I walked, still in the wet clothes, thinking the action would warm me. It did not, and at last I had to relent to the freezing cold, and clumsily put up the tent for the night. Snug and warm and dry again in silk pyjamas, reeking of expensive French perfume — clutching at symbols of the civilisation I thought I was trying to get away from — I lit incense and thanked God for having safely crossed the river.

I wondered if this was it — the French tourists' guide had only talked about 'one' big RIVer. Yet others had talked about many, and I suspected that the others might be right. Whatever — for now I was in my tent while it poured with rain outside. Clothes absorbed the leaks as usual and I myself became absorbed in the re-reading of *The Way of the White Clouds* until daybreak. The wide and far-reaching syntax matched the vast spaces that surrounded me, and I was anchored to my portable home unfolded by the sweet light odour of the rice straw mat, the incense and the warm candlelight. I was somewhat perplexed by the author's perpetual assertion that it hardly ever rains in western Tibet; but even with the rain falling just as perpetually outside, life was quite simple, undistracted and perfect, and everything else that I read made sense. The wind blew stark realisations across the plain, echoing the remote spaces that had always blown about my bones whenever, throughout my life, I had read anything about Tibet. And here was my actual body transported, breathing that very same high air through which so many subtle bodies had flown, from which so many legends had emanated. Every second in Tibet is vivid with the sense that man is here only as the guest of unknown forces.

Due to traditional Tibetan xenophobia, only a few foreigners had made it along this road until recently; and there had been a time when no Tibetans came this way either. During the ten years of the Cultural Revolution, all pilgrimage was actively discouraged. It was even harder for Tibetans to travel in Tibet during that time than it had been for foreigners for millennia; suitably disguised, photographic and surveying equipment well hidden, stories prepared and interpreters where necessary nervously to hand — at least a handful of these dreaded interlopers had been able to penetrate the Favoured Realm over the centuries. Under the paternal dictatorship of Mao, even the Tibetans lucky enough to live at Kailash could only do koras of the mountain by explaining to the People's Liberation Army that they were looking for their yaks.

The first recorded foreigners to travel along the southern road went, though well bundled up in sheepskins sewn in Shigatze, neither in disguise nor in fear of their lives. They were English and Indian, and travelled equipped with letters from the Central Government advising the local chiefs they would meet to help them in any way possible. They were the members of the punitive Younghusband expedition which had whipped up from India in 1904. Worried about Russians, possibly paranoid that they had an eye on the wool trade, they'd confidently marched up to Lhasa and in true British spirit negotiated a trade treaty; the Tibetans, a bit taken aback by the power of the foreign bullets against their protective amulets, conceded them three trade stations. One of the trade stations was to be at Gartok in western Tibet, so the enterprising party decided they might as well go and sort it out right there and then, although it was October and rather chilly. Accordingly they cut up the same Tsang Po valley as I was now walking, and returned to India via Kailash. With several dozen ponies and over a hundred yaks to carry their gear, from time to time they were able to jaunt up hills and valleys in passing, and apply their surveying equipment to the unmapped terrain. Though they had come ready for war they left in peace, and the stunning beauty of Kailash greatly impressed them. They did not linger, however, as they had pressing bureaucratic duties to discharge before slithering down snowy passes back to the social life in Simla.

I was recalled from reverie by the apparition the next afternoon of a small family striding across the plain, heads held high, a small flock of burdened sheep galloping in front of them. They stopped to pass the time of day, and to examine my things as I was packing away. There was a father in the beginning of his old age, with son and daughter; the father carried a folded black umbrella which he used as a walking stick, and all three trailed prayer beads from their hands. I gave them a packet of 761 biscuits each, glad to lighten my own load. They tucked them into the pouches made in the breasts of their wide belted robes, and said they'd just come from Kang Rinpoche. Was I going there? Yes, I was. We all saluted in the direction of the holy mountain. They said it was eight days' walk to there from here. Did they mean my snail's pace or their brisk half-trot? Still — it was an encouragingly low figure, which in any case blew into insignificance when they put their hands to their chests and solemnly assured me: 'Choo chembow'. I did the same back to them, ominously aware that my suspicions had been right.

But they had come through. Watching them stride off across the plain I was struck by the uncomplicated purity of their intention. Every Westerner who goes to Tibet feels compelled to write and tell the world about it; yet wonders and hardships were everyday to these people, and the things which I regarded as obstacles were for them matters of fact. Swift and unquestioning they sped off into the landscape, merging into the inner sea of pilgrims who over the centuries had all trodden this sacred path. The wave of devotion was alive, and already, as I watched them, invisible again.

14 - Rivers and rain

THERE FOLLOWED a period of several days dominated by either lack of or too much water. I would have to wait a couple of hours in the morning while the wet clothes and tent dried out in whatever sun appeared. Then just as rain threatened I'd pack up and walk on, and by the time the rain fell I'd be parched with thirst. Suddenly there was water, lots and lots of it collected in creamy turquoise pools in the tufted sand. It was full of tiny wildlife which I purified away before drinking. No, I'm not one of these people who drinks the water everywhere, believing *they* won't get sick — I believe the agent of my hepatitis was a steel tumbler of water meant for washing hands, inadvertently drunk one long ago hot day in Pakistan. I've been careful about water ever since, and now had with me a stash of white purifying tablets from a clean Hong Kong chemist where all the cockroaches had been swept under the counter. The Mickey Mouse watch told the minutes as the visible population of the water fainted away to the bottom of the water container — Om mani padme hum. It was self-defence — them or me.

Strength returned with the water. Walking on, determined to sleep either when it got dark or when I next came to water, whichever came first — it seemed inevitably that, though I'd cross streams or pass pools in the middle of the day, by the time it got dark I wouldn't have seen water for hours, and my water bottle was empty. Expectations of water elasticated over the wide and apparently waterless horizons, and days were condensed into the moments of thirst-slaking. Camped amidst scrub-covered sand-dunes, which every night seemed the same as the night before, I put out cup and plate, and in the morning was able to drink the rain they'd collected while I slept.

One day the thirst became so demanding that I dumped my luggage and walked up a hill in order to locate the Brahmaputra. There it was, oozing flatly across the plain. I walked a mile or two down to it. It was swift, impossibly deep, coloured a dark rich brown borrowed from banks of velvet mud. But it was water. I bathed in it, drank it, rejoined my rucksack with a whole new purified bottle of it, and, full of the vigour it had given me in the face of a strange insistent wind, walked on.

The wind became demoniac. I strode on and presently met a nomad, prayer beads trailing. We went through the usual interchange, in which it was established that he lived somewhere invisible nearby, that I was going to Kang Rinpoche and that I was alone. Then just as I was about to shoot off again, he called me back. 'Eah!' — 'Eh?' — 'Choo!' — and as he said the word of double importance, his hand was at his waist. There was no doubt about it in this case, then.

Soon enough there was not one river but many bands of muddy water strewn across my path. The first two were only knee-deep, but the third was narrower, speedier and darker. No time to stop and think and whip up a fear — I chanted 'Hare Krishna' and walked across, following the line of the current. It was waist-deep and fast, but the floor sandy and smooth, easy to tread. At the far bank I hauled myself ashore but did not stop to take breath — there were half a dozen more mucky streaks to cross yet. None proved as deep as the first. By the time they fell behind me, freezing cold rain had begun to pour and the icy wind was blowing furiously.

As the rain continued, I didn't bother to change into dry clothes. Numb fingers put up the tent in the rain in the middle of the draughty spaces, with only a gentle sand dune for protection, and no water but the rain. All my lighters had disappeared into the wayside hands of the people who had offered me food and shelter, flashy thanks for plates of tsampa; there wasn't much point in trying to light a candle as all the wicks were wet, and it would take more than the three remaining matches to light them. But there it was again — complete luxury to be in clean dry silk pyjamas, utter joy to be on the way to Kailash, paradise on earth to be alone.

So when I was awakened at daybreak by a nomad standing outside and going: 'Oo-er! Oo-er!' — my reaction was to tell him to piss off. But I opened the zip of the tent and let him peer in. No, he didn't have any matches … when he left, I left the tent flaps open. Sometime in the night it had stopped raining, and there was a thick dew on the grass. Through these diamonds that grew at eye-level I had a clear view of the snow and blue of the Himalaya way beyond. What a beautiful morning! A pointed change from the usual blue-grey overcast skies before noon.

Because of the weight of my rucksack, I was obliged to watch every foot-step that I took in the direction of Kailash. The first hour was always the worst, the hour in which muscles, joints and back rebelled at their exploitation; after a few hours however, things would usually calm down, and my body would cruise steadily along as the mind drifted free-range from one pleasant daydream to another. But today was different. That morning was beautiful and that night was beautiful, yet sandwiched in the middle was a long day of low pressure, quixotic thunderstorms and a matching bad humour. Thunder bellowed all about like a herd of angry bulls, mosquitoes buzzed and I sweated in a muggy, unpleasant fashion as I forded a dozen or so small muddy rivers. Rain jacket, sweater and hat were on and off in various combinations all day — and twice there were storms of hail so thick and harsh that they clipped me violently on the ears and left the ground and mountainsides sparkling white.

Access to the daydreams was lost. My mind threshed and snapped with the weather. With no distractions to keep them down and with all the climatic encouragement, an assortment of demons leapt up from the subconscious. A devilish master of ceremonies conjured up a past I thought was past, and carefully pointed out every injustice. I'd thought my mind was quite free to dedicate to Kailash, but no, here it was, having another go. The mind distorted so skilfully that, under its tyranny, it didn't help to know that the tyrant was an illusion. Mood black as the sky, I walked on. And then there was a moment in which a sudden trick of the heavens killed more demons than my feeble mind could have done in a million years: wanting to strangle the rain that fell so endlessly cold down my neck, I turned around to set on it. And there out of the black sky to the north arched a perfect rainbow, and framed inside it was a magical other sky and landscape of translucent blue, where clouds swam in golden islands to another land. Sitting down suddenly to watch it, it didn't matter that cold rain continued to pour down my neck, didn't matter that the wind still skewered my ears. For however long I sat staring, the demons were arrested. All that mattered was this magnificent reminder that what really matters is far beyond the complaints of the physical body, including that overrated organ, the mind. Even pleasant daydreams paled.

There is a human tendency to put names to the formations of nature. Tibetans have wisely named peaks and other outstanding features of their landscape as gods, and venerate them. This vision of other lands without names was rising now from the Trans Himalaya, so named by the Swedish explorer Sven Hedin. A pugnacious and single-minded man, he had travelled this way to Kailash the year after the Younghusband expedition; he was fully aware of the sacred implications and was the first Westerner to do a kora of the mountain. His journey up the Tsang Po valley was only one of numerous expeditions across the Tibetan plateau over several years: most of the time he spent determinedly dodging local officials and crossing and recrossing the Trans Himalaya, all in the cause of geographical research. He was an unapproachable man, severe on the large caravans of hired Tibetans and yaks that accompanied him, reserving his affection for his dogs. Despite his self-imposed isolation, he was obsessed with a desire for international recognition and fame for having been 'the first white man ever to....' Though he ranged the Trans Himalaya for years, though he found the source of the Indus and was responsible for filling in square inches at a time on the maps, his attitude prompted the Royal Geographical Society in London, whose approval he particularly sought, to discredit many of his findings. Feeling rejected by the establishment, he later became a Nazi and died embittered and unacclaimed. Yet it seems he was genuinely and deeply touched by the intangible and unnameable beauties of Tibet. In this landscape hovering over the mountains which still retain (for maps published in the West, at any rate) the name he had given them, lingered intact and indestructible some of the memories he must have forgotten.

One forgets very quickly. During the second hailstorm — just as I'd yelled (to no avail!) at the thunder to shut up — I met a man with two pigtails and four horses. He had an open face — like so many Tibetans, immediately cognisant, defenceless and obliging. When I asked him for matches he said he hadn't any, but that in two kilometres I would come to a place with matches. He jerked his head sideways and shut his eyes several times, indicating that I could also sleep there. I thanked him, and ploughed on through the hail, imagining a snug stone house, carpeted beds and cups of hot tea. Dream on! I forded the last river of the day — this time a clear knee-deep flow over smooth, rounded, white stones — and came just before nightfall to two small nomads' tents. The sky, after all the tempers and humours of the day, was now a clear turquoise. Nearby a group of people, who scarcely looked as if they came from this planet at all, made unearthly noises as they penned in a herd of sheep with ropes. The tents were very thin cotton, with scorched slits through which smoke came pouring out. Out of one of the vents also popped the gorgonian black head of a woman, and from the light of the fire leapt strange orange reflections ran across her startled face. She responded to my request for matches by looking at me as if I were the one who came from outer space. Then with a high-pitched yelp she called over one of the sheep-tenders. He had a stylish haircut which reminded me of a South Sea cannibal — short back and sides and very long wool on top that shot up to the sky. He gave me a handful of matches with tiny inefficient-looking green tips, and I filled my ragged box. He did smile, but everybody else stared at me so hard that I did not feel disposed to even put up my tent in the vicinity. With neither question nor explanation, I wandered on.

That night the full moon rose above the mountains beyond the direction of the nomads, and reverberated through the greenish night with a piercing white light. Using nearly the whole box of matches I was able to light one candle. The demons of the day were gone. Sky and mind were now permeated with a luminous, guileless air.

15 - The choo chembow

MORNING GLIDED IN on a magical lavender breeze and I read a passage from the *Bhagavad Gita*, as demon-substitute fodder for my mind. Here I was reminded that the mind should be steady whatever the weather, rain or shine. Though intended as metaphor for transcendence, I could not help but take the reference quite literally. For the moment, it was a happy association. The road changed, and rose in a steady incline out of the plains. Sun shone, the sky was blue, the clouds high, and though lightning flicked in the distance, no rain fell. Sweet scents sweated out of a net of purple flowers thrown over the grass, and sandy rats scampered in and out of holes at my approach. There was a sharp-eyed beauty to the day; a stream of fresh clean water accompanied the road a short walk away, and the whole of nature was buoyant.

Rocks stuck out of the sand, prehistoric teeth of the antediluvian inhabitants of this empty land. The inclination levelled out in a new table, over the edges of which the mountains of the narrowing valley peeped with a child-like curiosity. Was that smoke on the horizon or a mirage? No — yes? I didn't know till I came to it, about half an hour before sunset. Yes! Three solid black yak-hair tents surrounded by a flock of sheep. Inside the nearest I found ten nomads around a fire, and nineteen eyes surveyed me in somewhat astonished but not unfriendly reserve as I drank the lid-full of fresh yak's yoghurt they gave me. They also gave me a box of matches, far superior to the ones I'd begged the night before. Late evening sun streamed through the small cubes in the black mesh of the walls, and the Dalai Lama photo I gave them went straight away on the altar behind the fire. A one-eyed man presided, smoking a long cigarette made of chopped tobacco rolled in newspaper. With the other hand he scraped patterns in the dusty floor with the horn of a yak. What about the choo chembow? he asked. Wasn't I afraid? A woman on the other side of the fire made a cut-throat gesture with her index finger, indicating that I was liable to die. She threw back her head and roared in delight at the thought, and the whole lot of them joined in loudly. Even the baby at its mother's breast seemed amused. I smiled politely, polished the lid with my tongue, Tibetan style, and left shortly afterwards.

I walked on through an incredible wind to a spot sheltered by scrubby sand-dunes, with no water nearby. That night I dreamt I died, and in the morning I found nearby what seemed to be a gravestone on a mound of earth. But the Tibetans don't bury their dead in the earth, and surely no Chinese wanted to be buried here. Probably it was just an association produced by my churchyard-conditioned brain. I left promptly, not wishing to court any doubt, with the words of the day's reading from the *Bhagavad Gita* in my head: 'As the use of a well of water when water is to be found everywhere, so are the use of the Vedas to the man who has knowledge'.

At first I was glad to see it. Ashen blue-green with an iridescent sheen of lilac tumbling over white granite, the river appeared from nowhere and ran innocuously alongside the road. Seeing as it was Sunday, hair-washing day, I meandered down to the river, and delighted in its edge. The water was fast, and I was glad it didn't seem as if I had to cross it. Just as all was clean and purged, a biting wind nipped in and egged me on, worried at the socks that hung to dry from the straps of my rucksack. Feeling quite strange and dreamy, devoid of the usual savage determination to do nothing, once I'd started walking for the day, but put one foot in front of the other, I drifted off. Presently I looked up to an unwelcome sight: before me the vague tyre-tracks that were the road plummetted down to the river's edge, and reappeared on the other side.

This happened at a point where the river ejected in a sharp curve from the mountains. It gushed out and unbraided in lots of small rivulets, some shallow, some on cold boil and deep. Long straggly islands of pebbles intervened the flow. For about twenty minutes I tried to go island to island, through the shallows, in which the water was very cold and my feet and ankles lost all sensation. But there was no getting around it, however much I trailed up and down — there was this last strip to cross. It was not so wide — perhaps seven yards — but the river bed was invisible under the foam. It surged in front of me like some great wild green animal, terrifying and powerful. But I was obsessed with getting to the other side. I plunged in. Immediately the water was up to my chest, and all confidence left me as I felt its real strength. It tugged violently as my feet slithered over huge stones, groping for holds as I slipped in the direction of the flow. Eddies wrenched my sense of balance, and then I was down; the water tumbled me over the stones on the river bed, and under the water I opened my eyes to a fast wet white world, thinking, 'I'm down,' thinking that this was it, thinking of my body floating all the way down the Brahmaputra to Assam.

'Hare Krishna' — somehow my legs were stronger than I'd imagined, and by a reflex action up I shot again. The rucksack was all skew-wiff, pulling me down once more; for a second I tried to dislocate it, but before the second was up I realised how little I could afford to do this; things like passport, money, tent and warm dry clothing had no say in the matter, but what occurred to me was that the belt buckle took a few seconds to undo even when I was on dry land, and anyway the weight of the load lent me some stability. Even if I was precarious, I was upright, and while I was still upright I'd better move. The water was icy cold, but I was oblivious to that; all that mattered was propelling myself over to that far bank. Down again, up again, all backwards and dizzy and full of water, stumbling with the flow — somehow I jumbled across. I caught on a crescent shelf of caved-in bank where the cold water skimmed over my shoulders and rucksack; but I was out of the main drag, greedily blasting air in and out of my lungs. I stared at a tiny fly who skated on one of the pools of water that dripped from me into the sand. He had perfect shiny little wings in pale green and gold. He's alive and I'm alive. Life, life, life, I thought. Thank God.

After a couple of smaller channels I was through with the choo chembow, though I didn't realise it then. Piercing rain fell, and for the first time the close red walls of the hills seemed somehow cold and unfeeling. In full blast of the wind I changed into warm clothes, which, all sub-wrapped in plastic, had remained dry despite the dip. I carried on as usual, but was in a state of mild shock. My desire to be alone appeared as an absurd self-indulgence, and I'd be glad of somebody with me now.

About a kilometre up the road I came upon a group of wonderfully charitable nomads. They insisted that I should camp with them that night, and energetically helped me put up my tent. Afterwards they surveyed with satisfaction the job they had made of it: poles and guy-ropes projected at a selection of rakish angles, giving it a somewhat unconventional appearance, but more welcome than ever. One family in particular adopted me; they gave me tea and made sure I dried my shoes and socks. They made enquiries about a stove, and I replied that yes, a fire was no problem. I think they were eagerly awaiting me to conjure a space-age cooker from my rucksack; but when I did no such thing, and began picking up pieces of dried yak dung, they stopped me and led me to their fire. Here I cooked potato starch noodles with garlic. It was the first hot food for a week, and every soggy bland strand was exquisite. The family were a warm and quiet brood; patiently the man and wife explained new words of Tibetan to me, and the man drew maps on the floor of the road from here to Kang Rinpoche with a twig. This was the last choo chembow, he assured me. There were perhaps a few more small rivers, but none any deeper than the knees. And it was only five days' walking to there from here, or seven if I went *'kali, kali'* — slowly, slowly. As he traced diagrams of Kailash, of the koras and the surrounding gompas, something quickened, and the mountain seemed almost tangible.

In the evening rain I showed the children how to put water colours on paper, but they didn't seem to see any connection with what they put there and their surroundings — they just copied me. What amused them most was to help me do whatever I was doing, and to watch me wash my face and brush my teeth, to watch me drink tea and smoke a long cigarette of the local tobacco. They were astonishingly dignified and humorous, magical people of Arthurian honour and fairytale courtesy. Seven bowls of water sat on the wooden altar to a smoky picture of Guru Rinpoche, and a sleeping baby rested its head on a fat red cushion of yak meat.

That night I stayed awake for hours, pondering about Life. Opening *The Upanishads* at random, I read, aptly enough, about the question of which are the different powers that hold a being together, which keep burning the lamps of life, and which among them is supreme. The powers are space, air, fire, water, and earth, represented in a human being by voice, mind, the eye and the ear. The sage doing the talking describes how these elemental senses believed it was they themselves who lit the lamps of life, that it was they who united a being; Life, however, tended to disagree. 'Do not fall into delusion,' said Life to the bumptious senses, 'I'm the one who keeps you all together.' But the powers didn't believe him.

At which Life got offended, and rose aloft to leave the body — and the powers had no choice but to follow, just as a swarm is compelled to follow the queen bee when she moves. Then when Life relented and came back to rest again, the voice, mind, eye and ear realised from the jolt that they were mere servants of a far greater power than themselves. In joy they sang this song of life:

'Life is the fire that burns and is the sun that gives light. Life is the wind and the rain and the thunder in the sky. Life is matter and is earth, what is and is not, and what beyond is in Eternity.'

I wondered and marvelled at Life, at the thought that I might be now a bloated lump of meat dragging down the floor of the Brahmaputra. The senses were indeed powerful; they all converged upon the king sense, the mind, with their complaints — the weight of the rucksack, the obsessive desire for green vegetables, the stale grievances with which it agitated the luminously clear open spaces of Tibet. Yet now that senses, king and all, had been shocked into seeing how dependent they were upon Life for their being, these pathetic complaints sagged in a sorry

heap of dust at the bottom of my head — for the moment. I hoped that
they would stay there.

In the morning I ate tsampa as if it were the most delectable dainty
available on the globe. The woman seemed to catch the speciality of the
moment, for she had combed her hair so it hung in two loose plaits either
side of her head, and long loops of freshwater pearls appeared in her ears.
Life oozed beauty everywhere; the slow distilled movements of my
nomad hosts unfolded from a secret pattern and opened up every
moment, and every look and every gesture bloomed vivid with loveliness.
These people had not always lived here, like this: though they had
traditionally done so, there were dark years during the Cultural Revolution. All the nomads were forced into collective herding whereby they
served not the household, as before, but the communes. Wealthy nomads
were denounced as exploiters and dispossessed of surplus animals and
food-stores. Vigorous self-criticism and public abuse sessions disin-
tegrated social boundaries, and the communes were generally led by the
ones who had been poor before. Worthy as the Robin Hood approach
of communism was in ideal, in practice the system was undermined by
lack of enthusiasm; at one point the nomads rebelled, and the People's
Liberation Army was called in to quell them. Sullenly the nomads
complied; the men were cropped of their traditional pigtails and bushy
fringes, and many other features of their ethnic expression — such as the
private and public practice of religion — were suppressed. Then in 1981
the more enlightened policies of the post-Mao era dissolved the whole
commune system; every nomad was given an equal quota of livestock,
altars were reinstated in every tent and they reverted essentially to the
way of life they had known for centuries.

I couldn't even begin to guess at the full vicissitudes of their recent
history. Yet they exuded the spirit of an unbroken chain of ancestry living
in full joy off this barren earth, and their simplicity was no ignorance, but
a clear-sighted recognition of what is. Their sophistication was unique
even among Tibetans, and I thanked God for throwing me in the way of
these good people at this moment. Glad to be alive, scarcely feeling the
weight of my load as they lifted it onto my back for me, I bid them a very
grateful 'Tashi Dillee' and skipped off on a new wave of expectation.

16 - Up the pass

THE VALLEY AFTER this point narrowed into a long corridor. To the foot of the high cliff-walls great cubic monoliths had fallen, engraved with the universal mantra. They burned a wet gold in the rain, and quartz twinkled in the mud under my feet where shoals of stones swam, green and orange, red and purple. The river that yesterday had been my enemy ran today as my best friend alongside the road, and the road was scarcely more than a couple of faded tyre-tracks in the grit by now. Sometimes even these had been swept right away; I scrambled warily over the wobbly line of muddy rocks that edged the riverflow at the base of the cliff.

There was a close and strangely cosy feeling in the narrowing valley, presaging human connections. It seemed to have invited quite a population. After the first few kilometres the riverbanks widened into small sloping meadows, and from the first group of black yak-hair tents I was greeted by a woman gliding down with a smile, a friendly jerk of the arm and the happy sound of: 'Cha dhoo!'

So unexpectedly soon I found myself sitting by a fire again in the raw homespun security of a nomad tent, drinking a never-ending cup of salt and buttered tea. With the same quiet and regal hospitality as my hosts of the night before, the woman brought out of some box two chapattis and some yoghurt, and put them before me. I was grateful but disbelieving, and wolfed them down quickly, in case they should vanish back into the ether whence they had come. The mother watched me, and seemed to approve.

The whole family approved when this weird-looking guest of theirs brought out a small photo album full of pictures from my brother's wedding. The nomads clustered about with fascination at the absurdities of life beyond Tibet: high white heels stabbed the turf of an English churchyard, a white wedding dress belled out in immaculate cleanliness, beer cans hovered, captured and poised by the shutter. Out of context, these tableaux of middle-class English convention were already so curious to me that I could have had sartorial attacks on the theme of being and nothingness; fortunately, I was kept so busy answering their questions that there was no opportunity to indulge.

'Are these Inji clothes?' they asked. 'Are these Inji shoes?' 'Inji' is the loose definition of nationality Tibetans generally give to Westerners, and as an explanation can justify all mysteries. The fabric of my rain-coat was

'Inji cloth', my tent an 'Inji' tent. When I replied yes, these were all Inji things — here the Inji temple and there the Inji lama — they nodded, satisfied, and told each other about it. They were particularly interested in which were my parents, and at the sight of my father in grey morning suit and my mother in a natty netted little hat — yes, this was an Inji coat and that an Inji hat — they jerked their thumbs up and down in the Tibetan gesture of approval: 'Yagadoo, yagadoo!'

When the mother and father of the household had finished with the little red book, a whole gang of ragged children pounced upon it to fight for the honour of turning the pages, of telling the others which was my mother and which my father, which my brother and which my sister, that this was an Inji temple and these were Inji shoes.

This was another family of the sort I had begun to believe had ceased to exist. They stared, but not much; were courteous, did not touch my things unless I offered them, asked for nothing and seemed only to give out friendliness from their gentle eyes. They were intent on offering me whatever they had that might help me, and when the crowd of children dwindled away they continued to fill my mug as soon as I'd sipped half an inch of tea. I produced some jars of creams, which interested them greatly. Especially captivated — and captivating — was their son, Guang-cho, a boy of ten years old who ran around in a pair of ragged trousers and flimsy shoes, finding humour in everything. Into his naked filthy torso he rubbed handfuls of sweet-scented Avon and aloe vera Forever Living, over and over delighting in the way the murky unguents swilled about his brown skin before suddenly disappearing right into it. When his parents had to go out to attend to the sheep, they left me with strict instructions not to move till they came back. Guangcho was in charge. Again and again he competently rustled up the sheep's droppings which burnt in the rusty cylinder of the fireplace, so as to keep the tea perpetually hot; and never did I have less than half a cup of tea before me. I smoked another of the long cigarettes of the local tobacco, and no disapproval stained the enjoyment of it. I gave them a bottle and a half of the scented factory potions, a Dalai Lama photo for their altar, and, feeling completely rested and revived, set off again up the valley.

Then for hours my only society was the river. Side by side with the beautiful coils that had nearly killed me I walked, and the higher I got, the more refined and clear the water and its song, till I was hopping over, drinking from, washing in — a small clear stream. The grasp on Kailash quickened; for some reason, today neither back nor hip ached — or, if they did, I didn't notice it. My legs went under me like a couple of pistons, despite the fact that now I was palpably climbing for the first time, and I felt full of the living force of the mountain. The magnetism drew me up and on over the vague path, rarefied my brain, and enlivened the whole day.

Somewhere in the long evening I passed another nomad encampment; but this time the people scarcely greeted me, being primarily concerned with establishing whether or not I had a lover with me. 'Roga? Roga?' they asked, several times, flipping their wrists as they directed alienating stares at me, refusing to take my 'Mindoo' of denial as a satisfactory answer. And then when just as night fell I had the temerity to approach the occupants of more tents, and to ask them if they happened to have any tobacco — the dark shape of a man turned ferociously on me. 'Lama Lama!' he yelled at me, throwing stones at the dogs who simultaneously howled about their fire. 'Mindoo! Mindoo!' — meaning I was barking up the wrong tree. He was quite right of course. It was the first time I had asked for anything beyond matches, and it would do me no good to acquire a taste for this local tobacco.

So I hurriedly rattled up the track in the dark to find my own spot by the scintillating stream under the cold stars. That night it was chilly, but I slept well, feeling finally as if I was approaching an introduction to the spirit that had drawn me this far.

Yet, having decided that, the constant rain of the following day disinclined me to get up till the middle of the afternoon. Perched in my nylon capsule with the tent flaps ajar I luxuriated pleasantly in solitude, reading and feasting. It seemed a suitable day to dig out a packet of cheese that had come all the way from the supermarket in Hong Kong. The wrapper was mouldy from repeated duckings and I couldn't even read what sort it was any more, and the mould veined the cheese with wiggles of verdigris; but whatever sort, mixed with tsampa, the last of the butter, Vegemite and streamwater, it was exquisite.

When I was finally up and packing away the more or less dry tent, a spritely old Tibetan man popped out from behind a rock. He sat and chanted 'Om mani padme hum' as I sorted and buckled, and he salvaged the withered plastic Hong Kong supermarket bag I'd been going to bury under a pile of stones. He was absolutely delighted with the treasure, and thanked me three times. Then the politest Tibetan I ever met vanished as skilfully as he had arrived.

There was not much time to go too far that day, but the elongated evening of sunshine brought me over a pass riddled with streams and buttercups. The main stream was the one which had accompanied me for the last few days, guileless parent to the ferocious adolescent flood below. Finally even that was just a frail emanation of waterdrops seeping from the green hillside, and I gathered by the map that this was one of the three major sources of the Brahmaputra. It became absorbed in the past; the hillside jetted up now into a *lha-tse* of stones, where prayer flags flew to mark the top of the pass in the thin air. I did homage to whatever spirits had brought me safely here by putting up a stone and circum-ambulating.

In the twilight, as the road veered though a sort of space-warped gathering of mountains and decided which way it was going to take, I deviated to examine a strange outcrop. It jutted out of an otherwise green and gentle hillside, and was invested with natural turrets of red and green, sliced with white crystal, all grown about with rich crops of nettles — just the sort of rock a mystic should found his hermitage upon. Looking about at the ring of new mountain ranges it seemed impossible that the Red Army could have penetrated so far. Maybe there were still some ascetics tucked away in the dark blue creases? And even if all the caves were empty, the rare air that filled them was full of invisible vitality yet.

Camp that night was on the lower lip of a decline. The ground was stony, the wind cold, and the view over the direction I was going was of a new range of deep blue snow-capped mountains at whose dark feet seemed to flow a river.

17 - Past the salt lake to the first sight

THE WATER GLEAMED in the starlight, but by daylight assumed a modest, graphite tinge before blurring into the mild meadows about. It proved to be a large oval salt lake which took two days to walk past; and as for the deep blue mountains, they slid on at my approach to an indeterminate space ahead. They later turned out to be the Gurla Mandhata, the mountain range that separates the Kailash region from

Nepal — but I didn't know that then. All the same, it was evident that 'the land of the gods' was not so far off now.

The whole of nature contributed to the general clarity — days continued to be blue and sunny, sweet-smelling flowers bloomed, birds piped, and I was able to bathe in clear streams, feast my eyes on the beauty everywhere, and cook on fires of dried yak dung every night. I'd never expected that I could find packet soup and noodles so delicious, but here they were — days of miracle and wonder. The water was a great frosted sheet of blue-green black, depending on the sky. Deceptive distances separated me from the water's edge, and from their spaces came one morning a scattered herd of a hundred or so wild horses. I'd read about them in Heinrich Harrer's account, and was delighted to see that they still roamed here wild and free. *Kyang,* they're called. They were dun dots at first, and then they bucked, pranced and snorted into focus. Their necks arched as they cantered, with the same tight rocking motion as circus horses, into a curious wide horseshoe about me. Even in the midst of all this solitude, they still insisted on moving in a herd. If one should get separated from the rest, and then see me — its eyes would boggle out of its head and it wouldn't rest its hooves till, with squeaking noises that sounded like someone bouncing on a sofa, it had rejoined the gang.

One night I camped on the extra-green banks of a clear stream that fed the lake, but by the next night the lake was left behind. I'd descended to a land of deep green marshy meadows run with thick narrow bands of clear water, and the only raised ground was over-run with walls and sheep droppings. A stream ran by and prayer flags waved — but there was human offal too. Old sheepskins, old shoes, a goat's foot, a yak's leg — these things seemed to get into the smoke and the taste of the noodles that night, and I did not feel so great there. By morning the valley and hills were white with snowfall, and I took care the following night to pitch camp in a place of open nature — not that there was any choice.

The road took me from valley to valley. Sun made gold the dull green hills underfoot and illuminated in unearthly splendour one mani wall that marked the meeting of two valleys. In a state of suspense now, my whole being was alert and efficient; the mind had done with brooding bad eggs and just quietly hatched plots for stories it would probably never write. As for the body, it simply walked. I'd been walking for nearly three weeks, and had covered several hundred miles; it had become painlessly mechanical, soothing as a mantra, to put one foot in front of the other. I had eaten enough of the weight to be able to raise my head and see a little of the mountains as I walked, and for the moment I was happy to walk forever.

That night the fire was a miracle worked by the one last match upon a tiny scrap of scratch, and in the middle of the night I was driven by thirst down to the river to fill my water bottle. As I squatted on the banks, the waning moon came out and formed a fine silvery path across the water. Oh, how beautiful were the days and nights now! Quite another universe from the grey cold rain of the plains.

Then the wide open blue of the morning turned to a thick bruise of rainstorm that never quite fell, and the road led down a valley which any moment or any day might open onto Lake Manasarovar. Two eagles flew up from behind a rock, and I saw small heaps of lha-tse ahead. Tibetans pile up these stones to mark the sight of anything holy — and there it was, a huge streak of turquoise blue ahead of me — Mapam Yumco, Manasarovar, Lake of the Mind — the highest and holiest lake in the world. I felt something cracking apart inside me, breaking and pushing through the flesh and the blood, running along the neurons with the insistence of a flood. It was a smile that crashed across my face, indelible and unstoppable, followed by a mild wash of hysteria. Grinning, I added my stones and walked rapidly on.

I was obsessed by the desire to camp by the shore that night, but the more I walked, the more innocently the lake hovered at the same apparent distance. I'd been able to see Manasarovar for hours, it seemed, but it was always a turquoise streak tied up with indigo mountains under a deep-pile Prussian blue sky. Then I had to ford another stream. Walking barefoot in case I should have to ford another, I ascended a small hill at the other side of the stream. Looking up for the thousandth time in the direction where Kailash should be, I saw the low dim clouds of the west split apart. Out darted an urgent light. There it was — a faraway regular dome of ice, scored with a great black cross. It could only be Mount Kailash.

I was stung in the solar plexus, the same pang one gets upon seeing a loved one unexpectedly — I burst into tears and threw myself, rucksack and all, down in a prostration to match the one with which the walk had begun, in gratitude for having been brought safely to such a vision, such a place. It was a major event in my life: I had seen Kailash. And having seen, could hardly take my eyes off it.

The greatness of Mount Kailash was obvious, even from this distance. It rose up out of an ordinary-enough looking mountain range and stood alone, a little back and aloof, surrounded by gold-lined clouds that threatened any moment to wrap it all up again. Kang Rinpoche, the precious Jewel of the Snows, was protected. Everything was justified, everything was just as it should be, quite in its place in the quiet realm beyond.

To mark the occasion, there then happened the most flamboyant sunset I have ever experienced. I did not just see or witness it — it was all around, a multi-dimensional event. The split in the western clouds widened, opened up a great abyss of ethereal blue light. Golden clouds sailed across that — but I've seen golden clouds on ethereal blue before, especially up here; no, these were extra-surreal. Not the mere gateway or touchstone to heaven, but heaven itself, floating above the indigo lake. Every direction poured forth colours that shone with an intensity such as I'd never seen before: the snow of the Gurla Mandhata, binding the southern shore, took on the patina of dusky roses rustling out of deeper shades; strands of luminous gold-pink clouds festooned the mountain peaks, and swords of green gold separated their feet from the violet depths. I turned about in all directions, hypnotised, unable to even take the time to remove the rucksack, saturated by the changing colours.

I did not reach the shore that night, but camped where the river flowed at the foot of the escarpment I'd been following for the last couple of days. The river was now miles away, and snaked at an even greater distance into the lake; by my tent eeled a tangle of sandy bedded streams. The wind howled like crazy but I slept peacefully and entranced, aligned in mind, body and spirit, to the light breeze.

Part Three

18 - First bathe

THE STREAK OF Manasarovar beyond the open tent flap was an elusive turquoise. The green grass was lightly overgrown with pom poms of wild garlic, and the early morning light of the sky stunned the moment with its electrifying blue. Feeling weightless as the air, I dashed up the escarpment for a view of Kailash. I had entered the *dharm*.

Dharm is the Sanskrit word for a place sacred not only because it is a centre of veneration, but because it is inherently holy. According to the Hindus, Kailash is an embassy of the spiritual world, a reception room on earth for a higher mode of consciousness. There are certain ways of thinking which, in accordance with this belief, must be avoided in order that the dharm be appreciated as the dharm. For example, it is an offence to consider Kailash as an ordinary place, located in Tibet or China; Kailash on earth is a manifestation of the Kailash to be found at Shiva's planet, Shivalokha. It is an offence to consider people who live in a dharm as ordinary people, an offence to break any regulative principles while in the dharm (such as gambling or eating meat), and any pious activities performed in the dharm are a thousand times greater in effect than any performed outside. Entering a dharm is like entering the spiritual world. It was easy to see how such beliefs had sprung from Kailash. A vast harmonious balance of earth, water and sky encompassed the white peak. No reputation for splendour had ever been so richly deserved. Just to look at it was to forget about anything else, and even when Kailash itself wasn't visible, the air was charged always with its presence.

It was Sunday, appropriately enough, for Manasarovar is the lake of the sun. The sun in turn represents the mind, and with it all positive, masculine, creative forces. At last I was able, not only to get out and wistfully study, but to actually use, the photocopied map of the Kailash-Manasarovar region that the Frenchman in Shigatze had given me. It was a map drawn by Swami Pranavananda in 1949. The Swami made many trips to Kailash, and explored the whole area more thoroughly than anyone else; he combined scientific enquiry with mysticism as he merrily sailed his rubber dinghy *Janma Bhoomi* across the waters of the holy lakes, taking soundings. His book *Kailash Manasarovar*, which I had not yet then been lucky enough to read, amounts to a comprehensive geographical and spiritual guide-book. The only differences on the map between 1949 and now had already been marked by the Frenchman, and they were

not as great as they had been: about half of the monasteries destroyed by
the Chinese in the Cultural Revolution had been rebuilt and were
operating again today. The roads and paths remained the same.

Had I continued walking along the road — which in any case I'd
abandoned a couple of hours before nightfall yesterday — to Kailash, I
would have gone along the northern shore of the lake in an anti-clockwise
direction. Though not personally allied to any form, it seemed only
respectful to accord with the religion of the country and do a clockwise
kora of the lake before approaching the holy mountain itself. In any case
— once I reached Kailash there was the possibility of encountering
Authority; if I was to be sent off with a flea in my ear, I wanted to have
had some experience of the holy land first. Also, there were hot springs
marked on the map, somewhere up the bank of a river that ran into the
lake on the eastern shore. Hot springs would be nice, too. Accordingly,
that morning I cut off diagonally leftwards and headed for that hovering
southern shore. The river story was still not completely over — shortly
after I set out it was necessary to cross one more. The swift current
dragged at my shaking pins, breath came fast in and out of the dry tunnel
of my throat. I turned mid-stream to look at Kailash; it was an axis of
security, and maybe the dependence just a placebo — but in any case, it
worked. I was calmed instantly.

The clouds hadn't yet got to the sky above the lake by the time I finally
came to its shore of sand. The water shone its magic mirror in the sun,
and I tore off my clothes in a flash. In a second I was in the water which,
despite the sun, was very cold; but it was a clear sweet nectar, just as the
Hindus say it is. They also say that to bathe in the waters is to absolve
the sins of a lifetime. I wasn't quite so sure, but carried on ducking myself
under in a primitive baptism, marvelling. The sins of a lifetime? Really?
Sins capered across the inner eye, and I'd plunge below the surface again.
The forgiving lake splashed away the shadows. What, even that one too?
So it would seem: the water dashed the memory-slate clean. Whether or
not I was absolved, at least the follies of the past didn't seem to matter
very much any more.

I wondered if those sands were the golden sands of which I'd read,
held by tradition to be compounded of the dust of precious and semi-
precious stones. A scattered group of people flowed over the hill,
whistling at a herd of yaks. They took no notice of me. A little further
on I passed mani walls on hillocks, which, I gathered from the map,
marked the recessed presence of Seralung Gompa. Soon I came upon
two children who were praying on their knees by the lakeshore in the

direction of Kailash, now fast disappearing behind the clouds. They sprang up at my approach with bright spontaneous smiles and 'Tashi dillee!'s, and told me they came from Seralung Gompa. They invited me back there with them, but I was happy by the lake. There was something astonishing about their self-confidence, about the profundity of their devotion as they saluted the mountain before shouldering their baskets of roots and yak dung and taking their leave. Tibetan faith seems to have nothing in it of fear or evasion, or even the passion of transcendence; rather the believers, regardless of age, school or station, are flooded with the clear light of simple open good nature.

Sharing all these qualities was a Bon-pa I met later. The Bon-po (*'pa'* refers to an individual, *'po'* to the whole lot of them) are followers of Bon, Tibet's primordial, animistic religion, and many of their practices have been taken and married with Buddhist doctrines to form the distinctly esoteric streak that characterises the Buddhism of Tibet. The Bons in turn have taken and incorporated many things from Buddhism into their own rites. I'd never knowingly met a Bon-pa before, and knew little about them except that they practise black and white magic, and that they circumambulate holy places in an anti-clockwise direction. The associations seemed vaguely sinister, but this happy man dispelled them all. We walked towards each other on the lakeshore, and stopped when we met.

'Why are you walking this way and I that way?' I asked him.

'Bon-po, Bon-po!' he responded, waving a staff to include all fellow-believers in his mission. He was dressed entirely in maroon corduroy with a woolly orange hat on top of his shaved head, and seemed to carry no luggage. It's often surprising what Tibetans manage to tuck into the pouches of their robes, however; perhaps he was carrying a kettle large enough to slake ten people's thirst at once, plus bellows to speed up the process, and I just didn't see them. Planting his staff in the sand he demonstrated for me his mantra upon the white prayer beads strung about his left wrist. There was neither vocabulary nor inclination for theosophical discussions, but we established our mutual adoration of the mountain before continuing on our ways with smiles. I followed his bare footprints in the sand at the lake's edge for miles.

Small black flies flew in clouds out of the low scrub that covered the hills about the lake's edge, and great brown beetles rose up with abrupt helicopter whirs. The sand turned to rocks, more difficult to tread, and I walked towards nightfall in a rattling dream of hot springs. Then I came to another river. Cold, thick, murky, fast and wide — I took one look and began to shake again. Terrified, I began to walk upstream, determined to walk to the source rather than wade it — when lo! A bridge! Rickety indeed, the wide gaps between wooden slats sometimes filled with stones, sometimes not — with prayer flags attached to the steel wires that held it all together — but it was a bridge. Beside it was a small lha-tse decorated with yak skulls and flags, and joyfully I circumambulated and added three stones in gratitude.

That night, dissolved in a sort of solitary bliss that pervaded every dimension, I camped on a patch of sand in the scrub-covered dunes up above the lake. When I awoke it was Monday morning, the eighth of the eighth of '88. I began the day by putting into my cup the last of the sack of muesli I'd brought from Hong Kong, mixing it with streamwater and finishing it off. Kailash was completely invisible under heavy green-blue clouds, and under a similar sort of torpor myself, I proceeded quickly before it should begin to rain.

That day was heavy going, at first. So much for absolution by ablution. Triggered by a dream, vengeful demons tore bitterly through my mind, so I had to sit down by the lake where occasional sunshine snagged at the waves, and here I tried to reason with myself. Tibetan Buddhism reckons that the greatest demons that we can encounter are the negative thoughts that arise out of our own minds. They thrive on the negative face of ego, and the vilest things do best in the corners that the conscious mind squashes them into. Alone in such a place it was obvious that I had no-one to blame for these disruptions but myself. Gradually the demons were absorbed by the lakewater. How long for I did wonder, but now was now and eternal in the land of the gods.

Here on a hill facing the hidden mountain were many more mani walls. They were always a reminder of the intangible good company of all those who had trodden here before me and of all who would tread it after. Looking at each of these stones — some carved with the mantra, others simply humble stones picked up from the ground and placed there, and imagining each one of them as representing the eyes of one who has stood on that spot and looked at Kailash — I felt one of a great congregation. A congregation with the natural priest of Kailash to preach wordless messages from the high white pulpit of the gods — no fire and brimstone here, but only fresh air and clean clear water. It was raining. Slowly I moved on, towards the great blue-purple mass of the Gurla Mandhata rising above the southern shore.

19 - Thugolho Gompa

I NEVER DID find those hot springs. Instead at mid-evening I was surprised to come upon an odd arrangement consisting of a tractor, to which were attached the guy ropes of a tent, and a row of eight concrete houses. Outside the last room a man in a baseball hat squatted over a puddle, and near him played two children.

He looked like he might smoke, so I asked him for a cigarette. It was the first since the local tobacco a week ago, and tasted pretty uninteresting by comparison. As for matches — well, it was raining, and as I obviously wouldn't be able to make a fire tonight I didn't bother begging any further. We sat in companionable silence, watching the rain. From time to time the man spat into the puddle he was guarding, which raised delighted imitation from the two children. One child was quite smart, with split pink knitted trousers — the man's daughter. The other was really ragged and spare, with a pinched knowing face and lively black eyes. Spit, spit, spit they went, shrieking with the joy of achievement. Then the laughter turned to tears and screams; the little smart one lay howling while the ragged one stalked off with a superior air in the direction of the tents.

The mystery of what these rooms were doing here was solved as soon as I rounded the corner: here was a small gompa, undergoing renovation, and the rooms must be attached to it in some capacity or another. Actually, though I didn't know it then, they could be rented from the gompa for ten or twenty kwai a night. Peering into one of the rooms of the gompa I saw men at work. The ceiling of the room was hung with printed Rajastani sheets from India, and one bright-eyed young man in maroon robes presided over the installation of a huge prayer wheel in the centre. Absorbed in their work, they cast me friendly glances of recognition, and got on with it. I was glad to be insignificant again.

Inside the monastery itself, round a tiny courtyard, were built a few mud rooms. A cat prowled about with kittens in her mouth, an old man in a corner chanted mantras in a state of semi-transport, but it seemed otherwise deserted. The meditation hall was closed, and a carpet hung over the door. But the guardians of the four directions were faithfully, simply and beautifully painted outside. As I stood regarding them, drinking in the first bit of established religion I'd encountered for weeks,

I was invited by a young monk into the kitchen to wash it all down with some tea.

The kitchen was a dark room that extended the length of the second floor, reached by an uncertain flight of wooden steps. The walls were matt black from the perpetual smoke of the fires. One end was il-luminated by orange lashes of flame that leapt out of the fire, presided over by a small old woman who made sure that I got the warmest fireside seat. This seemed to displace a nun there, but when I protested, the nun threw a sheepskin at me and gave what was evidently a convincing discourse on how she was hot and tired of sitting right next to the fire. I allowed myself to be convinced, brought out my tin mug and plate, and they were filled with hot butter tea and tsampa, seasoned with sugar. They asked me how this tsampa was different from that which we eat in England, and they were amazed and horrified to learn that we don't. No? What do English people eat, then? — and meanwhile my cup never ceased to be filled with hot butter tea, and I noticed that my name was 'Acha' — the name used for servants, without the honorific 'la'. I've been in many rich and sumptuous houses, but even with all honour and all their gold-picked cornices and polished mahogany staircases — this was the most impressive of them all, certainly the perfect place for that rainy moment. Every grain of tsampa and crystal of sugar was registered on my tongue and I gloried in the luxurious warmth of everything.

The old woman answered to the name of 'Ama' — mother — and the kitchen was her kingdom; anyone that came in there was immediately her family. She was constantly in motion, constantly singing mantras with an unqualified joy. Now she'd be puffing up the fire with a pair of sheepskin bellows, now pouring hot water into the great butter tea-churn as she yelled: 'Atta — ah — on!' with the full force of her lungs, grinning hugely, now filling up everybody's tea-cup, now pausing to listen atten-tively to something someone had to say, to stick out her tongue in full recognition of what they were saying — not for one second was she unoccupied, yet a competent precision stilled her every action.

The nun's smile was equally wide and generous, but she limited her activities to fetching the water and chanting 'Om mani padme hum'. A woolly orange hat sat upon her shaven head and she, like all nuns in Tibet, answered to 'Ani-la'. I gave her the remains of my jar of Tiger Balm for her knees, which she had bruised while crossing the same swift knee-deep river that had shortened my breath with fear yesterday morn-ing. This delighted her so much that she showed me, wrapped in many layers of ragged cotton, a small silver cross which she said had fallen to her out of the sky in Lhasa. '*Tok-cha, tok-cha,*' she repeated over and over as she indicated the heavens. Somehow she was the easiest Tibetan to understand that I ever met — it wasn't just because she spoke the Lhasa dialect, but had to do with the fact that she took the trouble to speak slowly and clearly, would repeat herself if I didn't seem to understand, and simply would not entertain for a second the concept that I didn't speak her language.

Other people drifted in and out of the kitchen: an old mad mute proclaiming in fluent gestures the virtues of Instant Noodles; several novice monks in ordinary clothes; the bright-eyed young man in robes who had presided over the prayer wheel. He had obvious authority; when he came in the others all leapt to their feet, and he it was who invited me to stay there that night in the kitchen. Perhaps he was also the Rinpoche who the others kept talking about; when one of them rushed in with some candles from Rinpoche they all expressed their delight, and when a cup of consecrated tea also came in from Rinpoche we all had to smear a bit on our foreheads before the rest was poured into the pot, that the precious prashadan could be shared by all. Prashadan is a Sanskrit term that means food which has been blessed by being first offered to God; in this case it was the lama who had sanctified what we ate.

So I stayed sitting there all evening, watching the rapidly failing light through the rough rectangle in the roof out of which the smoke sometimes went. Ama-la kept filling my cup with tea, Ani-la chanted on her beads beside me, and the two young novice monks kept me entertained by drawing maps and two kinds of indecipherable Tibetan scripts in my diary. One of them came from Kumbum, near the big blue lake of Koko Nor. He took such a fancy to the Mickey Mouse watch that I gave it to him — Mickey didn't tell the time very well nowadays in any case, but his head could jerk sideways as engagingly as ever. Enthralled, unable to believe it, the young man fastened the bright plastic gimmick to his wrist and went on kneading at a basin of dough. Like a couple of children the pair of them divided their basin of dough into long strands, which they looped about their left wrists in the manner of prayer beads when not in use. Then, working in unison and with a stunning speed, they nipped bits one after the other off the end of the loops, and hurled a tirade of dough-pellets into the pot of boiling Chinese leaf on the fire, grins splitting their faces to see my entertainment. I took a strand, and joined in. Later the owner of the new watch presented me with a large picture of Dolma (He said it the Tibetan way, 'Droma') Kermu in red and gold, and wrote a long accompanying piece in Tibetan to go with it. When the candle died he shone his torch so I could write. These attentions, if inspired by Mickey Mouse, were nonetheless pure in their content.

I slept in a sort of trough running along the back of the kitchen wall. From the room below infiltrated the sound of a woman chanting mantras all night. The gompa was constructed of burnt orange earth, and the walls reverberated gently with the sound, as if it was the earth itself that was speaking.

It was the repetition of mantras that awoke me in the morning as Ama-la rolled indefatigably in, throwing water all over the floor and reviving the fire. I went out to wash and to bring back water from the lake's edge. Kailash across the water was still under a cloud, but sunlight leaked out in three places and shone thinly onto the dark morning surface of the water, sharpened the tridents that stood guard on the roof in the exact chestnut shade of the bands that ran round the upper rims of these squat cubic constructions. Water weed had sculpted itself into equally matching heaps about the lake's edge. My vision was hazy with ignorance: what did I know of the messages encoded in the mantras? But it seemed pretty obvious that here, religion was a natural expression of the environment. Where else could it have come from?

This gompa was a rare place. Everyone present there seemed pervaded by a constant awareness of the holiness of the very earth they trod on. Everyone was happy to serve in unspoken co-ordination a power transcending all the limitations of the self. Everyone perpetually worked and sang, everyone was happy; and in the flux was the same stillness, even amongst the bustle of the many, as characterised Ama-la's perpetual motion. Now she was scraping a pot — I sat beside the fire digesting a hillock of tsampa, and surveyed all the various activities going on in the kitchen. In the corner by the door an ancient man was trying to light a cigarette, and having endless trouble deciding which of two boxes of matches to use. Another woolly-capped Ani-la had appeared, and her sharp and mobile features followed her restless eyes about the room in a silent battery of comments, as she and Ani-la dipped long pink proboscises in and out of their bowls of tsampa. The two novices gleefully fought one another as they chopped up firewood in a corner, and now Ama-la was feeding the fire. She seemed to animate everything she touched — the shaggy sheepskin bellows breathed with hearty life under the sure clamp and release of her black fingers; the fire roared up in response; the huge black pot of water began to sing. It was as if the very earth had come alive alive-o — floor, walls and stone were composed of the earth, and the colours of the people and their clothes unified with it. As Ama-la put her tsampa back on the shelf, a stab of sunlight lit up the red sash around her *chuba,* with the same surprise as when the sun comes out and picks out the vermilion hills. The old man abandoned his cigarette and took to winding raw wool onto a rough stick, with the same persistent pull that controls the clouds across the skies. Yak dung smoke swirled up the blade of sunlight with the liquid irregularity of water, and voices perpetually murmured. The mantra rolled on and on from the depths of throats young and old, uniting in its vibration the deeper connotations of the original sound; the people, in their whole-hearted devotion, were devoid of self-consciousness; their faith simply annihilated the common diseases of humanity. This was no euphoria of separation from ordinary, mundane matters, but rather a complete integration of spiritual with material. Through the humblest activities was the highest bliss invoked. Time as the world knows it was registered only by the engaging but inaccurate plastic Mickey Mouse watch from Hong Kong. They seemed conscious that they were vessels, sent to convey the spirit of God through the song of the earth.

20 - Gossul Gompa

THE KAILASH MOUNTAIN range was a dull line of bashed pewter that morning, Kailash itself mugged throughout the day by accumulated clouds. A pity, as I wanted to paint the sight of the white peak across the blue of the lake, but it was a sight I never saw. Still, here was Manasarovar. In *The Way of the White Clouds*, Lama Anagarika Govinda mentions how the sun always shines over Manasarovar, and indeed this seemed to be the case; as if by consent to the wish of some invisible vortex in the sky high over the centre of the lake, all the clouds left the sky clear here and collected only at the rim. The sun was free to ply all its riotous tricks upon the water and the variety of hues conjured up between blue and green was eye-consuming. Here was the deep decadent ultramarine velvet of a sixties pop star's pants, there the worthy green of all the marble quarries of Connemara after the rain, there a sensuous swirl of smuggled jade where a river curled in. A strong wind tore at all the surfaces of the water, the sun caught every turning, and the scintillation of the lake set subtly afire all the wild colours there.

Many people have correlated colour to mood, and there has been quite a lot of academic talk about how the language of colours can transport us to the Antipodes of the mind. The subtle intensity of the Manasarovar colours penetrated to inner regions not usually considered by conscious-ness; trying to pin the colours down with descriptions, they would change even as the words fell into place. Here was enacted the full parable of illusion: here was the beautiful distracting play of the material world, illuminated by one all-pervading light. It was better not to think, better to just keep walking in the practised way, and dance with the flux.

A river from the Gurla Mandhata splayed into a delta of rivulets through rich green spongy marshes bordering the southern edge of the lake. Furry grey stars of edelweiss and the yellow trumpet flowers grew in the long grass, and I ate quite a few of the latter. As the southeastern corner is somewhat chopped away, this is the shortest shore. Soon I was turning northwards, and the corner curve encompassed the edge of an extra lake, shining with pink gravel, adding another slant to the fantastic colour scheme. I began the straight line towards Barga along the western shore, which here was littered with hundreds of dead moor-hens. I did not stop for lunch — of the interminable 761 biscuits and strawberry jam — until I'd passed the sinister flotsam, and even then I found a dead waterbird lurking behind the rock I chose to shelter me from the wind. The water was innocent of pollution, so I could only conclude these deaths had been the result of a storm. They were a sorry contrast to the legendary swans who are supposed to glide over the sacred waters.

The Gurla Mandhata mountain range is known as the Swastika Mountain, because this is the shape it takes; the northern arm, which divides the two lakes of Manasarovar and Rakastal, rose now up to my left, completely eliminating even any possibility of seeing Kailash. Walk-ing today, I saw no-one, and the only human trace I came across was a torch lying on the path. Having no torch, I picked it up. Several hours later I came to some caves in the pudding stone cliffs that now bounded the lake's edge. They were quite large, with a couple of chambers strewn about with piles of clean dry water weed from the lake. The ceiling was in a halfway state of petrifaction and the bubbling conglomerate of stones embedded there shone black from many past yak dung fires, freckled with pale brown patches where bits had dropped down. Though many people must have passed through here over the years of its formation, the only visible trace of their passage was the dry waterweed. The mouth of the cave framed a view of the lake that lit up the inside, and the accumulated tranquillity of all who had slept and opened their eyes to this view pervaded the air.

At the top of the cliff a small flagged chorten marked the presence of a gompa. It had to be Gossul Gompa. I ascended a very steep path of moving scree to the top, and came upon the small squat monastery. I later saw a photo of the ruins to which the thorough purge of all things old by the People's Liberation Army had reduced the former building. Renovation under religious reform had been successful, and it now sat as peacefully as ever in its remote patch. Not so peaceful was the dog that yowled and screamed from a stone kennel by the entrance, but his tantrum did alert an old man from the kitchen, who came out and invited me in.

First he ushered me into a lovely temple room lined with silk-spun Buddhas and hung with coloured cloth. A couple of monks, one young and one old, sat and chanted from block-books of sutras. They ceased after a while, to mildly quiz me with the usual questions. At each answer the older of the two had a way of looking me up and down, and laughing derisively, though not unkindly. He must have seen the warped illusion and vain dreams that dripped from my not so subtle body, but he did take me on a short tour of the temple. It was a quiet retreat, composed of symbols I understood little of. What I liked best was the vast wide blue view of the lake through the glass windows, where the white frilled curtains fluttered on the outside lids in wild eyelashes.

Entrusted then to the care of the old man I was taken to the kitchen and given several cups of hot water, to which I added cocoa mix. The old man chanted his rounds on his beads and, apart from offering me more hot water from time to time, seemed indifferent to my presence. It was clean, neat and well-equipped here compared with last night's gompa, quiet without the raucous laughter of the mob.

For an hour or so I sat upon an old rug of intricate design, drinking cocoa and writing. The fireplace was a tin can with a cylindrical chimney, and on it clustered a whole crowd of pots. Phoenix and dragon-decorated thermoses stood in a line, and as water boiled the old man would fill them up. A digital clock sat telling time upon a small wooden stool; a bowl of Chinese leaf, almost fresh, sat on the floor of swept earth; china cups with brass lids, dragons flying about their sides, studded spare surfaces about the room; and in the corner stood a clean wicker basket of brushwood — not yak dung. Daylight still poured in strongly through a glass window, and I judged by the clock that I had about four hours in which to go and scour the hillsides for the hot springs marked by the map.

Leaving my luggage there for the moment, I bounded all over the ridge between the two lakes. I scanned every likely area for wisps of steam — there were only the smooth heaped rumples of orange earth, plummed with fist-sized pebbles of granite and scented not with sulphur but with ethereal odours from clumps of shrub. The last sun sprang out of the clouds — I saw a turquoise curl of dull gleaming water set in the orange stone valley beyond — and that was Lake Rakastal, the lunar lake of the darker forces that no-one goes to visit. I laid a stone on top of the lha-tse that marked its viewing, and hurried back down in what I thought was the direction of the gompa. Clouds from the Himalayan side rolled off the snow-pockets caught in the peaks on a level with me. I descended, collecting yak dung in my silk scarf as I went, light and frivolous without the rucksack.

The frivolity wore off when by nightfall I still hadn't found the gompa. This was the night of no moon, and only one star came out to help me at all. Fortunately I came to the lake shore, so did not have to fear falling off the cliffs in my confusion — but then I didn't know which way to go, and was charging up and down the lakeside for about an hour in both directions. The great round pebbles lurched uncomfortably under my feet and I recited every mantra I knew — until, as so often happens, at the moment of despair I came to the cave and the monastery. Where the dog leapt out as if to kill me and I managed to beg a box of matches. It had the picture of a blonde witch with a long nose on the cover; later, people seeing the box, would shudder with delight and energetic *'yaga-mindoo!'* s, though no-one would ever tell me anything but that it was 'no good'. Well — whatever the package, the matches worked. With the torch I'd found that day, supplemented by the light shone down to help me by the younger of the monks, I negotiated my way down the vertical path to set up camp in the cave. With the matches I set light to the yak dung, and cooked Maggi Oriental Sweetcorn Soup with potato starch noodles from Golmud market and sage from Germany, which was all quite delectable.

The atmosphere turned odd and itchy here — moths flew out of the waterweed and crawled through everything, including my hair; in the morning I had to break through nightmares to open my eyes upon the vast reaches of the lake, dulled with rain today, and no longer felt like staying here to meditate. But there was a pleasant surprise amidst the oddities; today the monastery dog rolled disarmingly on its back at my approach, inviting me to scratch its belly; I did so, rather cautiously at first, suspecting a trick — but the dog's soppiness only increased. Then in the kitchen the younger monk, plagued with hiccups that didn't seem to cause him any disquiet, came to stare speechlessly at me as if I were the latest movie. There was only one solution to my unrest — to move on, to approach a little nearer to Kailash.

21 - Chiu Gompa

MY WALKING DAYS were so much shorter now that they were measured by gompas, the regular rest-stops of the majority of the pilgrims. I walked along the scrunchy white granite pebbles of the lakeside and came in wind and rain to a high red cliff, over which a fine narrow path led me. The lake spread out in a fan of wind-ruffed blue below on a scale so vast that every horizon I'd ever known was embraced and melted therein. Feeling was rarefied to integration through isolation. Mine was such a small figure on this stone, everything I held so precious no more than a crawling crushable fly when compared to this natural expansion of rock and water.

On the other side I descended into sight of what had to be Chiu Gompa. It was built most cannily into a great rocky clump that rose out of the pink plain. Ascending to it, I was accosted by the shouts of two children — a boy and a girl, dressed in religious maroon corduroy. Compelled to answer such definite cries, I went over. They both had a hand raised, all five fingers splayed out on each, and were eager to inform me that I could hire a room for five kwai that night. One room, all for me, they told me urgently, over there — and they gestured to a compound that stood on the opposite hill, and would have marched me over to see it right there and then but for my insistence that I looked at the gompa first. To this, on the promise that I would immediately after go and take the room, they reluctantly agreed.

From the outside, the gompa resembled a stony extension of the horn of rock upon which it sat. Inside it was radiant with rainbow colours — contained in silk *thangka*s and hangings, painted beams, calendar pictures of the Potala around the skylight, sutras wrapped in brilliant cloths, and offerings of brightly dyed sculptures of butter and tsampa set before the altar. This monastery is dedicated to Padmasambhava, and it was in a cave about which this monastery had been built that he had, in the company of his female counterpart, spent the last seven years of his life before ascending to the heavens of clear light.

I did not know this then. Then the children waited impatiently for me in the doorway. They rubbed lambskins ceaselessly between their hands, presumably to soften them, and seemed to think my examination of the place quite unnecessary. I did manage a good long look at a white-faced Guru Rinpoche made of papier mâché, but as soon as I'd stuck some crumpled Chinese money there, they decided I'd snooped around quite enough, and it was time to go and install me in one of the promised rooms.

An enormous dog snarled guard at the entrance to the compound, but the family threw stones and shouted at it to prevent it from attacking me. They did indeed give me a room to myself — with a flat cracked earth floor and a glassless window, through which people peered from time to time. But what interested me first was the fire in the family kitchen. They made a space on the stove for my pot, and into it I put noodles and a packet of Japanese seaweed, which I found hard to explain away.

There was a large heap of lambskins in the corner, and the whole family was at it, rubbing and worrying at the skins with their hands as if their lives depended on it. Even the mother, in between various culinary preparations, had a skin to hand. I felt it — it was soft enough for a pair of fine gloves. But still it was not soft enough for her, and she continued to screw, twist and generally torture the thing whenever she got a chance.

Before eating the food I went out for a wash in the stream that flows between the two lakes. Sometimes, in the times that are good for Tibet, they say, the flow from Manasarovar to Rakastal, fifty feet lower, is completely above ground. In bad years it is not, and seeps for the most part under the dry river bed. The flow has not been complete for many years now. I washed in a semi-stagnant pool while watching a tangerine and orange sunset rage over Rakastal.

Coming back unannounced, the good people of the establishment were not there to stand between me and the dog when I crossed the yard; delighted, the dog sank his fangs into my leg. But I didn't care — the feast I'd prepared was flavoursome, sleep good, the morning bright. After some yoga, which revealed how painfully stiff my body had become, I again set to the task of consuming. Most of the family and their friends sat out in the sunshine, kneading their skins and hooting with laughter. I sat in the kitchen where sun flew in at the open door and lit up the long brown folds of the mother's skirts, pulled out of their grimy skin the bright colours banded on her apron, illuminated her torn ear as she moved through the steps of the stove and lambskin dance. I brought out a withered sachet of sugar from a Hong Kong 7-Eleven, to add to the cocoa with which I concluded the meal, and was surprised when she said the Hindi word for sugar: 'Chinni'. But the muddy rut I'd passed the night before was the main road to Nepal from here, and she had probably seen plenty of Hindu pilgrims. Unfortunately I lacked the vocabulary to ask her what I would have liked to have done, and she just carried on with her routine. GET WHAT YOU WANT WHEN YOU WANT IT, read the message on the sachet from civilisation.

But this place was civilised too. There were telegraph poles, though no sign of electric light, and tucked behind the compound walls that morning I was shocked to find a bus. Even more startling was the nonchalance with which its one occupant reclined there. Then just before I left, the family unlocked a room, and showed me their shop, hoping I'd buy something; I stared at canvas Chinese plimsolls and the White Rabbit milk sweets, and couldn't think of a thing I wanted. Resigned, they locked up again, and let me go.

22 - Across Barga Plain

Today I left the shores of Manasarovar, leaving the northern shore unwalked and my kora not quite completed. I had heard that there were meditation caves set into the deep bronze cliffs I could see rising up there, and I decided to return and find a cave for myself for a few days, later, after I'd been around Kailash. For now — I followed the rough road that runs down the spine of land intercepting the two lakes, thinking it would lead me to the village marked on the map — Barga. But then — which exactly was the road? Suddenly there were lots of roads, dashing out in different directions all over the hillsides — and trucks, what seemed like an army of them, but only three in all, I believe — all going different ways. None of them passed me, and anyway I certainly wanted to walk this last bit. It rained heavily. I put my head down and walked in what I hoped was the right direction, and missed the right road completely. When I put my head up it was to find myself wandering over trackless hillsides tufted with scrub, and nothing of Barga or a road to be seen.

The compensation was that Kailash, after being veiled for nearly a week now, suddenly popped up most unexpectedly from behind the clouds. It was still far away, but much nearer than when I'd first sighted it. The holy mountain stood there like a great milestone with no number written on it, for Kailash is the ultimate earthly destination, and once one has reached it, what need is there to go anywhere else?

These last steps, in which I was closing the gap between dream and reality forever, should have been laden with significance. I should have been pondering the grace that had allowed me this divine vision, I should have been high on the euphoria of my own achievement, on the greater bliss of its subsequent absorption into the power of the mountain. I should have been tasting with every foot-fall the glorious confirmation of all the sacrifices I had made for this, should have been relishing the realisation that what I had relinquished for this opportunity was all rubbish compared to the jewel that stood before me. But through the sense of all this cut the demons of the mind. For no apparent reason, except that the skies above me were overcast and pregnant with an electric storm — I was in a bad mood. Having reasoned out all causes for complaint a few days ago, I was unsure what to take it out on; looking around for a scapegoat there was only my rucksack, so I thumped it. Then I felt so sorry I felt better. It was interesting, watching the causes and effects rising up and down in my mind, but on looking up at Kailash again they all seemed pretty unimportant. The white triangle loomed up clearly on the horizon, an immovable and unchanging reproach to my paltry preoccupations.

I was walking over many rumpled hills that crease the northern shore of Rakastal, feeling rather tangled, when all of a sudden a figure appeared, striding purposefully towards me. It was a lean and brown male figure, dressed in well-patched black corduroy trousers and a knitted sweater of natural homespun wool. He carried a small khaki rucksack from which protruded a crackly sheepskin. Upon reaching me he threw himself down in the bristly grass and pink stones, and in an amicable fashion said:

'You Manasarovar going?'

I gaped a bit, surprised to hear English. 'No, I'm going to Kailash.'

'Ah. Kailash temple going. I Manasarovar going.' He was a conversational character, and chirpily told me he came from a mountain village in Nepal, three hours walk from Simlikot at the border. He had come on a pilgrimage to Kailash temple — by foot and by truck, and had been on a *parikarama* (Hindi for 'kora') once about Kailash; he had *rudrakshas,* which are seeds sacred to Shiva, about his neck, and saluted the great three-eyed one: 'Om nama Shivaya'. Then there was a river just outside Barga which was high in the mornings and low in the evenings, and did I like Tibetan cheese? A rummage in the rucksack produced a Gurkha knife, a torch, some cigarettes and matches and a goatskin bag of hard dry crumbly cheese. *'Churra,* Chinese cheese,' he said, though the Chinese have no liking at all for such stuff. It had a sharp flavour which yielded slowly to saliva, to become the most delectable thing I could remember eating for centuries. He however had other things on his mind. 'You marry?' — 'No, I no marry.'

'You like sex? — I very like sex. You try?'

I gaped again, washed back to the streets and hotel receptions of Kathmandu. Still, there was something almost charming and innocent in the way he uttered this last; and he was, despite the convention of his words, quite an unusual looking Nepali. The vivacity of his slender features and the profundity of his deep olive-brown eyes betrayed a knowledge of life that transcended the slim trammels of his mountain village. Why, at Barga there was a Tibetan woman who would sleep with him for no money. He didn't need me. But would I care to marry him, and go and live with his family in his village? All his younger brothers were married so it was time for him to do so too. We could fly to Kathmandu sometimes.

I declined. We had, after all, only just met. He galloped cheerfully off in the direction of Manasarovar and I continued in the line of his vague gesture to Barga.

Neither hide nor hair of Barga appeared, as I floundered over the pink hills through the rain, past the turquoise streak of Rakastal. Then the lake was out of sight and I was wandering about marshes, leaping from tuft to tuft, wading through black slime which exuded a strong smell of yak with every squelch. Jigsaw pieces of water reflected a dull sky and Kailash took to slipping in and out of the clouds. Always the mountain was directly ahead, and though it never seemed to get any nearer, it was interesting to see how, as I unstuck eventually from the marshes and reached drier land again, a filmy white gauze in the distance slowly turned into a huge flock of sheep.

The shepherd herding them walked out of their midst towards me across the plain. When I asked him where Barga might be, he said I'd passed it, but that Kang Rinpoche was right there, and there was Darchen at its foot, so why bother with Barga? We looked towards Kang Rinpoche, just then making a momentary appearance. The nearer I got to the mountain, the more its presence seemed to dominate, the deeper its silence seemed to penetrate across the wide land. He had a point. Of what possible use was Barga?

He also mentioned a 'choo chembow' between here and Kailash, but I pretended I hadn't heard. Walking ever on and on over those im-measurable spaces over which every step seemed so tiny and futile, I came just before nightfall to a line of telegraph poles, a ditch, and a rough road. The road shortly brought me to a river, a far-flung sprawl of tangling shallow rivulets through the grey sand. Tucked in between scrub-topped sand-dunes somewhere amongst the waterstrands, I set up camp for the night. I scrubbed my body with the gritty grey river water, hoping to dislodge some of the dirt with which my skin, despite frequent washings, seemed to have become impregnated; it was too dark by now to see if it had any effect or not. And just as I was dry and dressed and ready to put up the tent, it began to rain heavily. No matter — I was a nimble pitcher now, and it was all up and I inside before I was even half soaked. Tomorrow I might be arrested, fined large amounts of FEC or deported from the land of the gods. For now I lay in a cosy candlelit cocoon of feathers, silk and the drench of French perfume.

23 - To the foot of Kailash

JUST AS I set off that grey morning there spluttered over the river towards me a jeep-full of what appeared to be Indians. We stared incredulously at each other, and went our ways. Soon I came to what must have been the Nepali and the nomad's 'choo chembow': the river had well over-spilled its banks, and an abandoned truck was embedded at a rakish angle in the centre of the joyous rush. This choo was not quite as chembow as I'd feared, and soon I was across.

Kailash was again invisible. From the point ahead where the mountains rose out of the plain loomed an elusive grey ectoplasm, which I presumed to be the smoke of the fires of Darchen. After a few hours I met a group of about ten Tibetans. The women streamed long strands of turquoise, and they walked singing, arm in arm, in a line that spanned the road, while the men leapt about the scrubs and feverishly untwisted branches with which they'd presumably make a fire later. 'Tashi dilleeeee!' they all shouted together, as if they'd been expecting me. I returned the greeting at full pitch.

Blobs of grey and white appeared under the haze of firesmoke, and my feet slowed as I came into sight of Darchen. It seemed to be composed mostly of tents pitched amongst broken walls and stones, but the first building the road brought one to was a small grey compound of suspiciously Chinese-looking concrete. Blue paint announced in crooked letters on the gate-posts: WELCOME TO DARCHEN REST HOUSE. In the yard were heaps of firewood and a dog, but there was nobody around. I dithered. Perhaps I should forget about declaring myself until I'd been round Kailash — the kora started from this village, and there was no reason why I shouldn't just go now. The decision seemed to be an especially good one when round the corner ambled the unwelcome olive and gold of a Chinese army uniform. I shot off around the other corner.

Round the corner however were a crowd of Tibetans. They were just hanging about and passing the time of day by a few squares of cloth, on which enterprising traders had spread their wares. There was also a bright green tent made of Inji stuff perched upon a ridge, a bit apart from the main tent-village. I approached the people. After a friendly welcome, they were all insistent that I must go up there — they pointed in the direction of the green tent. A young Tibetan man led me up there. My attention was bewildered, divided as it was between the double attraction of seeing what there was to buy, whether or not there was soap powder, and the possibility of someone to talk to in English. The kora could wait a bit perhaps.

It was a long lean American who loped down the ridge to greet me. 'Hi!' he said. His name was John, a laid back and matter-of-fact follower of the Dharma. He'd been here three days, waiting for the clouds to clear off the mountains, and had only seen Kailash for the first time that day. But now of course it was hiding again. The Tibetans gathered about to umpire, applaud and comment on our meeting, and the young Tibetan man took me down to a stall upon which were spread the luxuries of civilisation — cigarettes, matches, bags of soap powder and a few jars of mouldy and disintegrating orange slices. Dizzy with the happy choice I bought some of each, and sat on the hillside for an hour or so, with all these people bombarding my senses. Rain fell a bit, wind blew, but no-one took any notice. The cigarette tasted stale and no better than the one at Thugolho Gompa, and I was very amused to hear how John had arrived here. He was easy-going and seemed to attract easiness — he had chanced to be dining in the Lhasa hotel one day just over a week ago, where he encountered a party of three. They happened to be leaving for Kailash in the morning, in a jeep they had hired at great but apparently unimportant expense. Over onion soup with cheese on top he'd hitch-hiked a ride to the holy mountain with them, and, six days later, here he was. As for his benefactors — they had stayed an afternoon, in which Kailash was invisible, taken a dip in the lake, and gone off to Kashgar.

Because he'd been in a jeep, check-point officials hadn't bothered to ask him for such things as Alien Travel Permits. But — 'Have you met Dorje yet?' he asked. Apparently Dorje was a Tibetan man, the 'tourist liaison officer' here, and for 105 FEC he'd made John legal. Reluctantly I allowed myself to be led down to declare myself.

One room at the rest house was occupied by a couple of Tibetan men who sat on carpeted beds and talked busily with one another over butter tea. They really didn't seem to want to bother with dealing with me, so I just sat in the yard. They invited me in to sit there on a bed, and I too was served many cups of butter tea while they carried on talking. An old woman with short hair and a sour face kept a warm fire crackling and I wrote up my diary. After a while one of the men asked to see my passport. I went to unearth it from the bottom of my rucksack, left dumped in the middle of the yard.

The two Tibetans seemed more interested in the lion and the unicorn, emblazoned on the cover in imperial gold, than anything else. It was funny, looking at the beasts chained to the Queen's crown, pondering their relevance to my present situation. Crossing the river, I would happily have let the passport wash away in favour of life; but having crossed it, it was not on the physical presence and capabilities of my live body, but upon this navy and silver symbol of imperialism, that depended whether I could stay here or not.

Of the two Tibetans, one of them wore a floppy hat, spoke English, and turned out to be Dorje; the other wore a blue tracksuit, spoke no English and was a policeman. The wearer of the olive and gold Chinese army uniform sat in the corner smoking cigarettes and appeared to have no clout at all. Dorje explained to the other two what I said about the lion and the unicorn, and they nodded as if they understood. They could have drawn dark cynical parallels between the chaining of Scotland, Ireland and Wales to the English crown and the forced fastening of Tibet to the silken apron-strings of China, but no grudge seemed to inspire them to do so.

They were very surprised to hear I had come by the southern road. Weren't there rivers? Well, yes, there were. How had I got across then? My presence seemed to puzzle them. Everybody knew it was impossible to come by the southern road in the rainy season. And how long had it taken me? I wasn't sure whether to count the journey from Raka or from when trucks ceased to ease my walking, so said the first auspicious figure that came into my head — 'Twenty-seven days.'

After some consultation, the policeman disappeared into the next room with my passport, and Dorje mentioned to me that it was illegal to walk by the southern road. The policeman was now deciding how much to fine me. I nodded. I'd expected to be fined for something, though I hadn't know the southern road itself was illegal. I also wondered why — I hadn't seen any ballistic missile silos or nuclear waste pits that the Chinese might keep hidden. Anyway — I had 1,000 FEC especially for this purpose; its saving had added piquancy to my teaching in Hong Kong. Whenever I wondered what was the point of all this prancing about like a dancing bear, lodging the simple past and present perfect firmly in the heads of my students — I would remember the future and how I was saving up to pay my fine, and then every step in the dance was worth it. The future was now, sitting safe and snug in a buttery smoked room at Kailash; Authority was this spry Tibetan man, writing 'Om Nama Shivaya' in Hindi under the picture of Shiva in the front of my diary. I drank butter tea hungrily and gratefully, and carried on writing. Dorje was not an old man, but he had cataracts in both his eyes, which gave him a slightly faraway aspect. He had been born here at Kailash; Darchen was his village, and he had spent most of his life here. He said that when he was a child, he didn't speak Tibetan like the other children, but some strange language that no-one else understood. His parents took him to a high lama for a consultation. They were told that their son was speaking Sanskrit, the classical language of India, and the reason for this was that he was the reincarnation of a high Indian Brahmin, whose spiritual attainment had been such as to earn him his desire — to be reborn at Kailash. Later he had forgotten the Sanskrit and taken to speaking Tibetan, but when he was sent to India for seven years to study English, he had had little difficulty in learning Hindi. Upon returning to Tibet after the Chinese take-over followed dark years; when the People's Liberation Army overran the plateau even to here, all the monasteries were destroyed and koras of Kailash were forbidden. But now, with the new religious tolerance, Dorje worked for the government, using his linguistic abilities in his post as KAILASH MANASAROVAR GUIDE/ INTERPRETER — so his rubber stamp announced him to be.

John came slipping in, and Dorje went on to tell the story of Padmasambhava's last days on earth. As he spoke, he filled his cup butter tea with tsampa and kneaded nuggets of dough which he passed to us. 'Hakko!' he said. The hakko tasted delicious.

After quite a long while the policeman returned, and he and Dorje fell into discussion. I returned to my writing. Eventually Dorje turned to me again, and said that they were afraid they had to fine me, as I had acted against the law. The last people who had gone this way were some Japanese who had come in a jeep in May, and they had fined them 100 FEC each. But, because I was a woman, because I was alone, and because I did not 'make a lot of noise' — they would just fine me half that. Then there was the question of legalising me. For another 75 FEC they furnished me with a travel document which validated my presence in the whole of the Ali region. I wasn't sure how far that extended, but it covered at least from here to the town of Ali, a few hundred kilometres to the north, which was what mattered. For suddenly, after all my furtive fears of authority, I was completely legal from here to Lhasa. I was quite unable to believe this good fortune, and handed over the thin wad of paper notes with pleasure. And then, after the happy outcome, we all went to the 'dining room' — one round table stuck in a rather unsavoury atmosphere of kerosene, where a Chinese cook produced a slop of noodles and boiled cabbage.

Darchen was not, upon inspection, a very idyllic place. Broken glass and excrement crashed and splashed the stony ground all about the conglomeration of tents, broken walls and occasional mud-covered buildings that formed the village. An uprising of rock guarded the valley that led right up to the very foot of the holy mountain, and in it was a cleft. Prayer flags hung across the narrow gorge, out of which shot a cold river that ran past the village. I meant to pitch my tent on its banks, but when Choying Dorje suggested that it would be nice for me to spend that night in the guest house, I did not disagree.

John came to visit me with his petrol stove. It leaked all over the floor, and eventually we had to ask the Tibetans in the next room if we could heat water on the fire they had going in there. The fire smoked so generously that tears streamed down my face, but after a couple of hours we had a cup of cocoa followed by a cup of Celestial Seasoning each. Technical difficulties only made the situation more interesting — I forgot all about the joys of solitude in the novelty of society, of the indulgence of speaking and hearing my own language again, and we chattered away for hours. After the long silences the easy communication tumbled through my head with the bewitching fascination of an acrobatic display. It was not utterly idle chatter. The extremity of the circumstance and place seemed to cut away all necessity for pretence or distraction, and there was nothing of importance to talk about but the threads that had led us here. It was as if through the years we had each followed a trail of clues, not understood at first, staked out by apparent coincidences, difficulties and strokes of luck. Through dreams and hindsight the thread had become clearer and stronger — and here we were, still locked in the human viewpoint, amazed to be here, here, at Mount Kailash.

24 - Now what?

So here I was at Kailash. Now, what? Would my life stop dead here, could I just finish the story now? I'd bathed in the waters of Manasarovar and seen Kailash — for a devout Hindu, this would be more than enough. Many a Hindu *sadhu* (ascetic) never goes nearer to Kailash than where he caught his first sight of the ice pagoda. To be within eye-shot is to have *darshan*, which means sharing the company and thus benefitting from the transcendental qualities of a holy person or place. Even at a hundred miles distance, the sadhu could go into raptures, do his puja, and go back and tell everyone he'd been to Kailash. And he'd be right, for indeed he would have had darshan of the holy mountain.

Hindus believe that pilgrimage is purifying. Though individual Hindus may go with different motives, they all believe implicitly in the merit of visiting holy places. Kailash is difficult to attain and thus alluring; it appeals to the romantic silk and pearl devotion of the Hindu approach. Just to have darshan of Kailash is to secure an excellent rebirth — maybe, if they're lucky, with Shiva on a heavenly planet — and the more pious activities they perform in the region of the dharm, the more release they'll receive from the bondage of karma. Some are doing business with God, hoping to prosper in the next life as a result of this pilgrimage; Shiva is known to be very generous, paying off all your bad karmic debts, and grants boons very quickly. One can ask Shiva for what one wants, at Kailash, and get it. Others go out of unconditional gratitude and adoration, because there's no question about it that devotional things are good to do. The intrinsic austerities of pilgrimage — especially one as taxing, whichever way you go about it, as journeying to Kailash — produce, they believe, forgiveness as well as purification. *Praiscitta* is the word, and perhaps 'atonement' is a better translation than 'forgiveness'; by concentrating on the object of the pilgrimage, come-uppances due from the past fall naturally behind and the individual is granted the liberation of a clearer, more subtle state of mind than ever before. This is the mental purification necessary before one proceeds with meditation. Meeting other pilgrims on the way, even of other faiths, is regarded as auspicious, as it uplifts and confirms individuals in their devotions.

I of course am no Hindu, and was never meant to be. But from India I'd come to Tibet, so to speak. Whether one understands the mysteries of the deepest teachings given in the elevated language incomprehensible to the majority of Tibetans — or not — the image of Kang Rinpoche is an integral part of every Tibetan's education and value-system. The Jewel of the Snows is represented by swastikas, by triangular blobs of white paint on doors, by the central bead in every Tibetan rosary, in pictures and paintings on walls and rocks, woven in with clouds onto carpets — from one end of Tibet to the other. Whether the Tibetans sitting on the carpets still ponder the significance of the mountain as knowledge rising out of awareness is not for me to say — Tibetans are inherently transcendental anyway. Laughter arises from living conditions which would have Mrs Bloggs-Smith fainting in her shopping trolley, from lips that could, if they didn't believe it unlucky to talk about bad things too much, tell stories to curdle the very bone marrow. But this is the Favoured Realm, where skeletons dance....

Tibetan Buddhist practices at Kailash are similar to those of the Hindus, though they lay less stress on bathing than do their neighbours. Certain spots and caves are sacred because some great mystic lived there, and it is customary to visit these places and pay tribute. Rituals are attached to places dotted all over the vicinity of Kailash: odd little actions, such as touching a particular stone, offering grain in a certain spot, or squeezing between a hole in the boulders, are energetically enacted by the Tibetan pilgrims as much for fun as for merit. The most extreme prostrate their way around the koras. And all of them pile up stones in votive lha-tse and on the mani walls, and never cease chanting 'Om mani padme hum'. Some spots are believed to be powerful in assisting prayers for ancestors, others for sharpening one's own chances of a good rebirth and so on. Dorje could whet the appetite for hours as he talked about the lakes and caves, gompas and hot springs where certain things did, could or might happen.

Every Hindu or Tibetan or Bon-pa who had made the pilgrimage to Kailash would do at least one kora of the mountain, and most would go round Manasarovar. Nobody seemed to go to Rakastal, the lake of dark subconscious forces whose few gompas are destroyed in any case, and few seemed to do the other koras possible. Kailash is surrounded by smaller mountains and hills, many of which are encompassed by the usual circumambulation of the mountain. This is about thirty-two miles long and takes three days to do comfortably, though there is a special merit attached to getting up early and whizzing round the whole circuit in one day. Starting from Darchen in the south, one spends a night at each of the cardinal points and at the same time is supposed to enact a psychological unfolding — from hope to triumph, through loss and death, to the joy of rebirth.

As well as the main koras of Kailash and Manasarovar, there are the inner koras of Kailash. One is reputed to go right around the base, but as it would be more or less impossible to hop over the icy shoulder that juts to the east, one presumably has to go via the pass of Dolma La to get around it. Another inner kora does not go around Kailash, but loops clockwise up to the base in the south, girdling the mountains that divide the two streams running from the melting snowcap. There is a gompa in each of their valleys, and further down these streams unite to form the river that foams from the mouth of the prayer-flagged gorge behind Darchen. It is high in the valley of the eastern stream that the 'black and white lakes' are to be found, but one is not supposed to visit them until one has done thirteen koras of Kailash. Dorje did say that he thought the qualifying number should be reduced to three for foreigners.

For now that the Dharma is spreading to the land of the Red Man, the Red Man is coming to the Land of the Dharma. Concessions are being made to Westerners in Tibet as they are in California, where ear-whispered teachings kept secret from all but a privileged few for centuries are now available in any Dharma bookshop.

We were Westerners, drawn from dwellings where hot water runs out of taps, fire comes at the touch of a button and Celestial Seasoning teabags can be plucked from supermarket shelves. We came from education and belief-systems where stress is laid upon achievement. Hiram Bingham discovered Machu Picchu in 1911, so the National Geographic announced — but he asked the way up there from a Peruvian campesino cultivating the ancient Incan terraces as had his father before him; Edmund Hillary became 'Sir' for being the first person to climb Everest — but as he stood on the summit, Sherpa Tenzin was just a few inches below him. Tenzin, having come this far, still would not offend the gods by putting his feet upon their crown.

The woman in Shigatze had had a point: there's not much point in going to Kailash unless you're a Buddhist. What she meant when she said 'Buddhist' was 'believer'. You'd have to have faith that the sacrifices of getting there would be justified in the end. Otherwise it's just a pudding-stone conglomerate topped with ice.

The idea of sacrifice is part of all religious ethos. Hindu sadhus as part of their training go through a period of *tapas*, or austerities, in order to win release from and perhaps control over the minefield of Maya. There's many an 'average Hindu mystic' as Lama Govinda refers to them, who have extended the duration of their austerities to standing for fifty years on one leg or a lifetime with one hand in the air. The Buddha on the other hand tempered over-zealous self-mortification by stressing moderation in all things. In his search for enlightenment, he tried renunciation and decided it led nowhere. Still, Tibetan Buddhism also deifies the great poet-saint Milarepa, who claimed that renunciation led everywhere. He distressed his sister to distraction by refusing to eat good food, and when his only possession, his pot, broke, he instantly composed a song saluting the pot as his guru for teaching him the lesson of detachment. Despite the wealth of pots and pans that cluster round every nomad's hearth, to take birth in Tibet is to renounce the majority of stuff surplus to existence before one even begins. Then Christ was crucified. The stress on asceticism and renunciation as a means to liberation is not dissimilar to that of early Christian mystics, who lived alone, dined on berries, wore scourging shirts and saw visions. But the Christian pilgrim's hymn seems to be more one of self-congratulation, based on this Western urge for achievement, than one of adoration. Tibetans stick to mantras when they're on pilgrimage.

John's English benefactors hadn't really minded that they'd gone all that way to see Kailash and it wasn't visible when they got there — they'd had a good trip and got a funny story out of it. One of them had taken a dip in the lake in deference to local mores, but it had been a bit too chilly for the other two. Perhaps they were Bodhisattvas in disguise, coming down from their plane of spontaneous goodness to take human form, in order to make John's arrival at Kailash, after years of failed attempts, a suddenly swift one. Whatever — their thoughtfulness coincided more with the Tibetan way than with the sweet sad smiles of the traditional Christian martyr. Tibetans, however crude they may appear in dress and hygiene, demonstrate a lofty grasp of the subtleties of the human psyche through the simplest actions. They manage to give and make the taker feel comfortable about the taking, and receive what they need with equal discretion.

The Tibetan nomads don't believe you when you say men have landed on the moon. They don't believe that machines exist whereby people can talk to one another across the world. No, no — you must be making it up. Ghosts, phantoms, demons, deities and telepathy are everyday matters to them. They never lost touch with the roots of existence but their lack of worldly progress prohibits them from believing in men flying to the moon. They'd like to believe you, but they've never seen it, so how could they? It was equally hard for me to believe that I'd actually made it to Kailash. And the reward was to feel the present in a jackpot of epiphanies, all the lucky numbers of the world landing up at your feet at once. Chance, say our Western instincts. Karma, say the Eastern.

Are instincts necessarily geographical? Perhaps they are. The earth is a living organism just like anybody else, and has her energy channels. In the northern hemisphere the water spirals clockwise down the plug; when a butter lamp is lit under a paper prayer-wheel, the hot air therefrom naturally sends it turning the same way. It was only right and proper that clockwise should be holy in Tibet, and only to be expected that an Inca would feel differently. The earth has a subtle body too, and Kailash represents the energy nexus found in the navel. To any Tibetan it is instinctively obvious that Kang Rinpoche is the umbilical link with the parent deities who guide and protect.

Then again — are instincts necessarily religious? Are instincts necessarily good?

Well, whatever the nature of the instincts that had drawn me here, here I was at Kailash. With all these wide spaces and magnificent views, the Eastern habit of circumambulation was particularly attractive. By walking, the whole being — body mind and spirit — is induced to consider in every aspect the object of devotion about which it walks. Through concentration, the sacredness is absorbed until it is a living experience. The ways of the country seemed only natural and practical.

What is engaging about Tibetan Buddhism is its appreciation of the present moment. Buddhist deities represent dynamic functions of experience. Whereas we Westerners experience them subjectively as moods, Tibetans transform this energy into something positive and beneficial. Whether or not all understand all the theory, they certainly as a nation have a remarkable grasp of the practice of transforming passion into compassion and anger into wisdom. Tibetans do not waste time bemoaning their lot. They are as stoic as the rocks they take and place in lha-tse as offerings to the lakes and the mountains, as flexible as the prayer flags they hang in the winds, as soft as the water they offer to the four cardinal points and as energetic as the thunderstorms that roam their isolated plateau.

Though I did not have their faith, I had conviction, and I was convinced that the basic Tibetan Buddhist rituals would be rewarding. It seemed practical to do as Tibetans do while I was at Kang Rinpoche, and not to forget Shiva, through whom I first came to hear of the mountain, while I was about it.

Having already done three-quarters of the kora of Manasarovar, I would do a kora or two of Kailash and then, I thought, in deference to my difference, a kora of Rakastal. It would be good to visit the gompas which had been rebuilt, and the caves unchanged from the times Padmasambhava and Milarepa had meditated therein. It would be good to cut up the valleys closer to the southern foot of the mountain, do the inner kora and maybe find the lakes. It would be good to go back to the northern shore of Manasarovar and to stay a few days in one of the meditation caves there. It would be good to view Kailash from every angle and to experience every mood and mode of worship.

But most of all, it was just good to be here. The moment expanded. Universes unfolded from grains of sand. Minutae boomed with significance. Existence was ecstasy, and I began my rites with a purification dip in the icy river. The object of devotion was no painted idol, but a heap of stones.

25 - European invasion

IT WAS WITH great domestic pride, dripping hair and frozen hands and scalp that I surveyed my clean clothes spread nicely out over the river bank to dry. Kailash was again lurking behind a sheet of grey; Dharma John's tent was gone from the ridge and the Chinese cook had finished serving breakfast by the time I arrived at the dining room. Wandering about Darchen I was invited into a trading tent, and here a pair of kind and beautiful sisters presented me with endless cups of butter tea. The hot tea in the cup thawed out my fingers, and as if that weren't enough, they then went on to pile into it tsampa, churra and butter, all of which was very comforting this chilly morning. One of the sisters was married, and it was her child who ran about the place in a pair of split Chinese trousers; he ran with the wobbly gait of one who has not long ago learnt to walk, but when he came running in with a cigarette in his hand, and proceeded to puff at it in convincing imitation of any would-be Mr Cool the world over — both mother and aunt laughed till they nearly cried.

Bright-eyed, the child played to their approval, blew with scornful competence on the glowing tip and, when he'd finished, threw down the butt with a lordly air; without condescending to stamp it out, he ran out, shrieking with laughter at himself.

They did not want money. I gave them a Dalai Lama picture, but they could always out-do me in generosity. The child's mother dipped into a sheepskin pouch hung up above the stove, and brought out a book. The cover was black and shiny with the yak dung smoke of its residence, and to my surprise it turned out to be a copy, in English, of the Dalai Lama's book: *My Land and My People*. I immediately set to reading it, but an old man who had hitherto been sitting quietly chanting 'Om mani padme hum' to himself now came and took an interest in the book too. He liked the pictures, and touched them to his head many times; maybe he had been one of the thousands of Tibetans depicted gathered about the Norbulingka summer palace for days in 1959, protecting the Dalai Lama against suspected kidnap by the Chinese. Whatever, it was a time in his country's history he would never forget; the old man disappeared with the whole book.

Just as I was packing up my things, I looked up to see three foreigners in woolly hats being ushered across the yard. Then I heard my name at top volume, and I was being pounced upon, kissed and hugged. It was Franca. She had been two weeks here now. 'So quickly you come!' she exclaimed. 'Where is your 'orse?'

I explained. 'But I was so sure you'd get an 'orse,' she said, looking around the yard as if expecting to see it tucked grazing behind the woodpile. I was rather sorry to disappoint her. As for her, she'd managed to hitch-hike here with no real difficulties, and for two kwai in Ali had obtained the necessary ATP.

The other two were a slim Dutch woman with an uncatchable name who I referred to in my diary as Question Mark, and Thomas. When I asked Thomas where he came from, he proudly replied: 'Bavaria!'. With his rosy red cheeks and big brown beard, he was the very picture of health and wholesome living.

I never did get to set out on the kora of Kailash that day. My excuse was that my washing hadn't dried yet, that Kailash was invisible and that it was windy and rainy — but what was new? In truth I was just wholly captivated by the drama these three brought with them, and so was entertained all afternoon and evening.

The three of them invaded 'my' room. I watched three rucksacks disgorge piles of typical stuff: plastic bags full of instant noodles, sugar, milk powder and tsampa all slithered into straggly piles of messy etceteras that spread across their three beds and spilled over the earth floor. Franca, having done koras of both Manasarovar and Kailash, was ready to leave. She had met Question Mark and Thomas at Manasarovar, from whence they'd all come just now in a truck; QM and Thomas had met in Kathmandu, taken a plane to Tibet, and on the plane had joined up with a group of Swiss tourists who also happened to be heading for Kailash. Once in Lhasa they had all hired, at quite great expense, two drivers and a truck to bring them all here. Their truck and companions had gone but they had remained, now arguing as to whether they should take all or half their bag of peanuts round the kora of Kailash; and even as they argued, Thomas cracked peanut shells and rushed the nuts down his throat with such utmost haste that the subject of debate was in danger of extinction at any moment.

These three brought with them the expectations of civilisation; in admiration I watched the imperious efficiency with which they managed to wrest two thermoses of hot water from the old woman who ruled Dorje's kitchen, ruefully comparing it to the labours I'd undergone the night before just for a couple of hot drinks. Franca proceeded to wash her hair with one thermos, Thomas to make milk tea with the other, while QM declared that the bedsheets were filthy and so went off to demand clean ones. Enthralled, I sat on my bed. After the uncomprehending and disgruntled hotel staff had reluctantly produced bedsheets of the same uniform grubbiness as those already on the beds, the two girls set on Thomas. They were going down to wash in the river now, and he'd better come with them, as he was really beginning to stink like an animal, and it was disgusting. He'd better wash all his clothes too, and it must be three weeks since he'd last washed his dungarees.

'But how can I wash them here?' asked Thomas dolefully.

'Quite simple' replied QM briskly. 'You take a brush and you scrub them.'

Sorted and equipped, the girls went down to the river to bathe and scrub. Thomas sat in full gloom on his bed. After a while he heaved a deep sigh, and began: 'They wash every day, and they never stop complaining because I only wash every four or five days. But that's enough, I think. It's cold here. Look at the Tibetan people, when do they wash? I think it is not so necessary to wash so often at this altitude. Man is an animal and he has his smell. Why do we have to wash it away? A dog smells of dog, a horse smells of horse, a human smells of human ...'
— and so on. Miserably he finished up: 'Besides, I have the beginning of a cold, and I do not think it is so good to wash in icy water when you

are not feeling too good.' So saying, however, he slowly gathered his things and sloped off down to the river.

The Dalai Lama's book fell back into my hands that evening, but it was hard to concentrate, as QM and Thomas bickered constantly over minutae — for an hour as to who was to go and fill the water bottle at the river, fifty metres away, till Franca yelled at them to stop. She meanwhile was doing her usual thing of dashing about with a phrase book in each hand, this time trying to arrange a lift for herself up to Ali. The room was squalid and cold with people-litter; tonight I couldn't do yoga, and I missed the solitude of my tent. The novelty of the European invasion was beginning to pall. Finally I lay down the book, swept the floor and went to the river to fill everybody's water bottles. Incense and candles were lit and new peace fell. We cooked rice and dahl on Thomas's stove and made a thermos of hot tea, spiced with sacred Dolma herbs that Franca had brought from Dolma La. Stars laughed over the great plains outside, and I realised that despite its petty intrigues, company and conversation could be just what I loved. It was fun to create a home out of nothing, to listen to stories and crack jokes. In one way or another we were united by a common purpose — even though we couldn't see it, there was Kailash hiding just up there behind the rocks and the clouds. Tomorrow would begin the kora.

26 - First leg of kora

THE SUN SHONE, the sky was blue, and the tip of Kailash was visible from the river. Everybody was in a good mood. Franca blew off in a flourish of kisses and exhaust to Ali, QM and Thomas settled once and for all what to take and what to leave behind. I had another tea and tsampa breakfast in the trading tent, and scampered off westwards.

I'd dumped tent, extra noodles, books and so on in Darchen, so my rucksack felt extraordinarily light. Feeling like an irresponsible fool I skipped along the sunny path, past the mani wall that marked the beginning of the kora. The scrubby vegetation hummed with bees, and Kailash was just to the right. The mountain was hidden for the first couple of hours by the guardian southern hills. There were mani walls and lha-tse all along, and I took to putting a stone on each, to wishing a prayer with each placement.

And then upon rounding the first corner — there was Kailash, edging out from behind a tall wall of grey and undulating rock, biting up the sky with its whiteness. Here a river flowed out through green banks from the valley that defines the west side of Kailash; the path led through wide stepped meadows, and I recognised from pictures in a book a tall pole standing firm in a dome of stones. This pole is erected in a ceremony every spring. It is bound with yak hide, and from its tip radiated many strings of prayer flags; and their flapping in the wind was the only sound in the vast and cavernous silence. Behind the merry flagpole I could see the tall sombre red walls of the valley leading north; but, while the sun shone, and this surreal vision was actual before my eyes, I wanted to paint it.

QM and Thomas wandered past presently, but they didn't notice me. After they'd gone the sound of singing streamed down the valley, and along came two Tibetan men who certainly noticed me. They sat down, and one of them began energetically exploring the contents of my rucksack. I gave them a picture of the Dalai Lama each, but that did not satisfy the one. He continued his investigations, looking for more Dalai Lamas. I painted rapidly, feigning an indifference to his forays at first, and fortunately finished just as he was becoming a little too warm — I only had two left. I slapped his hands as if he were a child, to regain control of my stock, and he grinned with good humour. We went our ways.

Again Kailash was blotted from sight, this time by the walls of the valley. The path followed the river. There was reputedly a monastery and caves on the other side, but they were so cunningly camouflaged in the shadows of the rock that I did not see them. The path threaded on, here through flat green edged with many mani walls, now keeping the river close company, now climbing up over steep banks mobile with scree. Strange animals with big eyes, swishing tails and golden fur, watched me as I passed. I believe they were a kind of marmot, and their high whistles haunted the air. At the height of the deep red cliffs loomed rocks which humped into an exact image of Nandi, the devoted bull who is vehicle and servant to Lord Shiva: had the myth sprung from the rock or had the rock conformed to the human imagination? There was no difference here between myth, imagination, divine fact and solid rock.

The narrow valley had a solemn aspect. Lama Govinda likens the gothic atmosphere to that of a cathedral, and he's right: the chestnut red valley walls soar with the impressive grandeur of cardinals swanning up aisles under celestial flying buttresses, to the sound of organ music supplied by the winds playing fluted canyon walls. They inspire the humble humans labouring up the valley at the hem of their flowing robes with a sense of trust in the establishment here, with hope and imminent triumph.

I passed a man who was prostrating his full length with every step he took. His hands were protected by Chinese canvas sneakers, and there would be a rubbery slap whenever he brought them together in supplication, followed by the long scuffling graze of his prostration. Then I passed a woman walking very slowly with one small child attached to either hand. She wore the usual dark rough skirts that touched the ground, and on her back was strapped a load of sheepskins, pot and bellows. There was a sense of a history so strong that it defied time; in any century this same woman and these same two children could have been here, compounding with their frail but persistent steps the pilgrim's path beneath their feet. How far had they come and what difficulties had they encountered on the way for the privilege of the intense peace they now enjoyed?

Somewhere further on I encountered a Tibetan man with an explosive hairstyle and a lop-sided gait which seemed to be due to the holes in his socks. From time to time he would stop to adjust the lay of his socks so as to expose new areas of his feet to blistering, but he never took a break from his guttural repetition of, according to the Tibetan pronunciation: 'Om mani peme hum'. He seemed to take it for granted that we should walk together, so we did. I followed his bobbing figure for a few hours, chanting in an echo to his chanting, resting when he rested. At one point we came to a natural armchair in a rock, and we took it in turns to sit in it. Further up we came to a point where the protective cliffs part in a great butterfly, and Kailash was visible, rising as the pinnacle atop a sheer jet of stone. This brief vision, the only glimpse one gets from the western valley, was less regular than the views I'd seen before: the lower faces were laterally striped with dark purplish grey and veined with snowlines. The peak was as white as ever, cutting now through the rambling clouds that had begun to gather there. And the many forms of Demchog, with only a slight nudge of the imagination, evolved out of the moving mists above. Demchog is the Tibetan transformation of Shiva, the protector of Kailash and all the mountain stands for: ringed with fire and crowned with skulls, stamping on desire and dining on brains, brandishing implements of detachment and united with his female energy counterpart, mingling with skeletons, dressed in tigerskins and dancing with death — he glorifies in erasing the limitations of conventional thought and finds liberation in destruction. Vividly he tore at the veil of duality, and to stand in that spot indeed heightens the feeling of organic unity which permeates the whole Kailash-Manasarovar region.

When only that morning it had been high spring, by the time we came to the north face of Kailash it was cold midwinter again. Muted green and grey slopes now prevailed. To the north, a thick mist clotted the valley where the source of the Indus is to be found; to the south, the mountain reappeared, in a new aspect. Behind the delicate cross-weave cut the roughened shape, savage and capable as a stone-age flint. The mountain here had stark and primitive associations. It cut to the quick, cut right away all the frivolous thoughts of the civilised mind; it spoke to the bones, to the first instincts of worship, and stood like a ghost behind the division of two smaller hills guarding the approach. The Tibetans name these two smaller hills after Vajrapani and Manjusri — two favourite Bodhisattvas who fight darkness, decay and ignorance, with their diamond thunderbolt and fiery sword of knowledge.

This was the north face, where individual expectation must be shed and forgotten along with the priestly associations of the preceding valley. This was an entirely new way of looking at the mountain. It is at the north side that the devotee, if he performs his rites with sustained devotion according to his tradition, may be blessed with a vision of his favourite deity. Next time around, maybe I'd have a vision of Shiva; but not yet. Meanwhile, Kailash slipped enigmatically in and out of the clouds without even moving....

My companion interrupted his chanting a bit to murmur about tsampa at Diraphuk Gompa, and I was all in favour of the notion. We had already eaten up the very last of the 761 biscuits. There were shadowy dapples that could be the gompa on the other side of a rushing river, so in the cloud-dimmed light we leapt from tuft to tuft, rock to rock, waded small waterfalls and slithered on slimy boulders. Half-way across we noticed a bridge a little way upstream, hidden before. It began to rain hard. I thought of how nice it would be to eat tsampa by the gompa kitchen fire, but when we came to the gompa, the monk in charge admitted my walking chum and shut the door in my face. I pleaded to be allowed in, to see the gompa at least, and reluctantly he held the door open just enough for me to squeeze through, pointing all the time to some building down below. He told me to put my rucksack down in the mud in the entrance. I did not, but put it on a platform of sheepskins where my footsore companion was making himself at home. By the light of a feeble torch I was allowed into the tiny womb of the place — butter lamps before pictures of the Dalai Lama and various gods and Taras (female embodiments of compassion, 'Dolma' or 'Droma' in Tibetan), and then, tucked into a small cave behind, was an image of Pad-masambhava, with one butter lamp burning before it. I touched my head to the stone, and wondered what saints had meditated here over the ages. But there wasn't much chance to wonder long — the monk marked the end of my brief visit by pouring yellow holy water from a kettle into my hands. I slurped it and wiped the dampness over my head. It tasted of yak. And then I was more or less kicked out.

27 - A night at the north face

SMOKE STRAGGLED THROUGH the drizzle from the outcrop of stones indicated below. It came from the roof of the kitchen, the last room in a building of about seven rooms in a row. The walls were of stone and the floors of mud, damp, littered with sheep droppings and smelling strongly of ammonia. A woman and several children appeared, eager to rent me one of the rooms for ten kwai. Despite the rawness of the weather, all of them were in a state of semi-undress; in fact I had never seen a family more abandoned to the natural order of things. The head of each child was crowned with a flyaway birdsnest of hair, while the mother's locks fell in long matted ropes. A thick sheepskin chuba, stiff with dirt, unpeeled from her shoulders to reveal two large breasts, heavy with milk. She was apparently too disinterested to be exactly friendly, but she did puff a set of bellows to a fire of juniper roots, in order for me to cook some noodles. Apart from the brief fire, it was a rather dismal place. The fire was too small to warm wet feet or anything; the place was dark and dank, with just a few very dirty sheepskins thrown about, and what was conspicuous was the complete absence of an altar or any religious pictures. The children cracked apricot stones and fought over the kernels; when the mother was out of the kitchen at one point, and one of the children offered me a kernel — and another child whacked him on the head, warning: 'I'll tell mother!' — I declined. In the corner of the kitchen another child nursed a tiny skinny baby, French kissing it with a hideous lasciviousness which I supposed was intended to give it the illusion of suckling on the absent mother.

The father turned up on a horse with a sack of potatoes he'd brought from Darchen, and then Thomas and Question Mark appeared. QM cooked them nettle soup on Thomas's stove, and we all sat about drinking hot tea, which our hosts made delicious with very rancid and very precious butter. Thomas coughed and sneezed as he counted how many vegetables grew in his garden in Bavaria, QM nursed the baby, the children fought and cried and the mother stared into space. The father squatted in the doorway, smoking Chinese cigarettes and gazing in the direction of Kailash, which was completely neutralised by a grey swab of cloud. Finally he started out of his contemplation, as if smitten by a revelation, and shooed us off to our rooms.

As a matter of fact, QM now had a name: Purnima. It means 'full moon' and she had been given it in India, where she had spent the last three years. For visa reasons she was studying music at the University of Varanasi, but actually she was doing her *sadhana*. Sadhana is religious practice, and can take many forms. I wondered what meant for her. 'Oh, I can just stare at the river all day,' she said. She and Thomas had the room next to mine and she came in to express her frustrations about Thomas; she insisted she wanted to do the kora in 'moan', and Thomas didn't seem to know what she meant. What she meant was that she wanted to do it in silence; even eye contact with other people should be avoided. The idea of circumambulating in moan is that the undistracted mind is better able to meditate on the holiness of the mountain. And he would keep speaking to her! Thomas coughed innocently and painfully in the next room. Eventually, having voiced every aspect of her desire for silence, she proposed that we spent the evening reading to Thomas from the *Bhagavad Gita*. He'd never heard it before, and it would be good for him to be reminded of the illusory nature of his discomfort. Accordingly, we brewed up pots of hot powdered milk on his stove, lit Indian incense and candles, and took it in turns to read selected passages. The invalid drank hot milk, stifled his coughs, and if he would have preferred sympathy and medicine to a reading from the *Bhagavad Gita*, he never mentioned it.

Again, trivialities vanished into a new calm. Kailash might be invisible, but Kailash was present. The valleys around were dark and filled with mist and the vast silences roared with the power that lurked there, uninterpreted and not even half-heard as yet.

28 - Dolma La

THE MORNING WAS cold and severe, and a heavy mist obscured everything except the foreground of broken glass, rubbish and shit. I was quite used to dirt — but there was something particularly squalid and repulsive about this place. I lay in bed for a couple of hours, reading and writing. People and mice kept coming to see what I was doing, but the only welcome visitor was Purnima, bringing a cup of hot water with which I could mix milk powder. Later, after they'd left, I sat on the verandah, waiting to see if Kailash was going to appear, watching how the mother and children spent their day — in simply sitting and scraping up distractions from the meanest things; the most savage child insisted on going naked and another tried to force a coat — or rather, the raggy remains of a coat — on her. The naked one objected with loud wailings, and clambered onto the mother, who kissed her back in an amiable fashion. She reminded me of an orangutan — heavy, ponderous, guileless. Other children played and scrapped in a similarly futile way. I gave them some small pieces of Danish small change, which pleased them so much that each child immediately set to hiding their coin — which touched off new arguments, heated and hysterical. These people lived in the dharm, at one of the holiest spots on earth; Hindu tradition would consider it an offence to even consider them as ordinary people, for they must have been elevated souls in their last lives to have been reincarnated here. If they themselves commit offences in the dharm they take rebirth as animals or plants; if they live piously then they return to Shiva's spiritual home, Shivalokha. But there seem to be an awful lot of offences in the spiritual penal code of the Hindus. Buddhists certainly wouldn't criticise, and would revere these people. From their teachings and folk lore, they know how often the sleazy old man in a torn coat, picking lice from his unwashed scalp and throwing them in the fire, turns out to be a great teacher. Doubtless they were demi-gods in cunning disguise, but I, seeing with material eyes, found them all slightly repulsive. The mists thickened, and I set off.

After a hundred yards or so I met a Tibetan man whose cratered face I recognised from the trading tent in Darchen. With him was a Tibetan woman whose open face generated friendliness. I carried her small bag, he carried my larger one, she carried his empty one; at least, it was empty to start with. Very slowly we began the ascent of Dolma La, stopping every hundred yards or so for her to dart off down through the rocks to collect scrags of sheep's wool. The path led up through a bleak blend of green and grey. Only the brown shoulder of the hill of Manjusri slipped out of the mists around Kailash, and soon enough, even if it had been clear, Kailash itself would have been out of sight. My companions were not particularly devoted to any ritual save the circumambulation itself; the man smoked a cigarette every time we stopped, and the woman chattered about the cardigan she would make of the wool she'd gathered. Their society was good and easy-going.

The hillside was dotted with stones balanced one on another, and small streams wiggled through the turf. We came to a place consecrated to the memory of the dead, where people leave relics of the departed and pray for their well-being. The death can also be that of one's own ego. A damp ragged jumble-sale of old clothes and shorn-off hair stained the hillside. Discarding something here is symbolic of shedding an old skin, of detaching from the corpse of one's former self, of stamping on a mask which was more trouble than it was worth to wear. I'd even seen a photo of a child left lying dead, but saw no skeleton. Above the heap, when you looked up to the grey sky, all that could be seen was a stone forest of lha-tse: the knobbly stelae reached out of a primeval spot in man's subconsciousness, into the grey present undisturbed. Here history was renounced in favour of more urgent currents. My two companions left me, and I threw a pair of favourite old trousers onto the heap. The dissembling is supposed to prepare one for the gruelling, death-associated climb of Dolma La. I carried on.

I was alone, following the slender well-trodden path up through the deathly grey silence. The presence of Kailash was compelling even without the physical vision, and as the altitude rose, so feelings of individual glory fell away. The forest of stones thickened. I lit incense, put up stones, and carried on. I knew at one point would come a big rock, on which one must lay down and renounce one's ego. I did at least lay down on a big orange rock, which by a chance in several hundred may have been the right one, and take a look at this elusive ego thing. It wouldn't appear to my mind's eye, but its numerous supporters were there: old attachments shed in well-plotted theory but hanging on ... for the moment they seemed very unimportant. I was almost mindless. Things of the past had no place here.

On I walked, up into the future. Behind a rock I found a party of Tibetans — one Ani-la and four men with silk-tasselled heads, who gave me a cup of tea with some tsampa added. Refreshed and fortified, I moved on. Slowly slowly up the dreaded Dolma La. The actual ascent was, as Franca said, 'not too bad'. The altitude is 18,600 feet, and it was a bit of a problem getting enough air into my lungs. Swami Pravananda describes with relish the blue-lipped rigours of the pass, and indeed many have died on the windswept way; but with a few rest stops I was soon there. A great flagpole marked the top of the pass, hung with thousands of coloured flags that streamed off it in all directions. All the rocks around were painted with red, green and yellow 'Om mani padme hum's, swastikas and Sanskrit. Coins had been pressed onto the rocks with butter, and grain was everywhere in this barren place. The flags flapped like a fire in the wind — and all around the area were scattered old clothes again, old shoes, tin plates, broken cups, long black tresses of sacrificed hair, coins and yak-skulls.

I breathed deeply there. Despite the cold, the altitude and the inhospitable weather — concentration was instantaneous and profound. Rainbows of hope streamed out of the *chakra* where Kailash was situated, and when I opened my eyes, snow was falling, and a small red-breasted bird hopped about between my knees. I was alone there, and it was a long way down to anywhere to sleep. Feeling indeed disembodied, I circumambulated the flagpole, put up a couple of stones, and began the descent.

29 - Down to Zuthulphuk Gompa

ONCE UPON A TIME, Shiva had a wife called Sati. Sati's father held a fire ceremony but offended Lord Shiva by omitting to invite him. Sati, outraged, went to the ceremony. Here she protested the insult to her husband by throwing herself on the fire, where she perished. Hence the name *'sati'* is given to the traditional Hindu practice of a widow similarly immolating herself on her husband's funeral pyre. Anyway, Sati was reincarnated as Parvati, and was determined to win back Shiva. This was not easy, for Shiva, in the grief of his bereavement, had retired to Kailash, and there spent his time entirely in deep meditation. Parvati had high standards to maintain, especially with a god for a husband. So she followed him to Kailash where, indifferent to heat and cold, she would immerse herself in an icy lake for days at a time, chanting the name of her Lord, hoping that he would notice and recognise her. For all her austerities, she finally needed Indra's help in waking him out of his sadhana, but it all came out right in the end. Now she is reinstated as Shiva's *shakti* (female energy counterpart) somewhere behind the veils of cold mist at Kailash, where they live happily ever after with their two sons, Ganesh and Kartikeya.

The name of the lake where Parvati would bathe is Gaurikund, meaning 'Parvati's lake'. On the other side of Dolma La there were waves and waves of cindery grey rocks, falling away downhill as far as the eye could see; and, at the bottom of the first fall away to the right, not so far from the summit, was a small pool of deep emerald green. This was Gaurikund. I have read that the waters are frozen all the year round, but, though the edges were crusted with snow, wind rippled the surface.

And then it was snowing — snow and rain together, driving down in icy blasts, and the path was lost in a sea of boulders — but down, down, down anyway I jumped, chanting 'Om nama Shivaya' all the way — until finally, after a couple of hours, the sun came out, and Purnima surprised me by appearing on a grassy bank and saying in quite a natural voice: 'You want a snack?'

Yes! I hadn't liked to disturb her moan that morning, but she seemed disposed to talk. She had, by some magic, a packet of Indian cumin-spiced fries and peanuts which we shared with a Tibetan of indeterminate sex who, when he or she had feasted, hared off down the valley. The sun was brief, and presently we followed the androgynous Tibetan. Walking, we did not talk; but I think we were both glad to have the other there when we found ourselves near dusk on the wrong side of a swift-flowing river. It was not too deep but fast and cold, with a bed of slippery boulders; we held hands to cross it, and how different it was to have the stability of another human being there!

Rakastal came into sight, and the sky over it was a luminescent blue, the sky above and behind us an orange and apricot glow of cloud. Soon before nightfall we came to the gompa of Zuthulphuk.

This gompa is built over the cave where Tibet's beloved mystic, Milarepa, sat and meditated for many years. Milarepa was originally sent by his mother to learn Bon magic, which skill he learnt so successfully that he was able to revenge the wrongs done them by his wicked uncle. Having wreaked the havoc of retribution, however, he was then so overcome with remorse that he went to the great Tantric sage Marpa, in order to learn the holy Dharma. Marpa treated him very cruelly, but Milarepa stuck it out and was eventually rewarded with the sacred instruction. He spent many years in this cave here in the eastern valley of Kailash, dining on nettles and composing songs in praise of the joys of renunciation. Numerous legends surround his name, a popular one being that his diet of nettles eventually turned his skin green. His sister referred to him as a 'human caterpillar' until she finally saw the light of his way and became one of his most dedicated disciples.

The vertical slash of the swastika on the southern face stems from Milarepa — it is said that, once upon a time, a Bon priest challenged Milarepa to see whose magic was the greater. The issue was to be decided by a race to the summit of Kailash. It was very early in the morning, before daybreak. Well, the Bon-pa set out, and began to scurry up the rocks and the ice with great speed. As for Milarepa, he just sat around in his cave. His supporters began to get worried, and urged him to set out, but Milarepa would not be hurried. Then, just as it looked as if the Bon-pa was about to win, the first sunbeam broke across the sky; and on the sunbeam, quick as its flash, rode Milarepa right to the summit. The Bon-pa was so surprised to see Milarepa whizzing past him that he dropped his damaru, his ritual drum, and it went bouncing all the way down the mountainside, scoring the ice with a vertical line of steps which are plain to be seen by anyone. This is the only recorded instance of anyone ever reaching the summit of Kailash.

To the cultural heritage of Tibet, Milarepa left a hundred thousand songs, written down by his favourite disciple Rechung. The Kargyupa sect of the old school leads through Milarepa, from Marpa and Naropa before him; this is the ascetic line, whose teachings depend not so much on doctrines and texts but on the austere practices of a hermit's life and on the realisation of divine truths through meditation. The Hindus identify Milarepa with Shiva, because both are ascetics with long matted hair and bodies coloured like Manasarovar. Milarepa is still adored today, and he is always depicted with his right hand cupped to his right ear, his head tilted sideways as he listens to the song of the soul which he loved so well.

After the forbidding sobriety of the northern valley and the gaunt rocks of Dolma La, the air was light and happy here, even though it was just about dark. A high mani wall glowed deep orange with the last of the daylight. First we went to the monastery itself. It was tiny, and all was black inside except for a few brilliant flames from the kitchen fire. Two men sat there, and a solitary monk loomed out of the dark to greet us. He was willing to oblige us in our request to see the gompa, and unlocked the door for us. Inside was first a scarcely-lit shrine, and then a low-ceilinged cave — the cave of Milarepa! His image, right hand cupped to right ear, was there, laughing in bronze out of the dim butterlight before him. On the ceiling was the vague imprint of his hand — apparently he once found the ceiling too low for the summer, so he pushed it up to allow more air in; then in the winter it was too draughty, so he went up above the cave and stamped it down again, and it is said his foot-print is still up there too. The low ceiling of the gompa blended with the blackness above the cave, and we crouched below. Despite the cramped physical dimensions, it was a very spacious and open atmosphere that pervaded here. The monk stood by with his torch, so we could not stay long. We bowed, laid flowers, and sprang out into the stars.

Tonight's accommodation was a new heaven and new earth compared with last night's; again it was a long row of rooms with a kitchen at the end. But tonight the floor was clean and dry and smelt only of earth. A quiet and peaceful man lived alone there; he was friendly and spoke Hindi, and so Purnima was able to converse with him as he boiled up some hot water for us. Thomas had gone on to Darchen, and we were the only ones staying here. We consumed noodles and hot milk while he mended his trousers in the candlelight, and before sleeping I read to Purnima the third chapter of the *Bhagavad Gita*. This was a vibrant place — a mouse rooted in our rucksacks and the air was impregnated with the simple joy of being alive.

30 - Back to Darchen

THE DAY WAS cool and misty, and birds hopped in at the open kitchen door to peck quite fearlessly at the tsampa from our plates. It was a delightful place to be — very simple, peaceful and airy. Even the sun came out. I waited till Purnima had been gone an hour or so before I also took my leave of the place. The man wanted no more than one kwai for the lodging. It seems this is his devotional service — to maintain a pleasant rest house for the benefit of pilgrims' comfort, and so perpetuate the peace of Milarepa.

Hardly had I gone a hundred yards when I heard a yelping; looking up I saw a large dog with a smaller, live, object in its mouth. This I first took to be a puppy, and was just reflecting on how, when a mother dog plays with her young, it sounds like torture — when I realised that it was not a pup, and it was torture: it was one of the golden marmots which I had glimpsed many times, and the dog had the unfortunate beast by a hind leg and was mauling it about. I picked up a stone and ran towards them, and the dog, seeing me, ran away up the hill. The marmot lay on its side, panting in utter exhaustion and relief — and I, reminded of what it felt like to lie on the river bank in the same state, empathised with it. Standing guard I examined the creature: ears set into the head, paws like a bear's, with long black toes, golden brown hair and a long flattish tail. Eventually, having recovered its breath, it rolled dark gold bloodshot eyes round and saw me — at which it scampered limping up the hillside to its hole, dragging an off-hind leg that bled. I hope it had a mate to bring it food and generally cheer it up.

Kailash is not at all visible from the eastern valley, but it is a pretty, magical place. This is the happy valley of joy and rebirth, of release from the confines of out-dated coffins. From the hillside fell a waterfall, and I followed the stream up to investigate the cave behind it. Impossible to sleep in it — the cave floor was damp and sloping, and there was even a pile of twisted ice there. I found a giant puffball growing nearby, and salivated at the thought of what it would taste like, fried in butter … nettles abounded, and I gathered a bag full of their bright green heads before proceeding. I was beginning to feel woozy, as if I too was getting a cold. Well, it was good to remember it was all an illusion, but also good to lie down in the sun from time to time, to feel my body disintegrating into the grass and the space.

The path followed high above the river valley, and the rocks were coloured with a hallucinogenic verve — here red and green interswirled, and the green rocks were dark and hard, ribbed like broken chunks of glass, as if they were baked on another planet and had been shot here by hypersonic delivery. Then there was a gorge streaming with black and orange, vivid as fire and soot. I lay down again, suffused with their dizzy beauty, and was just drifting into a land of pure colour when a prostrating man and his small son appeared; leaving his stone at the extent of his last prostration, the man came to hassle me for Dalai Lama pictures. The son already had one in his hands — I later discovered that Purnima had given it to him — and he flapped it at me. 'One of these! Look, give me another one of these!' he was saying. It was touching, the perpetual responsibility the Tibetans put on the foreigners to provide Dalai Lama pictures, and poignant too how much they valued the pictures. Their reverence for their Precious Ocean of Wisdom, their God-King, was not debased but elevated by this photo-fixation. To give or to receive a photo is a poor substitute for reinstating the Dalai Lama, but it does show to some extent how much he, even from exile, still rules the hearts of his people.

Lake Rakastal had now come into view; the streak of intense turquoise was reserved by the certain sobriety that always hovers over its waters. This was where I wanted to go next — around the Lake of the Moon where the hidden workings of the subconscious hover. Then the path dropped, turned the last corner. The happy valley was out of sight, and, as slowly as possible, I walked the last leg along back to Darchen.

I picked up rocks which might have been meteorites, and laid them on the mani walls that waylaid the path. The sunset was silver, gold, orange and pink over the Gurla Mandhata to the south, and a new Shiva moon rode gently through a pale luminescent blue sky to the west. If one walks around Kailash 108 times, say the Hindus and Buddhists, one is guaranteed entry into Nirvana. I had been round only once, in a haphazard sort of way; to gain full benefit, one must walk about with a perfectly concentrated and devoted mind as many times as possible. But even in my one circle I felt that the natural power of the mountain was so strong, that to walk about it one hundred and eight times would in itself be heaven on earth.

31 - Hanging out in Darchen

NOW THE COLD had really taken hold, and I gave up the idea of a kora round Rakastal. Walking along the slender path at the foot of the mountains, with all the wide plains sweeping away to the south, it was not surprising to feel at one with the spaces of the universe. Back in Darchen the feeling was a little at odds with the everyday demands of the body. I ceased to fight, surrendered to the enemy within, and became immersed in the sensations and impressions which filtered through, as if from very far away, in response to these demands.

The old woman who tended Dorje's fire was a hag, dancing about in glee as she repeated: 'Mindoo! Mindoo!' — she meant there was no key to the store-room in which I'd locked my tent.

'Doo! Doo!' I cackled back with equal delight as I unlocked the door with the located key. I was homesick for the tent. The room in the guest house weltered water bottles, stove, petrol, plastic bags and food — I pitched by the river, and, by the multi-coloured radiance of the growing moon, spiked tent pegs through stones with waning strength.

Almost indifferent to the iciness of the water, my body washed clothes, hair and itself, all on fully automatic. As everything dried on the river bank I idled in the sun with a large book lent by Choying Dorje. The book was in German, all about Reinholdt Messner 'an den Spoeren Sven Hedin' (in the footsteps of Sven Hedin), written by his wife. The expedition went from Beijing to Kashgar via Kailash in about three weeks, and with them went a few useful people like doctors, and things such as a Landcruiser full of photographic equipment. Reinholdt Messner naturally wanted to climb Kailash, but Beijing fortunately wouldn't hear of it. One night the members of the expedition had a heated debate as to the ethics of climbing the sacred summit. Messner argued that there should be no taboos, that the foot of man is free to go where it will, but the others demurred: one should respect the beliefs of the people in whose country the mountain happens to stand. He consoled himself by running round Manasarovar in a day. The book contained many excellent shining photos; Kailash rose like a god from the page, but reality rose just there in front of me; what really captivated me was the photo of men paddling flat bread hot from the oven in Kashgar. I caught my breath at the sight: 'Bread!'

There was plenty of feasting. In the friendly traders' tent I was so plied with tsampa and butter tea that I seemed to perceive the people about me as if sifted through a high dry mountain of rough-ground grain. One woman energetically unpacked a wooden case of noodles and repacked them into a metal box. The child had lost his charming lordly air in a long whining mood of complaint, and an old man flowed fingers and voice over his prayer beads in a corner of the canvas folds. The vision crumbled, and was replaced by the figure of Purnima triumphant over a pot of vegetables, begged from an Indian *pujari* at sunset and cooked on Thomas' stove. The steam had no scent, my stomach was full of tsampa, and the vegetables so long visualised could not tempt me. In dreams however, all the senses intact, I was tantalised by a madman I once knew; he came up to me in a bar, and offered me a deep-fried puri. I sank teeth hungry for fat into its flesh, and woke up.

The people of the traders' tent sat out in the sun, devouring a large plastic bowl full of boiled yak entrails; the mother cut off a piece of soft dark grey innard for her son, and it fell off the blade like velvet; he crammed it into his mouth but a lot of it spilled out over his face again, worm castings over smooth turf. I fled. Then quite casually Dharma John produced packets of Nepalese biscuits, a jar of honey and a jar of peanut butter, wondering if I was hungry. There was a faint echo of something sweet penetrating the taste buds, and a dry distant crunch that cloyed before descending the gullet. A woman gave me an apple, and while eating it I enjoyed the sight of orchards reaching as far as the eye could see, felt the cool white crunch toying with Baltic breezes somewhere, tasted nothing. And then at sunset Dharma John appeared at my tent door and gave me not one, but two, deep-fried puris, still hot from a fire made by a group of Khampas. Dreams come true at Kailash.

John had a yak skull balanced on a pile of stones outside his tent. As we sat there in the sun we were visited by a steady stream of pilgrims. One of the visitors had a festering wound on his leg, and when John produced a plastic box full of medicines, pills, creams and ointments, he rapidly became the camp doctor. All those present immediately set to rolling up sleeves and trouser legs to display their wounds and troubles, each one in need of medication, and the flow of visitors thickened. John did his best, but when one rolled-up trouser leg revealed a knee with the hole of an old bullet shot through it, he had to admit his box contained no remedy.

Another visitor was a lama from Samye monastery; he wore a Shiva rudrakshra seed round his neck, and was able to point himself out in one of the photos in the big German book. At the photograph of the wreck to which the Chinese government have reduced his monastery, he could only shake his head over and over, speechless. A whole mountainside was scored with thousands of rooms cracked apart, and all the contents are offered to the empty winds. Doubtless had we shared a language he could have howled the spaces with tales of horror — but there was only this haunting speechlessness.

In the night I finished the Dalai Lama's book, and wept at the story so largely unknown to the world — of deliberate annihilation, brutal humiliation, compulsory sterilisation and cold-blooded starvation of the Tibetan race at the hands of the Chinese. I didn't know how long the story had lurked unread, like an uneaten fruit, its skin ripening black by the smoke of the fire — but now it had fallen into my hands and been opened again, I vowed to pass it on, with the injunction to pass it on and on, so that as many people as possible might be alerted to the plight of Tibet.

Since then, the world has seen what the Chinese are capable of doing to the Chinese, in the broad daylight of Tiananmen Square. If the government could perpetrate such horror under the full glare of publicity, what ferocities could not be committed out of sight? But then — no government really speaks for the people. The Chinese cook in the 'dining room' was friendly and kind. On the second morning I arrived to catch him making vast quantities of deep-fried dough strips; he piled my plate high several times, and, having cleared up, invited me to take my time and to help myself from the thermos of hot water by the stove. He went outside to pass the morning with a few soldiers who sat there, toying with their rifles: floppy and languid, they were just boys, sent thousands of miles away from home to twiddle their thumbs on this desolate plateau.

I sat alone in the sleazy kitchen, feeling the fat sliding down my throat. On the wall someone had drawn white graffiti of two copulating horses, grins on their faces. The surreality of my situation grated on my bones down here — rather than stay in Darchen with all its sordid broken glass, I may as well take my tent up to somewhere with one clear view. Though I had neither energy nor inclination to walk around Rakastal now, there were a couple of gompas up the valley close to the foot of Kailash.

32 - Silung Gompa

H AVING PACKED THE RUCKSACK with tent, giant puffball, noodles and a few sugary oddments found in the store-cupboard shop at the guest house, I climbed up the rocky wall that guards the southern approach to Kailash. The cold white water surged out of its gorge, the blood roared around my head, and the prayer flags wagged vigorously across the gulf in the early evening wind. Once over the wall, the incline was mild. After an hour or so, the river divided. Both tributaries come from the same source — the foot of Kailash — and stream out of two valleys, separated by a large hill. There is a gompa in each valley. I knew that Purnima and Thomas had gone up to Gengta Gompa in the right-hand valley, so I took the left-hand one: up here was Silung Gompa, and nobody went here because the monks were in a three-year retreat. It seemed a very good reason to go.

I crept up the valley, collecting dried yak dung as I went, taking rest-stops from time to time in order to simply sit and breathe in the very pale green air. I was feeling half delirious, empty-headed, and my body was an open pane through which streamed the environment: water poured clear and solid over great round granite boulders, silver syrup over the celestial sweets of an austere table. Horned blue flowers and furry edelweiss grew out of soft springy turf, and a few birds shot the clear air with their song. The chestnut cube of the gompa, clinging to the other side of the valley like a burr on an animal pelt, came into sight. The river was wide and shallow now, and I crossed it without difficulty. An interlocking pattern of hillsides and rockfaces led the eye up the valley, gradually preparing for the moment when Kailash sprang into view. Much nearer than I had seen it before, the assertive white spearhead dominated everything in sight, rivetted everything in the world.

Rivulets ran with gurgles under pavings of mottled boulders, popped up in dimples of spiralling water (clockwise, naturally), dropped down once more into the earth. By one such basin, on a soft smooth cushion of green turf, I pitched the tent. Here I was just hidden from the gompa by the incline that led up to it, and I aligned the tent so that the flaps opened directly onto the view of Kailash. That night I made a fire with the yak dung, and crammed the pot with noodles, nettles, spices, and the chopped-up puffball. Though the fire lit easily enough, it gave off little heat and a lot of smoke; the wind sheered in and sliced away the flames in a lateral direction, and every time I tried to shield it, the wind changed. Thus the bottom inch of the pan's contents cooked, while the top remained stone-cold; with much stirring and patience, the feast was ready and all hot in about three hours.

And then for the next thirty-six hours I lapsed into a state of delirium and dream. That night and all the next day I lay inert in the tent, eating only a vile chemical compound of sugar and orange dye, going outside only for the necessities. The mild fever which had prevented my kora of Rakastal now plumbed the deep forces of the subconscious the lake represents; images long hidden and suppressed by the solid overlay of the active mind now snaked up, permeated the flimsy stratum the latter had become, and gyrated about me in a surreal circus of impossibility and delight. Odd moments blossomed vivid again and coincided and col- laborated with one another to create a mirage bordering on lunacy. And when I opened my eyes, there, manifest and tangible before me, was the greatest impossibility of all. Mount Kailash!

Another day dawned, and I lay looking at the mountain, waiting for the clouds to clear. Up the valley came a singing crowd of Tibetans, five men and a woman, all carrying large bundles wrapped up in coloured cotton. First they all threw themselves and their burdens down on the grass about the entrance to the tent, and peered eagerly inside, demand- ing to know how many people I was. Finally they believed I was alone, and sat down at a short distance where they proceeded to unpack their loads. These contained prayer books and bundles of cotton. The books were orange loose-leaf, bound by string; in wafery sunshine, the merry crowd sang mantras and opened up the cloth. Then they ripped it into squares, touched the sacred books to their heads, and wrapped each one up in its individual floral binding.

A Chinese soldier who hung out at Darchen arrived, with his Tibetan wife: she carried a baby on her back and he a rifle over his shoulder. He spoke a little English, like: 'Have you been to Silung Gompa?'

'Not yet.'

'Let's go!'

So when the cavalcade proceeded up the path, I followed them. An old woman, who stuck her tongue out so far that she fairly strained it at the roots, ushered us in. She led us through a narrow corridor of earth and wood, up a narrow staircase to a tiny room on the roof. Here a long-haired lama sat in a kind of small wooden cot, and gratefully received from the party the gifts of veneration they had brought him. There were of course many kathas, and one kwai notes, two bottles of strawberry shampoo, a bag full of coloured silks and some Nepalese biscuits. The lama had a lively face and friendly eyes, and demanded to see my books. Carefully he turned over the pages of my diary, and brought out with long finger nails some pressed flowers of horned blue. 'Mendip!' he said — meaning they were used for medicine. I could not oblige him in his request for a Dalai Lama picture, and felt that he regarded the money I gave him instead to be a pretty poor substitute.

The room was stuffed with religious objects, crowded with people, and a stove burned in the centre which made it very hot. When a young monk who spoke English appeared and invited me down to the kitchen to drink tea, I accepted gratefully. He spoke English because he had been brought up in Dharamsala, the town in northern India where the Dalai Lama has set up his government in exile; with his foreign ways he was in a position to show off, and he did so with professional ease.

The kitchen was small and snug, with raised carpet-covered beds, walls and ceiling hung with a cloth of rumbustious Chinese design — red, with pink peonies, peaches, grapes, flaming green leaves and bursting pomegranates. It felt like sitting inside a cushion. And the window framed a perfect picture of the magic mountain. It was an ideal compilation of the two worlds — that of physical and spiritual needs, both answered together.

The Dharamsala monk explained that this gompa was of the Digung-kargyu sect — one of Milarepa's lineage. As part of their training the monks must spend three years in retreat. Surely there could be no better place in the world to go into retreat. Uncontaminated by the lower symptoms of human inhabitation — broken glass, old boots and fag-ends, for example — the place was occupied only by such elements as build up the spiritual stairway. In typical Tibetan grace however, the stairway was flexibly constructed — though the monks were officially but one year into their three year retreat, they opened up every day at one o'clock to visitors; for an hour they could talk, laugh, interchange news, eat and joke — and then they would return to their silences, to their sutras, to their mantras, to their realisations within the raised womb of the protective earth.

The Dharamsala monk and two young novices brought out big Tibetan books to show me; the pages were covered with the flourishing formal script developed from the Sanskrit, and into them were slotted many loose leaves of pictures. Red-faced gods huffed and puffed their appled cheeks, stood in stalwart stances with swords brandished against the forces of evil, embroidered chests inflated against the winds that

swept off the painted mountains. They told me their names, knowing I
would never remember such a list, but telling me anyway, that I should
be touched by the divinity contained within their sounds.

It was lunch time. They dished out plates of rice, heaped them over
with yoghurt and sprinkled them with coarse white crystals of sugar. It
was manna from heaven. Others of the Tibetan party I had come up with
crowded in, and, as I ate, an old man squashed up to the left of me picked
up a human thighbone fashioned, in the Tibetan way, into a trumpet. It
was bound in red and one of the novices blew it rowdily in my ear, while
at the same time banging a damaru with the other hand. There was
nothing of blasphemy in the act of teasing an ignorant foreigner with the
sacred instruments; rather, by their child-like conjury of laughter, they
seemed to translate all the deepest and most secret mysteries of their lore
to a completely innocent and human level.

There are few texts to the Kargyu line; religious development is based
on personal realisations evolved from individual practices. The practice
is essentially to sit, as Milarepa did, alone in a cave, leading an austere
life; the emphasis is on neither denial nor penance, but upon the sheer
reality of the joyful regions of the soul thus attained. This gompa was a
very cosy civilisation of the cave, the yoghurt and rice a very acceptable
substitute for nettles, the daily visitor's hour a wholesome concession to
the human urge for company from the original solitude. The door
between body and soul was flung wide open, and it was laughter, not the
cowed whispers of Christian cloisters, that issued the password between
the two states.

Lunch over, the kitchen suddenly vacated. I was left alone, sitting on
the carpet-covered bed, with just the tick of the clock, the flip of the wind
and the riddle of the fire for company. The elements danced, each one
peacefully in its rightful place. I wrote. One of the party dashed in, and
with a business-like air filled two wooden cups with bee-hive shaped
lumps of brown sugar. He gave me one and it fell between my teeth:
'*rungba kasa*' they are called. He shot off, presumably to offer them either
to the lama or to a deity. Shortly after that I was charmingly ousted from
the monastery. 'Tomorrow, one o'clock,' said the young monk.

My wits were gathering about me again, and that night I lay with the
tent flaps directly open onto the view of Kailash, despite the mild cold.
With a mind completely concentrated by nothing but the magnetic force
of the cloud-covered peak before me, I finished reading *The Way of the
White Clouds* for the third time, and read the *Bhagavad Gita* right the
way through. Krishna appeared in all the terrible glory of his universal

form; the river ran and gurgled on, the yellow flowers in the grass were now stars in the sky, and I delighted in lying so close to the earth, sky and water, as if in perpetual prostration to the sacred mountain.

33 - Gengta Gompa

EVENTUALLY, INSPIRED BY lack of food, I packed up the tent and went down the valley again to where it meets with the other valley. Here I met Thomas and Purnima, just coming down from where I was going — Gengta Gompa. We lay around in the sun on a grassy bank, talking. The lama at Gengta Gompa had spent many years in exile in the south of India, they said, so he spoke Hindi; and he had a beautiful wife. 'Far out!' said Purnima. 'Just far out!' They had both spent the last four or five days there, not doing much; just sitting, talking, and eating. 'I think we ate one kilo of yoghurt every day!' said Thomas with satisfaction, rubbing his stomach. He told me that I should present some money to the lama, wrapped in a katha; and if I had no katha with me, I should ask the young novice who stayed up there for one — 'They have many kathas!' he said, beaming at the recollection of abundance. The only problem as far as Purnima was concerned was that they ate meat. 'Their hands smell of meat,' said Purnima, 'so everything they touch is contaminated.' She played with a piece of turquoise and some coral about her neck that the lama's wife had given her.

Thomas updated me on the number of vegetables in his garden in Bavaria: forty-nine. I changed American dollars and Nepalese rupees into Chinese renminbi for them; and then they started an argument as to whether it would be better for me to stay up at the gompa that night or to descend to Darchen. 'Well, I'll go and see what happens,' I said, and did so.

The blue skies produced a sudden cold hailstorm as I approached the monastery. This valley was a barren cauldron of green and Kailash was not visible at all from here. Long mani walls and stupas hung with prayer flags marked the approach to the gompa, where coloured dots stood on the roof of the cube in the clouds, watching my approach. Finally I ascended a long flight of steps that led up to the rear of the monastery. At the top I was met by a sturdy boy in long brown robes and a felt cowboy hat, who was obviously the novice Thomas had told me about. He showed me to a room with carpeted beds, where I dumped my rucksack; and then he led me up to the top room, where the fabled far out lama sat with his far out wife.

They sat in silence before a stove in a room warm and cosy with deep-piled carpeted settee-bed, religious pictures hung with kathas, and all the coloured silk paraphernalia of Tibetan Buddhism. The pair contemplated me in bemusement. The wife was indeed beautiful; full fat loops of seed-pearls hung luxuriantly from her ears, coral and turquoise about her neck, framing a lovely delicate face; and the lama indeed spoke a bit of Hindi — and all he seemed able to say was, 'Where was I going,' in a way that seemed to mean 'When was I going'. A pot of tea sat on the stove, but I was offered none. Not to offer tea to a guest is a Chinese way of telling them they're unwelcome, but it was unusual for Tibetans to do this. I asked if I might be allowed to see the gompa.

The boy took me down and unlocked the door. There was a dim room hung with silks and embroideries of the Buddha, cobwebbed everywhere with strands of offered katha. Before the cupboard which contained many small statues and which was the altar, I placed some money as the standard offering. Now I remembered what Thomas had told me about offering to the lama, and asked the boy for a katha. 'Mindoo!' he said emphatically, arms akimbo. The lie was rather obvious. Oh dear — this was not at all the kindly reception I'd been led to expect.

Perhaps had I offered the lama some money, his attitude may have softened; but, still unsure as to what proper compromise with etiquette I could make, having no katha, having already given to the gompa — any excuse, in fact, to cover up for the fact that I did not feel spontaneously moved to give — I offered him nothing. It was perhaps the wrong thing to do, or perhaps whatever I did would have made no difference. He sat, twisting pieces of sheep's wool about fragile splinters of wood in order to form wicks for the altar lamps. His coat, off at one shoulder, was of saffron yellow Chinese brocade, and he wore dark brown old fashioned sunglasses. I saluted them with hands together, in their own silence, and made to depart.

But apparently there was some runnel of the milk of human kindness yet remaining — as I compiled my rucksack again, the boy ran down and said: 'Tea drunk — djo!' I translated this as meaning that if I would accept a cup of tea before leaving, everybody's face would be saved. So I trotted upstairs for the one symbolic cup of tea — taken again mainly in silence. A silence as thick and heavy as the walls, which allowed in only a couple of fractions of light — through one small window in the wall and another in the roof. Peering across the stove to try and discern some of the wife's fabulous beauty, I caught her eye, and like another gleam of light, she slowly smiled.

And then her mood changed as she minced about the newly-polished altar lamps in the corner, lighting them and mocking — me? Not just my paranoia nor crushed expectations — there was definitely a strange atmosphere. The boy then 'Djo!'-ed me downstairs, and with a quiet triumph watched me go.

I left with pleasure. I could certainly understand their desire to be left alone. There were still a couple of hours of daylight left to go, and I made my way back down to Darchen. Once the gompa was out of sight, I rested for a while in the wind. A beautiful view of Rakastal had appeared — deep blue round the sprawling edges, with a strong white mirror gloss in the centre. Clouds rippled off the Gurla Mandhata range like the shining peel from some gigantic celestial fruit, and the sky over the surrounding mountains was a pale clear blue, reamed with muggy grey. The scree of the slopes about me was green and purple, clear as the song of the river. The pale moon, a little bit broader every night now, sailed gently over the mountain tops. I forgot about the disappointment of the gompa as the unlimited regions of nature called much more congenial reflections to mind.

Back down in Darchen, Thomas and Purnima laughed at my story: the lama and his wife were probably fed up of foreign guests, after having had them stay for so many days. And now Purnima modified her reports, they weren't really all that far out, she insisted: after all, their hands smelt of meat. But it's dangerous to apply one's own values, or one's own notion of other people's values, to other people's behaviour; how do we ever know the exact motivation of any action, and is it really of that great importance? I knew that that lama had re-built the gompa from the ruins to which the PLA had reduced it, that the very walls were impregnated with his dedication and faith. It was only natural that he should want to shy sometimes from the superficial tourist eye.

34 - Padmasambhava puja

PADMASAMBHAVA WAS A shadowy figure to me. He was the founder of the Nyingmapas, of the old school of esoteric practices; he gratified all his senses and yet he simultaneously sublimated them through the magical synthesis which is the core of the mysteries invoked by the word 'Tantra'. His was a crystalline power, blurred by occult shadows and engulfed in dark maroon robes in the twilight realm halfway between myth and history. His name means 'lotus born' and he was a great sorcerer, one great enough to subdue all the demons of Tibet with his magic thunderbolt; he cut quite a figure in the Tibetan mind with his adamantine abilities. The tenth day of every lunar month in Tibet is sacred to Padmasambhava, for when he ascended from Chiu Gompa to the heavens, it was not for ever. On this day the beloved Guru Rinpoche himself might still come down to earth in some shape or another, and pujas are performed in his honour.

The mind is restless and hard to control. Ritual is a practical means of combating the demons that can slip into our minds wherever we are, and demons find the high imaginative air of Tibet a particularly convenient place to live. By performing pujas in honour of Padmasambhava, so his blessings and protective powers are invoked. By repetition and rhythm a state conducive to meditation is induced; energies are aligned and transformed in order to create a still centre, and the stillness is preserved by the very demons who before presented so many obstacles: the thugs are now converted to wrathful protective deities, swiping with all their might at the graspings of ego with slings and cudgels, mercilessly severing the bonds of attachment to worldly matters with hatchets and knives. If puja is performed with a fully concentrated mind, the individual is elevated from selfishness to selflessness. If not, it is possible that the ritual can become a pretence, a show behind which one is secretly hoping that, by the merit he or she gains, all wishes will be fulfilled. What was going on here?

Dorje had prepared for this month's puja a small one-roomed building of stone set apart from the rest of the compound, whose door I had never seen unlocked before. He advised me to attend, and I found the door now wide open and crammed with Tibetans, the window-shutters unhooked, and viewing space through the bars equally occupied. I pressed into the crush of bodies, inhaled a sharp bouquet of rancid yak and unwashed skin, all raised to a wholesome dignity by the wind, and peered out of the bright broad day into the shadowed interior.

About ten lamas sat in the little room, each one with a damaru in his right hand, bell in left, banging and ringing away, chanting sutras up to a grand crescendo — in which suddenly the damaru would be exchanged for a dorje, the bell for a human thighbone trumpet. Tarantara! Boys ran in and out, filling up the wooden bowls in front of the lamas with hot butter tea, bringing in trays laden with sculpted tsampa and butter, running out with them again and throwing the bits all over the roof, where they broke into bite-sized pieces for the gods and the winds. Dorje nipped about the room, taking photographs with the camera left to him by the Reinholdt Messner expedition, and the chanting went on and on with the soothing bubbling sound of an underground stream. Again it would rise up to a crescendo, again it would drop, and so slowly through the afternoon the loose leaves of the books were unpiled and sung.

The ragged bevy of girls about me began to get bored. I asked a question, and one sharp wit mimicked my even more ragged Tibetan. The rest followed suit, and they all laughed. I suppose they didn't mean any harm, but it bristled the atmosphere. And of course I was an intruder; I knew something of the ideals, as set out in books — but I was ignorant of the practical practice and of the exact nature with which they took the practice. A lama came out to bestow blessings, and they fought to bow plaited and turquoise beaded heads under his benedicting hand. I had the sense that they gathered about the puja from herd instinct rather than in full recognition of what it meant — but perhaps had they been kinder to me, in the manner to which Tibetans in general had accustomed me, I would have been thoroughly enchanted by the whole thing.

The ritual of worshipping Padmasambhava is a metaphor for raising consciousness, for transforming lower energies to a diamond determination to cut away ignorance. Magic lies in the inherent powers of transformation within each and every one of us — was I sufficiently detached from my ego, now that I'd been round Kailash once, to take these snide affronts and turn them into all-healing magical forces? No, not at all. Why, as it turned out, I seemed to faint at the very prospect of going to Rakastal and confronting the beasts inhabiting its gloomy shores. Perhaps, if I did another kora of Kailash instead, I'd gain a little more insight. I wished them Tashi Dillee, they returned the greeting with enthusiasm, and I was off.

35 - Start of second kora

I HAD NO INTENTION this time of sleeping in the sleazy rooms at the north side of Kailash. I was fully equipped with tent, mat, books and noodles. Except for a fire, I was self-sufficient. I set off in the early evening, but time didn't matter now; I could stop wherever I liked, in the old manner. If I had no fire for tea and tsampa, I could always eat biscuits. The skies were dull, but it was great to be alone on the path. Perhaps this time I could really empty my mind a bit into the bliss of solitude.

Purnima had set out earlier in the afternoon, equipped with a note written in Tibetan by Dorje for the first gompa, asking if she could stay a few days there. When I came to the place where the Barga plain greets the western valley however, the place where the flagpole radiates prayers to the winds — there she was, waiting to do yoga with me. There were a few nomad tents camped there, and she had begged hot water from their fire. We did not do yoga and she never went to present her note to the monastery; when she said she was thinking of asking the nomads if she could sleep with them, I immediately said she could share my tent, and immediately again regretted having made the offer. I wanted to be alone, didn't I? And so did she, didn't she? But despite our both doing the opposite of what we'd intended to do, it turned out to be a very happy alliance.

We pitched the tent in the shelter of some mani walls, watched by a never-ending stream of nomads from the nearby encampment. They brought us tea, and I handed round a packet of biscuits — or, should I say, of flat compounds of sugar and sesame seeds. These they accepted with a certain shyness, and then asked, diffidently, if they might have the cardboard box. They might — and a man with pig-tails tucked the treasure into the pouch of his robe. Children grew wide-eyed out of their parents' arms, and fixed us with stares that went on forever; and the eyes of the elders, though narrowed by age, stared with no less wonder. But we were hideous ghostly things compared with them. In the lessening light, with the shadows of their homespun clothes, they grew like natural outcrops of the earth upon which they stood. A quiet light gleamed, in their eyes and in the rows of silver coins sewn into the braids of the women, just as specks of granite shine from the block, just as the sun catches waves on dark water. Though their lives were hard by physical standards, though they were used to action, to labour and endurance, so they were also used to simply standing still and absorbing, with an attention unmolested by distraction, whatever would appear before their gaze. Their beauty lay in their stillness, in their acceptance, and their unquestioning generosity. Perhaps they could not even have articulated themselves what it was that moved and stilled their existence, but they had as little need to justify or to explain as the rocks.

Eventually, one by one, they drifted away. They had sheep to be rounded up, supper to eat, dreams to dream. Night fell, and I sat outside the tent, breathing in the clear dark air. A wind blew, and on it came the eerie, bird-like cries of the boys as they herded together their animals. The wind carried the sound around the rough rocks and the carefully carved stones of the mani walls. It was lightly laden with the penetrating marriage of now with eternity, powerful with a feeling of utter simplicity. Happiness was so easy here.

36 - Cosmopolitan day in Darchen

THE AIM OF THIS KORA was not to clock up another milestone on the way to Nirvana (only another 107 to go …) but to absorb a few more of the details that constitute the whole. Neither Purnima nor I wanted to go round Kailash quickly, and having joined forces, we also joined resources. When Purnima mentioned that she had packets of soup from Nepal, along with several other things she would need, all stashed at Darchen — I volunteered to return there the next day, to pick them up. So, after a breakfast of tea and tsampa, she sat and looked after the camp and I scampered off, back-tracking in a good cause: packets of soup!

As well as unprecedented supplies, I found Thomas surrounded by a group of Indians. They had brought sacks of food from India; an older woman brewed up cups of strong sweet spiced tea, and handed them out to us as we all stood in the sun in a place where, should the clouds move, we would be able to see Kailash. Her forehead was smeared with the three horizontal stripes of sandalwood paste that mark a Shiva devotee, for she had that morning performed their puja on the banks of Manasarovar.

Indians are not allowed indiscriminately into Tibet; the Chinese government had an arrangement with India, allowing thirty Indians to go on pilgrimage to Kailash every month. The trip was advertised in the Indian newspapers, and cost each member about a thousand pounds. This is a lot of money in India but, nonetheless, applications were so numerous that some of them had applied as many as seven times for the privilege. They were also quick to point out that they were not necessarily all rich; to some members of the party, this sum was a life-time's savings. Yet to a devout Hindu this is a trifling price for darshan with the abode of Lord Shiva. Money was not the only qualification needed — each of them had to go to Delhi for a medical check-up before they were accepted; and even when they set out, they had a doctor accompany them to the Indian-Chinese border, checking their blood pressure twice a day. 'We were really pampered up to the border!' exclaimed the City of London-trained lady editor who was telling me all this. From Delhi they had taken a bus up to Almora, and from there they had been provided with horses to ride through the mountains to the dividing line between India and Tibet.

'Was it beautiful?' I asked.

'Beautiful!' There was a spontaneous explosion of glorious expletives to describe the marvels of the journey: there were waterfalls and forests, streams and mountains, and valleys of flowers so thick that they had all alighted from their horses for the pleasure of walking upon them. 'Walking on flowers!' — eyes shone. Once at the border however, the altitude had proven too much for the heart of one member of the party — the poor man had been sent back to Delhi. And then they were in Chinese hands, having to pay extra for this, that and the other without respite. Again they were provided with horses, but their Chinese (did they mean Tibetan?) handlers had taken malicious pleasure in whacking the beasts, to make them jump so the Indians would fall off — and so on. Somehow they had endured, and here they were, waiting for the clouds to clear from the centre of the world.

Theirs was a religious party. The editor told me that she had come more from curiosity than for religious reasons, but she had caught the mood of devotion from her companions, and was joining in all the rituals with an unprecedented enthusiasm, feeling elevated in a way she could never have believed possible. They held prayers every morning and evening, and invited me to join them, and for supper too; I had to refuse

— I was after all doing a kora — but they dug out from their stores some bags of spiced Indian snacks, and made a present of them I had to accept.

Kailash suddenly appeared, and conversation dissolved in the excitement. Canon cameras were rushed out, lenses extracted from the socks that wrapped them. But the clouds swirled close to the peak still. 'Shall I ask Him to blow them away?' asked the editor. 'Shall I ask Shankar to blow them away?' Shankar is one of Shiva's many names, and though she was joking, Shankar indeed obliged by blowing the clouds away again. The Indians clicked happily away on their cameras.

Into the midst of the excitement drove a small blue truck, to the very door of the dining room, and out of it leapt four Europeans. They were French, three women and a man, and seemed little disposed to talk at first. They looked distracted, especially the man, and disappeared round the corner. But I was curious. Half an hour later I found them again in the dining room: refreshed by a combination of beer, cigarettes, soggy noodles and the discovery that I spoke French, they opened up like flowers in the sun. They were disciples of a Tibetan lama, reputedly on his way here with an entourage of two buses full of European followers, with whom they hoped to meet up; they had hired their truck privately in Lhasa and driven straight through Ali, so were nearly as illegal as I had been when I arrived.

Dorje appeared, and mildly enquired if they had their passports. 'Later, later!' they laughed, caught up in the story of how vile their Tibetan drivers had been. Ten minutes later Dorje asked again about their passports. 'They are in the truck,' they said, as if that explained everything. Dorje began to frown and insist, and so they finally and reluctantly did as he asked. I last saw them all trailing into Dorje's room, where they remained in heated argument until after I left. I later learnt that they had had to pay quite a substantial fine — because they made a lot of noise? But they were essentially inspired people, and I was cautious about getting smug about anything in the vicinity of Kailash.

It was a day full of sideshows. There were two Tibetan youths roaming around and annoying the Indians by peering into their rooms. An outraged matron appeared in a doorway and, to their evident delight, yelled at them. The boys picked up pieces of broken glass, hurled them at her, and ran giggling round the corner. As soon as she'd retired into her room they were back, eager to provoke another performance.

'Look at them!' exclaimed one of the Indian men in disgust. 'They really are ignorant people!'

I leapt to their defence. 'You can find boys like that anywhere in the world, I don't think they're that special.' Just a glance at the boys cast immediate doubt on this as regards any literal level — both the miscreants had waist-length hair, elaborately woven long-ago into two pigtails each, and thick fringes that bushed over their eyes; coral and turquoise hung from their ears, and heavy corduroy coats fell off their shoulders and flapped about their ragged knees; on a global scale, they were quite unique. 'No,' said the Indian with distaste. 'Nowhere do you find people quite as ignorant as these. Not even in Bombay.'

The Tibetans held the Indians with equal lack of love; as I was taking a butter tea in the friendly tent, a middle-aged Indian couple wandered in. The Indians had been made to change $100 each at the border, and, though the Chinese had already helped them as much as possible in the matter, they were still at a loss as to how to spend the rest of it. Perhaps they could buy some turquoise? The lovely sister, who was always so kind and considerate to me, stared at them with a blank face. I suggested where they might find turquoise and, as they left, my hostess began to nudge me, to make 'wide' gestures with her hands — referring to the corpulence of the Indian wife. But then she stopped, gasped, and pointed: the lady editor was now outside, conversing with the old couple, and what the sister was pointing at was her boots. They were a rather magnificent pair, padded, ribbed and cushioned in silk-soft leather that put my own river-cracked footwear to shame. *'Hamgo yagadoo!'* breathed the Tibetan lady, entranced. 'Hamgo yagadoo!' Good boots! Good boots!

Thomas insisted on lending me his stove; he was with the Indians now, and would be starting out with them on another kora tomorrow. He would be sharing their delicious meals for days to come — he had no need to cook. I had no qualms about accepting the wondrous loan. This, the genuine Nepalese trekking packet soup, and the knowledge that my tent was pitched in a rather unique spot — lessened the sacrifice of the Indian feast. I began again the cycle of Kailash.

37 - Nyanri Gompa and cave

WHILE I'D BEEN in Darchen, Purnima had had almost uninterrupted darshan of Kailash. But the next day a cold mist and rain poured out of the western valley. We made for Nyanri Gompa, the monastery pinned to the deep maroon cliffs above the river, still at the mouth of the western valley; the small cube merged with the earth from which it had been made, and only came into view when we were nearly there. We found it by faithfully following a path that led over the river and up the steep mountainside. The stones were jewelled by the rain under our feet, and red, gold, green and silver of every shade glowed up from the path.

Various robed figures stood on the roof, watching our ascent. At the monastery door when we arrived stood the two men who had bugged me the time before, when I was trying to paint — the ones who had combed my luggage for Dalai Lama pictures, strangely enough, though they had annoyed me before, especially the short fat one — now they were like dear friends. Perhaps our rather odd reception by the other inmates of the gompa exaggerated the importance of their smiles.

We were ushered to the roof, where we gathered in loose assembly with these others — a handful of rather detached monks, and a few teenage boys. One of the monks wore heavy black-framed spectacles, and a long irregular black stick protruded from his robes; he greeted us tersely, and unlocked and showed us round the interior of the inner sanctum. The stick pointed out from shadow and soot every statue, flag, stone and thangka there as he simultaneously delivered information in a practised rattle a Sacre Coeur tour guide would be proud of. A couple of the boys trailed round with us, and watched with sceptical grins. Suddenly the guide was standing by the door and jiggling the padlock, the stick tapping on the floor; we hastily made some offerings, and bowed our way out.

The rain had stopped, and suddenly there was a magnificent view of Kailash from the gompa roof — stunning anyway, and even more so because it was so high, for we were now looking straight across to the mountain. The colours of the prayer flags jilted one another in the wind, and the dome of Kailash was white and silent. While we stared at the mountain, all was peaceful and still also; but when I peered through the hole in the roof into the kitchen underneath — I caught the eye of a boy making rounds of dough. He stiffened at the sight of me and threatened with an expressive snarl to throw a dough-ball at me as if I were a marauding dog. I prepared to slink off, tail between legs. Purnima, feeling little inclined to produce her note of introduction and request for hospitality, followed suit. Leaving, we came again upon the two men from before. They were making new cupboards in a room ankle-deep in curls of pinewood shavings. A kettle heated tea on a fire of their own, and they offered us some. They sang and whistled as they worked, and the fire lit up their deep curly-pile carpet with a warm welcoming glow, somehow absent from the rest of the place.

We made our way to the caves on the hillside below the monastery. Here fresh water ran and nettles grew. There were several caves to choose from — some of them small, the entrances for the most part built up with walls of stone to keep the edge of the wind out, and a couple of them larger. We selected a larger one. The rock walls formed a natural altar which lodged a few offerings and piles of incense ash, and to the side was a bed of wood piled with dodgy-looking sheepskins and a litter of straw and stones. All the inner surfaces were very black, polished by centuries of smoke, and the atmosphere was profoundly warm and quiet. This was home for the night. I laid out mat, etcetera, on the flat floor, and Purnima made a nest of the bed and the sheepskins for herself. Having lit incense on the altar and put candles about the natural alcoves in the walls of the cave, eagerly we brought out Thomas's stove, anticipating a feast of dehydrated vegetable and preservatives. But it was no good — the stove began to leak jets of orange and blue flame; Thomas had said the flame must be blue, not orange. We pumped and pumped and pumped, but the flame still came out orange. We talked to it in every way possible — kindly, persuasively, indignantly, pleadingly — and the stove just spat out more orange. 'Pumpy pumpy pumpy!' implored Purnima — while I edged near the door and, afraid that it would explode, urged her to leave it. Finally she did, and we packed up the wondrous Canadian invention into its maple leaf box again, and dined instead on lukewarm powdered milk.

The body may not have been overfed, but there was plenty of nutrition for the spirit there. That night we sat on the rocks outside the cave and dissolved into our meditations. The focus was the perfectly symmetrical dome of Kailash, brilliant silver white tonight by the light of the nearly full moon. Again, as at the gompa, we were looking more or less straight across at the mountain. The tall red cliffs of the western valley formed a frame, and Kailash grew illuminated out of a great long-stemmed cup of darkness. Moonwashed rocks intermeshed with the fibres of the brain in the compelling presence. The dark hollows, set either side of the vertical gash down the mountain face, stared hard as the eye sockets of a skull; the human skeleton forms slowly from a tiny conjunction, grows flesh, supports a whole lifetime, till the flesh is withered and the bones pounded and ground, burnt to ashes, to dust again; and all the desperate attempts and failures, dreams and achievements of the lifespan are likewise reduced to so much dust in the face of infinity. The message was clear enough.

38 - Mist and wind

WE HAD AS little success the following morning with the stove as the night before; I attempted something with a pile of yak dung outside, but it was damp, and would not stay alight unless swamped in fuel from the stove — and when that was out, the dung sulked back to a smoking black lump. Tepid water was again the best we could do, and with this we made up a soft porridge of tsampa and milk powder. I ate with usual attention, but Purnima, who didn't set so much store as I did on the joys of the palate, had other things on her mind. She had a feeling she had caught lice. In the thin and chilly morning sunlight she stripped off her clothes one by one, scouring every millimetre with an eagle eye for parasites. I was halfway through breakfast when she made her first catch.

'Look!' she cried in triumph, bringing her vest for my inspection, putting it right up close to my eyes between me and my feast. I looked. Indeed, there was a tiny pale body, with microscopic arms protruding in all directions. A louse.

'You can kill it!' she said eagerly. 'You have the longest fingernails!'

One isn't supposed to kill anything in the vicinity of Kailash, but I had taken an instant disliking to the thing. Perhaps, if the tiny beast hadn't so much resembled a grain of my breakfast, I would have been less revolted. Anyway, I dutifully killed it. She brought me a few more, and again they were duly executed, till finally she abandoned the whole garment on a rock and went on to explore the rest of her clothes. I considered this sufficient grounds to dissuade her from bringing along the sheepskins, as she wanted to.

The cave by day was not as enchanting as it had been by night and was still cold inside. Outside, mists surged down the valley, plundering all views of Kailash. At least it wasn't raining. Just as we were packed up and ready to go, a party of pilgrims arrived. They had come from some remote valley in western Nepal, but were of Tibetan descent; they spoke a unique dialect of their own, and bustled in, bowed reverently and touched their heads to the floor in the place where an hour ago our beds had been. The women radiated stiff skirts and coats of bright lateral stripes, and their many-braided hair was well-stitched with shining coins that rattled as they ducked and swung their heads. Chattering and praying together, they tucked rupee notes under stones on the altar, and told us that this was a Padmasambhava cave.

We left, and descended the steep path to rejoin the main route around Kailash. The day was often veiled with mist or dashed with rain, according to the whimsy of the weather. We walked each with our own songs and according to our own pace, and I soon left Purnima behind, arranging to meet at the place where the rocks part, and Kailash is visible. Wind-driven mist swarmed everywhere, mixed up the dull olive greens of the grass and mosses with the fundamental greys of rock and rain. The tall red cliffs where Nandi sat were completely blanked out, but, when I arrived at our appointed meeting place, miraculously the clouds cleared, and Kailash loomed into view. It was a completely different angle on the diamond-sharp peak of yesterday — now I stood right below it. Residual mist made a moving net which interchanged focus with the snow-veined menhir, creating a mysteriously free border between air and rock.

Then a heavy rain moved in, and ended the vision. I sat and waited for Purnima, getting wet and eating from the bag of spiced Indian snacks. The exotica of India ran riot on my tongue. Purnima arrived, and it continued to rain. It made little difference now — we ate the snacks and talked. We were sitting in the vague shelter of a dry riverbed, and waited for several hours before realising that perhaps we wouldn't get another view that day, and that we'd better move on if we wanted to find some grass on which to pitch the tent. Here it was all stones, barren and bleak.

On up through the rain we went. Again, I fell into the lead, forged through a cold wet elemental tunnel and emerged somewhere on the north side of Kailash without seeing very much more. Here there was a crude shelter, a sort of shed made of stones where before I had seen Tibetans brewing up their luncheon bowls of tea. I stepped inside, and found that the black earthen floor was as wet as the ground outside. Meagre as it was, it would be better in the tent tonight than here. But what about a fire? I had a horror of being drawn back to the sleazy place across the river again. Anyway, I blinked the rain out of my eyes for the moment, and peered about. On stones were piles of equipment left by prostrators: leather knee-pads, mittens of leather-backed wood, and leather aprons. A man and his small son, three years old he said, appeared. We grazed a while on the everlasting packet of salts and spices of India, resting unfocussed eyes on the oblong of drab drenched colours framed by the doorway. Finally the rain abated, and at this the boy caught hold of my hand and, with the father following, pulled me out of the room and around the corner.

39 - Supper with the nuns

ROUND THE CORNER, at a little distance from the shelter, a party of women had set up camp. Four were nuns with cropped hair and maroon robes, and the other two had long black plaits that vanished into the dark folds of their homespun. All of them had a sort of third eye in the centre of their forehead — a pink bump, buttoned with black, raised by the thousands of times they had touched their brows to the earth as they prostrated their bodies' lengths about the mountain.

Despite the faint drizzle that still prevailed, they had just begun a fire. Three large stones supported a large pot of water, under which burned juniper roots. The women greeted me joyfully, made room for me, and threw down a sheepskin so I could warm my toes by the fire. They really were remarkable women, uninterested in anything about me but whether or not I'd been around Manasarovar, and how many times I'd been around Kailash. And the most important thing was that my feet should dry and that I should get out my mug in readiness for the tea they were boiling. There was nothing that they wanted from me. They only wanted to give. An eye conditioned by the demands of civilisation might say that they didn't have much to give — but as they had everything needed to sustain life, they had everything. Fire, water, fuel, tea, tsampa and shelter; the whole point of their living was justified by simply being here. For here was Kailash, and it was the life-force itself, not simply the means of sustaining it, that was celebrated. Who knew what trammels these women had encountered, for the sake of their cloth, in their lives, and who knew what bureaucracy they had been through simply to leave Lhasa: they had hitch-hiked here in trucks with their supplies, carried them in between full-length prostrations half way round the mountain, and shared everything that they had with instinctive generosity. No warlord in his bastion or tax-exiled pop star in his French chateau was as rich as they were.

Their own chateau was a simple white canvas tent, in which elongated triangles had been sewn together so as to flare out in every direction. The central pole was made from a natural branch, and the open doorflap was tucked up over a guy rope along which hung coloured prayer flags. The man and the boy had a similar tent at a short distance on the other side of the fire, from which they now brought out a pot of rice to cook. I decided to do my bit by operating the bellows, fanning flames into the yak dung that had been added to the roots. It was a different type from the ones I'd used before — where wooden handles would normally be attached, the mouth of the canvas bag was loose and open-ended. Once the bag had been filled with air, one had to tighten the cloth with a dextrous twist of the wrist and elbow, and then pump downwards with the force of the fore-arm. The metal tube that ran into the fire jumped and hopped a bit with my experiments, but I didn't think I was doing too badly at all. The nuns, however, yowled with laughter. This is regarded as the most tedious of tasks, and yet after a while one of them took back the bellows and good-naturedly showed me how I should be doing it, after which I wasn't allowed to have them back at all. All I could do to contribute was to bring out some milk powder to add to the tea when it was ready.

Just as the water began to boil, Purnima arrived. Space and a sheepskin were produced for her also. 'Have you seen how they go across the streams?' she asked me. I hadn't. The streams had stepping stones, and I would leap from one to the other. But these women, apparently, would even prostrate themselves across the water; the folds of their skirts were already tied into sheaths about their legs by strings upon the aprons that they wore, and so they would simply stand upon a stone and fling themselves forwards across the flow, like flick-knives. Their bodies just skimmed the water with the rigid bridge they made as their outstretched hands grabbed the next stone.

The nuns laughed away. Before tea was taken, one of them took a ladle and offered some of the hot liquid to each of the four points of the compass, with special attention to the direction of Kailash. Clouds drifted off the mountain and swam up the valleys, to be followed always by more. Here, near the centre of the perpetual evolution, vision was no longer limited to one view — here one was involved with the whole scale, aware of all angles, all 360 degrees; Kailash was the centre, and nothing beyond the horizon mattered. Ragged circles torn in the scrag-weave allowed here and there a rough glimpse of blue to appear for a moment, only to be muffled by the swarming clouds again. The new spots appeared with the converting powers of visionaries. 'Here it is!' shouted the patches of blue. 'Here's the clarity behind all the veils and mists of illusion, here's the infinite peace behind the gluts and the clogs — come and get it!' — and bales of cloud would hurl in on their crows and stifle them. This after all was the north face, the spot where one is supposed to renounce, not congratulate, the self.

Still — the rough smooth silt of the tsampa tea ran down my throat with all the joy of coming upon hot springs in a cold place, and wallowing in them. One of the women found a tiny fly in her cup, and removed it with floury fingers. 'Om mani padme hum,' she said as she did so. Never had I seen the principles of *ahimsa* (non-violence) enacted so naturally nor so particularly. Custom and circumstance have long been used to justify the eating of meat by Tibetan Buddhists; even now they were now throwing meat into the pot of noodles which had replaced the tea on the fire. All the same — a fly now crawled through the grass who might never have enjoyed the sensation of a green blade under his six feet again.

There was a squall of rain, and we retreated into the women's tent. The walls of the interior were shored up with sacks of tsampa, roots, yak dung, sheepskins, noodles, dried meat and a few treats. At the base of the pole a stone made a small altar to Guru Rinpoche, that is, Padma-sambhava. One of the nuns brought out something yagadoo from a sack — it was a tin of the brilliant synthetic orange sugar crystals that could be bought at Darchen guest house shop for six kwai a go. We all had to stretch out our hands, and into them she poured an even mountain each; and the little boy, having smaller hands, naturally had to have several more handfuls than us to compensate. We lapped up the stuff with quickly stained tongues, and by the time the rain had gone we all had an orange sun in the centre of our palms, and emerged marked as if by initiation into some feral rite.

All of them pitched in to help me put up my own tent; enthusiastically they each grabbed a corner of the novel blue nylon, and any peg or rope or stone they could get, and copied one another's guesses at how it should be done. I hovered, succeeding in injecting few hints on the usual procedure into the bedlam. Soon it was up, poles and ropes projecting at quixotic angles, just as when the nomads had lent a hand. I liked the arrangement — the oddities slightly softened the intrusion of the factory-blue on the pastel colour-merges and jagged rocks of the landscape. Then there was the inner furnishing to see to: the ladies oversaw the installation of the mat, and jostled one another out of the way like happy schoolgirls for the fun of putting their heads inside. The little boy dived right in too — and was caught mid-air by one of the nuns, who efficiently removed the shoes from kicking feet as niftily as she would shells from peanuts, before releasing him again. Everybody threw back their heads and sent echoes of their laughter rebounding all the way up the valley to the source of the Indus.... We went to eat our suppers: noodles with long-anticipated tomato soup for us, noodles and meat for them.

40 - Learning the Shiva mantra

WE HAD THE tent-flaps open to allow a view of Kailash. The nearly full moon sailed on its arc beside the peak, and illuminated everything with a brilliant light. It was profoundly still, and silence boomed through the radiant air. It is here that the divine moves upon the face of the earth uninterrupted, here that the devout may be blessed with a vision of their chosen deity. Purnima taught me a mantra, and we chanted the Sanskrit syllables till the air around us was saturated with their import:

'We worship the Three Eyed One (Shiva) who is fragrant and nourishes all beings. May he liberate me from death, and grant me the gift of immortality, even as the cucumber is severed from its bondage (to the creeper).'

In the resonance I went to meditate upon a rock. Shiva is a strange god to me. He belongs to another people, to a land of hot spices and cool rivers. India tantalises the mind of the Westerner by uplifting the spirit from the shackles of the usual, by filling the head with attractive opposites all quite contrary to the Christian values that originally, and however loosely, shaped his mind. In India, the quality of mercy is strained by the belief in reincarnation; the fat rich Brahmin can ride happily past the legless beggar because he believes that the beggar must have been rather a scum-bag in his previous life. On the grand scale it is quite just that he sits half-starving on a skate-board, like a glove puppet centre-stage in the middle of a roaring highway. The Brahmin's scriptures are the Vedas, the oldest on earth and written by the gods themselves; they stress the temporary and illusory qualities of this world, enjoin detachment from pleasure and pain. And even in the modern translation, there's still the same God-gleam in the eye of beggar and Brahmin.

Many other things are enjoined too; Hindus are able to splice the varied elements of their faith and, beaming, produce results which can appear outrageous to the Western mind. And from this same vein of apparent cruelty springs the image of Shiva. His skin is smeared blue by the ashes of the dead, poisonous snakes swathe his neck; surrounded by snow he sits in eternal meditation at Kailash. Of course, he also simultaneously inhabits many other places, where he may or may not be in meditation; and then again, he is always dancing, for everything that moves is part of the dance of Shiva, and when he stops dancing the world explodes. Shiva lives in dirty places, rich places, sad places, poor places. Shiva is the god of destruction, of transformation, of liberation. He is the comforting light behind the shadows of graveyards, the compensation to sorrow, the constancy of change. Shiva guards the last resorts, the old, the abandoned, the seedy and the derelict; he protects the ignorant, the decadent and the decaying. And instead of laying these things discreetly behind a black curtain on the other side of righteousness, the Indian scriptures enjoin that these elements should be recognised as an essential ingredient of the way things are. While Brahma generates the active royal fire of creation, and sweet and unsullied Vishnu preserves the balance of the created, Shiva systematically destroys. He is the necessity of death to life and night to day.

Shiva may have a somewhat unusual appearance, but he stands for obvious truths. The human mind, conditioned by the world to acquisition, equates the deadly snakes, and all the associations of loss and the unknown, with fear. But no-one can deny that life needs death and night follows day. Shiva is an ascetic, lord of loss and renunciation; his austerities are the saving grace to the hallowed space of horror between this life and its ending. By recognising the downs of fortune's wheel, so Hindu theology comes to terms with and transcends them. When one loses everything, then God is bestowing the greatest gift of all: for when one has nothing, there is nowhere to turn but to God; and God being all that is needed, so one has everything. The Hindus, for all the jewels and golden peacocks of the Maharajas, have a traditional respect for renunciation; while on other continents people work hard all their lives to accumulate and secure, insure, assure, and reassure comfort for their old age, it is still not unusual for a prosperous Indian businessman to retire at fifty and take *sanyasi,* renouncing family and possessions and wander as an ascetic in the way of Shiva.

The fat of good living must be cut off before the flame of Shiva can really burn. After this protection has been reduced to a thin layer of ashes, there is nothing for it but to draw on the innermost resources. The image of Shiva arises from natural impulses quickened by austerity; the joys of renunciation flourish in the barren and unfruitful landscape, and here is Shiva, vital and breathing in man's image, the god who knows and loves the mountains, capable and sure-footed. The strength of his nature inspires the believer's mind with the power of detachment.

Then the inner resources of Tibetan Buddhists would manifest Buddhas and Bodhisattvas here. Thousands of their subtle bodies are believed to populate the mountain, sending out rays of compassion and mercy to the whole of mankind. They reach out to the struggles of individuals world-over, and the cleansing healing light of their meditation helps the efforts of those fighting the demons of greed, hatred, lust, envy and ignorance. The air was lush and luminously charged with moonlight, and the earth responded by thrusting this frozen white point into the dancing midnight blue. At Kailash the whole of creation was perpetually conceived and renewed with this energy.

According to the Sanskrit scriptures, Kailash is a place full of jewels, minerals, myriad wildlife and vegetable abundance. Elephants roam in herds through the hills, and when they move, it appears that 'the Kailash Hill moves with them'. There are sandalwood forests, refreshed by coloured lakes and many different kinds of lotuses. The warm air is permeated by the sweet vibrations of peacocks and the humming of bees; mystics live in caves with their beautiful mystic wives, and demi-gods skim down regularly in their aeroplanes to bathe in the waters. Above all this, Shiva sits under a banyan tree that is 800 miles high with branches spread over 600 miles around.

Of course, this is not quite literally true. The region is austere, and the descriptions of the scriptures must be taken as an image perhaps of the fecundity of spirit that the mountain generates. Kailash is understood to be the manifestation of the spiritual world, and every molecule of air vibrates. Certainly there were elephants roaming in the long grasses … whether or not the elephants were psychological parables or liable to walk by any moment was quite a debatable point.

41 - Birthday

I AWOKE TO the same view, and Purnima gently singing 'Happy birthday to you, happy birthday to you' — she disappeared off in the direction of the fire, presently to return with a cup of hot milk into which was mixed — muesli! I was astonished. 'I've been saving it all week,' she said, with justifiable pride. I relished every nut and grain of it. And as if that weren't enough — as I was half-way through, she presented me with a colour photo of Kailash, wrapped in sheets of rice paper, bound with string and sealed with a buttercup. Round the edges of the rice paper she had written in yellow and orange, four deep, the names of God in Sanskrit, and in the centre was a Sufi poem:

> *May the blessings of God rest upon you*
> *May his peace abide with you*
> *May his presence illuminate your heart*
> *Now and for evermore….*

There was something surreal in the way the flames stormed from the roots and the ashes, around which the nuns were as high-spirited as ever. Today we saw how the nuns managed their koras; they would prostrate themselves full-length for a few hundred metres at a time, and then, leaving their stones to mark the place they'd reached, would walk on or back to the fire, for a tea and tsampa break. Then they'd return to their stone for another spell, and when they'd had enough they'd have another tea break. Labour was distributed throughout the camp, and they all supported one another. At one point they all went off together, to perform their morning puja somewhere, and we looked after the fire while they were gone. Which meant that, having eaten breakfast, we now prepared lunch.

The ingredients were rice and dahl, which we put in one pot under the optimistic name of kedgeree; after an hour or so of dedicated attention we had a pot of rice made miraculous by the gift of a spoonful of butter, lightly mixed with hard green pellets of dahl. The taste was rancid, crunchy, full of woodsmoke and delicious.

As I ate, there was a prod in my back. It was Dorje, splendid in pink-framed sunglasses, floppy hat and down vest, waving a ski-pole. He was escorting a party of Japanese pilgrims about the mountain; piles of shiny pink silk coverlets gleamed against the rough hair of their yaks, and here were the Japanese themselves. They were geared up in designer sporting clothes, tough and admirable, all in clean bright colours. As I was scraping a broken wooden spoon around a blackened pot, in order to extract every last drop of flavour from the feast, a Japanese woman peered in, and her fuscia pink lipsticked mouth asked me: 'Oishi desu-ka?' — Is it delicious?

I assured her that it certainly was, and she nodded and smiled as if with such great pleasure that I have no doubt she was quite revolted by the whole set-up.

Purnima rather wanted to stay there; and I, motivated by a restlessness that seems incomprehensible now, wanted to go over Dolma La. Before we set off, I went up to the lip between the two brown mountains that flank Kailash, marked by a mani wall and a chorten. I did not go to the foot of the mountain itself, but stopped at the wall and added a small stone collected at the beginning of the walk. On the chorten I hung a katha that Joan had given me in Lhasa, and the rough white cloth swelled up with the breeze — and clouds swilled about Kailash. The nuns were keeping this camp as a base for a few more days, and so could we — but in the middle of the afternoon, we left.

Purnima's foot was hurting in her borrowed climbing boots. At the forest of stelae where one does puja for the absent and departed, we encountered a group of Tibetans with a fleet of sturdy black pack-yaks. Purnima was able to put her rucksack onto one of their backs, and went on with that party. I stayed behind, to do a drawing of the hillside and to allow her to accumulate some distance. Strong angled rocks grew out of the green skin of grass and moss that covered the earth, and the loosed rocks stood up from the fixed rocks in beaded watch-towers over the souls of all those remembered here. Colours flowed from stone to stone, and the very path under my feet flowed too when I moved on. The earth was worn fluid by many steps, and little flowers floated down the river — splodges of lichen, orange and mustard and sunshine yellow. The startling sprigs were hurled high in the waves of green rocks that here and there rose up above and narrowed the path — and crashed together in cracks, spread far and wide across the wide grey overshuffle of slate before the final ascent. I dipped my cup into the streams of water that frequently underran the path, and its coldness shocked me on.

Some Tibetans were camped in the last inhospitable ledge of flat before the final ascent. They called me up for tea, which I drank gluttonously for the heat, but I did not accept their urgent invitation to spend the night there. I would press on. It would snow, it would get dark, they said. They were right, but I'd wanted to go over Dolma La today, and Purnima might freak out if I didn't catch her up.

Instead of dashing on at my usual pace and having to stop every fifty yards for breath, I walked slowly and evenly. All the way up, cold mists swirled through the snow-ribbed rock faces and sombre clefts that cut from the magnificent distances right to the edges of the path. When I reached the flag-stone that marks the top of the pass, Purnima and the party of Tibetans were just preparing to descend. A heavy cloud covered all the horizon now, isolating the place with a ponderous air of significance. The party of nomads were all women and children. Competently they gathered up their yaks. The beasts moved harnessed heads slow with submission, and clouds of resentful breath landed drops of moisture on the shaggy black hairs of their chins. The women gave me grain mixed with sugar and butter to scatter: coins and turquoise glowed from their plaits of hair as they moved among the boulders, colours stitched into their floor-length robes echoed those of the prayer flags flapping heavily in the slow wind. These robes were so dark and thick and dense that when they sat down, their armchairs were already prepared. A crow pecked at the grains they flung in handfuls before departure, and when

he cawed between snipes his cry was long and eerily distended. Silently
the bulk of the yak party poured out of sight.

42 - By moonlight down the happy valley

I MET THEM AGAIN a few hours later, at a place where the path frays into
many smaller paths, and I fretted in with them. Here was Purnima,
pulling a yak by a rope attached to its nose-ring down a steep incline,
swearing at it crossly. A few wild-headed children popped surprised eyes
over the edges of the baskets that lurched on the yaks' backs, or pottered
down on their own tough little legs. Purnima parked her yak in the first
spot that wasn't near-vertical, in order to record their wonderful innocence. I believe she took some excellent photos, but unfortunately
mothers began to get annoyed, to yank their children forcibly away from
the range of her camera and turn their backs on her. Someone repossessed
the yak in her charge, and they gladly returned her rucksack. They would
keep their images to themselves.

Not at all put out, Purnima watched them moving on down the valley.
'Look at them,' she said. 'They are strong, independent, brave, fearless
in fact, self-sufficient — how different from the Indian woman, who
always has to keep quiet what she thinks, always dancing around and
slaving for her husband and treating him like a god even if she despises
him, always casting her eyes to the ground. These women look straight
at you and they're honest and pure and strong.'

The skies cleared with the early evening. The women camped not
much further on, in a place where there was water and grazing. We
continued, hoping to find someone to beg hot water off for a cup of
noodles each. And just before nightfall we came upon the Japanese. Their
super-modern tents mushroomed over the hillside, and they had just
dined on Japanese noodles and dried fish from Osaka. They showed us
the packets and invited us to sit on their silver groundsheets while they

heated a pan of water, specially for us, in a clinically clean steel pot over a similar stove. They were certainly equipped for an expedition: each of them wore a heavy-duty compass about their neck, and the walls of the tent in which we sat were piled high with huge boxes of Japanese food. Our eyes popped discreetly: they'd be back in Darchen tomorrow — surely they weren't planning to eat the whole half-ton before then? They were not tourists, but pilgrims, they politely told us, Buddhist pilgrims, but typical Japanese modesty forbade them to tell us along which branch of Buddhism their faith inclined.

Though not wishing to detract from our gratitude for the hot water, with which we were able to have a very satisfying packet of instant noodles each, it was interesting to note the difference between these Japanese and the Tibetan ladies of the previous night. The Japanese had everything necessary to preserve their bodies through the toughness of the scene — yaks to carry their stuff, men to lead the yaks, stoves, pans, bright warm clothing, sleek sleeping bags and tents, knives of Hokkaido steel and leather-blinkered sunglasses. They had come here swiftly and at great expense, and their faces had not had time to open up to the landscape; they sought to combat rather than to greet the situation. The Tibetan ladies had given freely of their tsampa with no thought to possible future shortages, trusting that new supplies would be available when necessary. The Japanese pilgrims, for all their excess stock-pile, gave us exactly what we asked for — hot water — and offered no more. Well, to be precise, and to give them their due — they had two tinned peach-halves left over from their own dessert, and very graciously offered us one each. We guzzled them gratefully, and indeed the memory of that mouthful stands out well beyond all the birthday cakes and gourmet delights of my life. We voiced our thanks and bowed, and they made throaty noises to express their astonishment that we were to continue, even though it was now just about dark, and we parted in a civilised fashion — that is to say, as if we'd been introduced en passant by a mutual friend in Shinjuku station — as if we'd hardly met at all.

It was not dark for long. Soon the moon, just short of full, rose up above the dark ridges on the opposite side of the valley. The river below and all her trailing tributaries gleamed brightly, and, now that there wasn't a cloud in the sky, it was lighter than the day had been. Again the solemnity of the upper regions fell away into a new happiness and levity. We walked for several hours thus by moonlight, only stopping now and then for a drink of water. There was no hurry, for we had been late before we began; the night absorbed all possible anxieties. We were back in the happy valley, back where the reborn psyche flies like a phoenix from the ashes of the discarded past. We marvelled at the lovely silence and the peace of the blue-green night-light. And somewhere between two and three in the morning we came to the rest-house below the cave of Milarepa.

I only went twice about the mountain; but in the difference between the two koras I could see how the scale of 108 is used as a register to mark entry into Nirvana. The second time round, already acquainted with the terrain, the sights, sounds and experiences of the way synthesised to a slightly more cohesive perception of the magic and mystery that characterises Kailash. Perhaps by 108, one might really begin to see the light.

Part Four

Part Four

43 - Full moon below Silung Gompa

BACK IN DARCHEN, there was a note for me from Franca; she had been stuck eight days in Ali. No traffic was going through to Lhasa on account of the Brahmaputra being so swollen at Lhatze that the ferry was out of action. So she was going to go up to Kashgar, and then back into India via Pakistan, so could I please make a parcel of her things when I returned to Shigatze, and send them to London?

Tonight was the full moon, the moon on which, in India, thousands of Hindu pilgrims trek up to the cave at Amarnarth in the north. Here they worship the ice *lingam* (phallic symbol) of Shiva which, so I am told, joins the roof to the floor of the cave just for this one night. The occasion is known as Rakshabhandan, one of the major festivals for Shiva worship, and so it seemed quite an auspicious time to be, if not at the ice lingam which manifests once a year, at the great ice lingam of Kailash which is always there.

John, Thomas, Purnima and I all arrived back in Darchen separately, and over a thermos of tea we each told our stories. John had been around Manasarovar with his Tibetan porter, who had been able to tell him many things which he would otherwise have missed, such as where to collect the sands made of precious stones, where to find the dried fish on the banks and who had done what where; the north bank, which I'd not been along, was difficult and treacherous with rivers, marshland and dogs, he said; but he'd got round. He'd also had a warm reception at Gossul Gompa which I had found just slightly cool — probably because of his initiation into and knowledge of the Dharma. He paid off his porter, who, delighted, immediately wished us all a joyful farewell and set off for Kathmandu on the very next truck. As for Thomas — he had greatly enjoyed the meals with the Indians, but the delight he'd previously found in his position of being their Tibetan and Kailash expert had somewhat eroded by the time they'd got half-way round the kora. 'All the time they were complaining,' he complained. 'All the time they wanted to know how far it was till the next rest stop, and if I said I didn't know, they got angry with me, and if I said a time and then we weren't there by that time, they got angry with me again, and if I said a longer time, then they got even angrier.' He looked wounded: he'd only been trying to help.

Though we had all arrived here separately, each of us had come with the same idea in our heads: to spend the night of the full moon up the valley below Silung Gompa, with a clear view of Kailash. Purnima had a cold now, but when John suggested it might be better if she didn't come up, she was horrified. Of course she was coming up, and we made our preparations in a festive mood. I spent time waiting for the others by dancing with a nomad boy in the yard of the guest house. Dorje had his radio turned up high, and we leapt and pranced to the beat of a crackly Chinese musical stew with increasingly dervish-style gyrations. His pigtails and the tails of his short coat flew as he stamped the thick soles of his bright felt boots on the hard earth, and his white smile spun like a discus through the clouds of dust he kicked up. Finally the last knot had been tied in the last plastic bag, everything excess to a night out was stored, and we were away. This time, unhampered by any sort of illness, my body just skimmed along the path, up the gorge and into the higher valley. The water-polished stones shone pale greens and rose, buff and gold amongst the purple daisy flowers that replaced the yellow trumpet flowers. Upon nearing the camping ground below Silung Gompa, I picked a yak skull from a sprinkling of fluffy edelweiss.

The yak skull marked our camp, which was the place of smooth turf by the stream where I'd been before. The last gold of the sun illuminated the white slopes of Kailash as I put up my blue tent; and just as I'd done so, up came John to put up his green one. Then came Thomas with his stove, which he immediately set to boiling hot water for the milk powder. Somehow, once back in his hands, it behaved perfectly. 'You only have to pump it a bit more,' he said. 'Look!' And in less than twenty-five pumps he had the flame transformed from that ominous orange to a perfect blue. Ah well ... it obviously knew its master's touch. I went back down the valley to meet Purnima, who had lagged far behind the rest of us: here she was, looming like a ghost out of the dark, frail and shivering and powered only by determination.

While walking round the lake, a lama had given John some *ribu*. These are precious pills which lamas make, and they are highly sought after as a panacea by the laity. They are made from ingredients which may include anything from herbs and crushed bones to the lamas' faeces — they being so pure that naturally even their waste-products contain healing properties. These pills were cream-coloured and appeared innocuous enough; the lama had said they'd be 'good for the full moon', and so we dropped one each. Was it the rising moon, the nearness of Kailash, the clear fresh air, the good company, the complete lack of any distractions, the silence and natural holiness of the place — or what? — that accounted for the smooth uplift of tranquillity that immediately permeated the whole system as soon as the ribu was swallowed? Or a combination of all these things? Purnima said something that none of us doubted: 'We are really blessed to be here.'

Though it was rather cold, we sat for hours outside the tents. At first we talked — or rather Purnima and John talked, about Indian music, while Thomas made pot after pot of hot powdered milk and I wrote by the light of half an inch of candle that dwindled into moonlight. Then the talk became mantras and the mantras became silence. Kailash gleamed silver-white, and the eye of the nearby moon radiated perfect circles of russet and carnation, burnt umber and luminous cream. Here in the air were all the colours that man has strived so hard to squeeze from plants, grind from stones and manufacture throughout civilisations over the ages: here glowed the purples of emperors and the stained rags of beggars. John pointed out how the lingam of Kailash penetrates the feminine receptivity of the sky to create the *yab-yum* of Tibetan Buddhism. In the natural symbol of sexual union, opposites conjoin at their highest level; the union is not directed by simple animal lust, but by a basic need to integrate the two ranges of energy contained within all nature: the passive and the active. Alone, they are limited; joined, they form a circuit and produce limitless dynamite. The meanings behind the symbolism were exposed, softly raw and vibrant; this was the matrix of a million million souls.

I sat at a little distance from the others, and breathed; when I opened my eyes, Purnima was placing before me a cup of hot milk. A loose low cover of clouds drifted over the valley. They were unearthly — blobs of floating light, blooming whites surrounded by haloes of blue, violet, ochre and gold. Drinking the milk, I was astonished to see a brilliant green light descend in a flash this side of the clouds, to dissolve just over the tents. Perhaps it was a craft powered by mantric hymns, flying in denizens from the heavenly planets; for the scriptures liken their visits to clouds in the sky, decorated with occasional flashes of lightning. Meanwhile, the others were watching how the clouds had clotted at one point into a perfect Om symbol. What is magic, but the unexplained forces implicit in every atom of the universe?

44 - Gompa

Purnima and Thomas had arranged a lift back up to Ali with the police jeep that morning, so when I woke up, Purnima was gone from my tent and Thomas from John's. John was also gone, and I spent the day alone in my tent, sleeping and dreaming with immediate ease. Just as the time before, I was drained, listless, and disinclined to do anything but stare at Kailash in between dreams. It was strange that the effect of being so near such a power source should be to feel so wiped out. An hour or so before sunset I did manage to sit upright, and paint in some pencilled sketches with water-colours. Their transparency was the thinnest membrane between perception and reality, and the painted stones of Dolma La rose from the thick white page as the last solid symbols before the inexplicable.

John appeared. He'd been that afternoon up to the gompa, and had made great friends with the lama before heading up the left-hand valley to the very foot of the mountain. There he had been at the bottom of the staircase that scores the southern face; and at the base of that, he said, is a natural lingam formed by ice and scree that has tumbled down the staircase and collected there. He was a reassuring person to have around — instead of calling me lazy for sleeping all day, he remarked how important it is to catch up on sleep, and said that he too, the nearer he had come to the foot of Kailash, had felt his own strength ebbing away. Of course, it could also be due to lack of food. I had a packet of noodles which we ate dry between us; it was surprisingly good, but not terribly filling. John had eaten yoghurt and rice at the gompa that afternoon, and suggested we tried again.

We trotted up to the gompa with plates and high hopes but, as I'd suspected, we were not allowed in: apart from the one hour a day, the monks were in retreat, as I'd been told before, and the doors closed to visitors. Still, I got a hot shower. It was a pity that I had no fore-warning of the event and so no time to take off my clothes, and perhaps a little unfortunate that the water was a deep grey colour and full of dirt and kitchen-scraps — but when, as we stood outside the door wondering if anyone had heard our knock, and the kitchen drainage spout emptied itself right over my head — I did remember to enjoy the quick burst of warmth it brought. My yell brought out the old woman; putting her tongue out as far as it would go, she lent me a cloth to dry myself with, and explained in Tibetan: 'Tomorrow, one o'clock!' We returned to our tents in hungry silence, and John immediately tucked himself into his sleeping bag, to dream about tomorrow, one o'clock. Had we had foresight, we would not have been in this situation: we too had intended to return down to Darchen that day, and so had brought no supplies. But it was somehow impossible to leave. And John did have some supplies of a sort — a bag of rungba kasa, given to him by the ribu lama — the conical lumps of brown sugar. I crunched through a couple of dozen of the things, felt them hit and grind at my stomach, stared hypnotised at Kailash, and miraculously slept again.

The next day at one o'clock we were punctually at the door of the gompa again — but one o'clock on John's watch was an hour ahead of one o'clock by the gompa clock, and so we spent the intervening hour watching a herd of goats being milked. Heads were tied in a long slip knot that joined a couple of dozen beasts in a herring-bone pattern, and the Tibetan couple milking them squeezed two pails of milk from the outward-facing udders. This herd supplied both Silung and Gengta monasteries with the milk for their yoghurt, and the couple spent their lives driving the herd backwards and forwards over the hill that separated the two valleys in which the gompas lay. Thus one day Silung had milk, the next Gengta.

At two o'clock Beijing time, the old lady and two young novices appeared at the gompa door to call us in. We were the only visitors, and were ushered into the lower room where the lama sat. His long hair was washed and clean today, presumably with the bright pink strawberry shampoo I'd seen him presented with before. We talked of this and that. He was twenty-five years old, and the old woman was his mother; he was friendly in a natural way, and accepted the small folds of money that John and I had compiled between us, with thanks that managed to be at the same time appreciative and indifferent. John knew the correct manner in which to present money without an enfolding katha and knew the correct forms of address. Yet I am sure it was not money that made us welcome there; just as the yoghurt and rice — which, to be truthful, was what we'd come for — was finally quite a trivial detail in the visit. It was something in the serenity of the place, the gentle hospitality and the easy bridging of all our differences in face of the view of Kailash from the window, that made up that hour. The talk was nothing profound, but behind the small-talk, even the flames of the fire were aspirated by the mantras.

'Don't forget your hat!' said the lama as I left. 'Nobody else around here wants to put such a raggedy item on their head!' — or words to that effect. He gave me two pieces of cord that he'd elaborately knotted: I still don't know their meaning, but they are important. Then visiting time was up, and with great grace we were ushered out.

45 - To the base and the lakes

WE WENT IN SEARCH of the black and white lakes the Frenchman in Shigatze had pointed out so elegantly on the map. Of course, one isn't supposed to go there unless one has done thirteen koras, and Dorje had said the qualification should be reduced to three for foreigners — but it wasn't till later that I realised the heresy we committed in going anti-clockwise round the inner kora in search of these lakes, with just three koras of Kailash clocked up between us. Of course I was unbound to any system, but one should always respect the traditions of a place.

There was nobody checking us but our own consciences, which weren't a bit ruffled — no fiery thunderbolts, deadly hailstorm or giant locusts appeared to obstruct us, and indeed the lama pointed out the way. He said we could find them up the right-hand valley of the fork, over the lip of the rocks that rose steeply above the path. We started up the valley, following a stream across which we'd leap with increasing ease at every curve. After a few hours we lost each other, and I forgot about the lakes. Green turf and flowers gave way with altitude to a scree of cindery rocks and the stream withered to a thin trickle. The only vegetation that grew there was a sort of primordial flower which wore a silver fur coat from root to stamen. Its long stem insinuated up through layer upon layer of stone, and on this barren bed it flourished at discreet intervals. Gloomy boulders of pudding stone loafed about. Rocks continually loosed themselves from high shelves up on the valley walls to fall in with the rough cindery lumps that jostled underfoot with a dry, terminal rattle.

Here it was: right in front of me, nearer than I'd ever been before: the Jewel of the Snows.

John manifested from out of the shelves above. He had been looking for the lakes up there, and had not found them. It didn't matter. I sat down and did a drawing; John took photos of me doing a drawing, and then the click of his camera faded into the rattle of the stones, and we lost one another again. It was deceptively easy to lose someone in that open area of grey scree — as if magical vanishing sheets issued up from the emptiness, to whisk one out of sight at a wish. Not that it mattered.

John, I later found out, went down the valley, following the stream — while I went up, and maybe found what I was looking for. For an indeterminate space I grated over the rocks and eventually came upon first one and then the other of what I believed to be the two lakes. One was a small dehydrated round of black stones and damp sand; the other a muddy brown puddle about twenty metres in diameter. I imagined they were the lakes for several reasons — their position corresponded with landmarks pointed out by the lama; they were the only reminders of the element of water in the area, which I had explored quite thoroughly; they were not very far from one another, and were both surrounded by devotional piles of stones. In themselves, they were rather disappointing, for they didn't quite match the expectations conjured by 'black and white lakes'; but this was probably because I was unqualified to see them, and was still blinded by a certain belief in labels.

A very cold wind blew me down a path to where a bleak world turned gentle again. The stream-stones were muted pink and green and grey and Kailash glowed gold in the setting sun. And as I walked, I thought. Imagine, I thought, imagine everything that you know — all the people, all the houses they live in, the things that they do, the things they talk about — imagine everything which is familiar and known to you — the food that you eat, the clothes that you wear, the smells that you associate with your childhood — imagine all this, and then imagine it seized by a flood of ice; everything is turned over to the Snow Queen's realm, everything freezes till it is devoid of smell, texture, taste and pleasure. Even sounds are sucked into a great white icy vacuum of silence. Thought can find no foothold on the smooth and slippery slopes, and only wonder and prayer will do. This is Kailash.

46 - Darchen interchange and hot springs

IT WOULD HAVE BEEN too embarrassing to have gone to the gompa in expectations of rice and yoghurt yet again; in the morning we bounded down to Darchen with meagre chips of apricot kernels rattling in our stomachs. But once inside the 'dining room' I wondered if it was worth it, just to gratify hunger. A scratchy atmosphere prevailed: the Chinese cook was in a bad temper, his wife in a worse one; a crowd of Tibetans fought each other for the pot of soggy noodles he threw on the floor, having long since delivered the plates of vegetables, meat and peanuts into either their mouths or the folds of their dress. Nobody seemed to enjoy a mouthful that they ate. The copulating horses on the wall pulled back their lips and sneered in derision as stools were snatched away from people in turn, and laughed aloud when the cook raised the price of the meal from two to three kwai. This irritated John, and a scene ensued. If even John could be irritated, well ... the tale twisted to a dark room full of soft cabbages, where the cook's wife sat on her bed streaking the air with high-pitched venom. Dorje hopped into the doorway where I loitered, and out of the sour atmosphere he gave me a slice of red ripe water melon from Kashgar.

I set up camp for the night by the river, an hour south of the city. From here Darchen was put into proportion — a puff of smoke at the base of a line of mountains, out of which rose Kailash. But I returned the following lunchtime, wanting to take a truck back down to Manasarovar; my visa was due to run out in six days' time — meaning I'd have to be in Ali in a week. Preferring not to think of that now, I wanted to use up my last days by going to the meditation caves on the northern shore of Manasarovar that I'd heard about.

Darchen was swinging. There was a new party of Indians, and some Japanese and even an Englishman who had succeeded in hitching down from Kashgar. He, with his red cheeks, bright blue eyes and bristling black hair, was of quite startling appearance; he'd closed the eyes at check-points, and so they'd all come, disguised as Chinese, undetected down a route many had been turned back on. The cook was smiling benignly as he dished out plates of limp cabbage, at reduced prices today, and the afternoon passed in a long flourish of unpacking and re-packing on all sides. Every now and then there would be a flurry of handshakes or bows or folded or waved hands, a splash of 'Tashi dillee!' or 'Sayonara!'

or 'Namaste!' or 'See you!', and the Barga Plain was chased with lines of dust rumbling off to Burang, Ali or Manasarovar. And then for every truck that left for Ali, another would presently roar off in pursuit, to pull the first truck out of the river.

The truck I was on was going past Chiu Gompa. Also on it were Dharma John and a policeman, whose authority, alas, did not stretch to visa extensions. In a couple of hours we covered what had taken me a couple of days to walk before, and this time I even got to see the legendary Barga. It was simply a walled village, of mostly wall and very little village, stranded in the middle of the plain, at quite some distance from its location according to any map I ever saw of the place.

As it was nearly dark when we arrived at Chiu Gompa, it was necessary to spend a night there. John had cosy notions of asking the woman to 'cook up some vegetables'; I was suspicious of depending on the estab- lishment, and the suspicions were substantiated when it turned out that the rooms of the compound were full of maroon lamas. They flitted like moths about the twilight, and the woman was too busy with them all to say anything to us but: 'Mindoo! Mindoo!'

But it was luck for us that she turned us away. For, in seeking a campsite down by the bed of the dried-up Ganga channel that joins the two lakes, I came upon not just the pools of stagnant black water I'd found before, but also the pale sulphuric vapours of hot springs. To my delight there was a whole seam of them, glug-glugging out of a bubbly white sulphur deposits; none of them were much deeper or wider than a saucepan, and many were too hot to touch, but they were everywhere. Clean hot water ripped up through silver-black sand, trickled in falls over, and secret channels under, the rough stone into the tepid black pools below. I pitched my tent on a beach of coarse white grains, heated Roman-style from underneath by the warmth of underground springs. As for John — he installed himself under a large shelf of rock higher up the sides of the tiny Ganga valley, and lounged there watching shooting stars while I cooked those perennial noodles, enlivened tonight with the addition of a spicy Indian mix, on one of the hottest springs.

The tent-flaps stood open to allow the clear blue night to pour in; the warm floor accentuated the sweet odour of the rice straw mat, and, now there was no need to huddle or curl or even to meditate for warmth, the whole luxurious set-up enveloped me like a sudden gift from the gods. Surrounded by the misty spray of stars and splash of moonlight, by the peaceful poppings of the hot springs, creature-comfort had the last word.

47 - Chiu Gompa puja and the cave

THE HOT STEAM of the springs brushed the cold morning air like friendly ghosts, and though John shouted: 'Good morning!' into my tent before dashing off in the direction of the gompa, I went back to sleep. Slowly slowly, every bone aching, every muscle hanging limp and in dead weight — it was interesting to note my body's reaction to luxury — I eventually dragged myself up and out too.

The woman with a torn ear slaked my thirst with hot tea, for it was quite a way to the lake for fresh water, and from the gompa came the sound of a puja in full cry. I crowded into the doorway, and crouched there with dozens of locals and pilgrims. Silver bells, amulets, semi-precious stones and charm boxes swung as heads turned shy smiles at me. From inside came the frenzy of sutras, which built up with the rhythmic beating of the damarus to long triumphant blasts on the thighbone trumpets. I could just see a small veritable city of *thorma*s, pink and white, built out of tsampa and butter on a tray inside, and from time to time the crowd would separate, to allow one priest in a dusty maroon shawl to fly past. He bore the citadels of butter and bowls of tea out to where he could hurl them energetically onto the roof.

During a tea-break, John emerged with the crowds from the hall. Having arrived bright and early, he had a seat of honour from where he could see and hear everything. The lamas conducting the puja were the ones who had filled the compound the night before. They had come from all over the place, including many from Nepal; and, being gathered together here in this auspicious spot, the site of the very cave where their founder last meditated before ascending to the heavens, had decided to hold this puja. It would go on all day.

And here was Padmasambhava's cave itself, tucked just off the crowded passageway. It was a tiny little hole in the rock, with maybe just enough room to lie down; I knelt, and soon the master magician's bright electric blue eyes and thunderbolt sparkled out of the gloom. Kathas hung, but no lamps were lit and still, after all this time, and all the curious eyes that had peered here, a solid air of miracles prevailed. There was a black nugget-shaped hollow in the wall, and tucked into its bottom scoop was a small, black egg-like stone. Apparently this marked the place where one of the thermas had been discovered. These thermas are treasures left by

Padmasambhava as an inheritance to the people of Tibet, to be discovered over the centuries at the appropriate moments. A general cloak of secrecy obscures the exact nature of the treasures, how they are discovered and how they are made manifest; perhaps it was a scroll of new sutra that was discovered here, or perhaps a holy statue, made by no man's hand, but self-manifest, of pure crystal. And here was the hole in the rock which, before the time was right for the discovery of the therma, had been just an ordinary wall.

It was fascinating and vibrant in the gompa, but the call of the lake was stronger than that of all the sutras. I would like to find a cave — and with a bottle of blue from the lake returned to the hot springs to dismantle the tent, and to take advantage of the natural hotplates of water by softening on them a bag of beans I had carried from Hong Kong. It was an odd spot. Colours straggled with surreal intensity down the rocks and into the pools, and out of the steam materialised strange people: first a Tibetan and a Chinese driver, on easy terms with each other and the world, it seemed: they squatted on rocks and watched me with interest, asking questions from time to time; and, when smart German figures appeared on the rhino-horn of rock that carried the gompa up above this creek, the drivers called them over with whistles and waves of the brightest articles of my equipage they could find. The Germans dutifully came, eying me a little suspiciously at first, but, when I had established my respectability by speaking a little German, they relaxed considerably. One of them went so far as to doff his Tyrolean hat and shake my hand, and he and another helped me pack up the tent while their wives took a culinary interest in the bubbling beans. They had come in Landcruisers from Lhasa, and, though they'd only arrived yesterday, would be dashing back again tomorrow. It was a shame, of course, to come so far and at such great expense for just two days — but they had to fly back to Kathmandu on the tenth, and so it couldn't be helped.

There was magic in the air. The rainy season seemed finally to have departed, leaving in its wake cold clear frosty nights and clear biting wind-blown days. It was September the first, the start of a new season. Kailash stood stark and clear against blue skies, unchallenged by the faintest puff of cloud, defying new and old with a distracting indication of timelessness. Then Kailash disappeared behind the golden cliff face and the rocky shore clattered underfoot as I crunched round the pink sands of the top left hand corner of the lake. The stones were twisted by their different hardnesses into strange ribbed shapes of flatness, and were so smooth they almost squeaked as they rubbed together. And the water was as mesmerising as ever. As I approached the lake, it was a strip of pure deep blue; when I walked beside it, it was a bank of deepest jade green, hollowed with waves clear as glass.

48 - The cave

F ROM A DISTANCE, the golden cliffs appeared to be riddled with black holes. Closer, what one saw from below were not holes, but the dry stone walls built around the entrances of the caves, high up at the extremes of perilously steep hairline paths. Clutching at the wild sage that grew out of the dusty ground I scrambled up to one of the less inaccessible ones and quickly installed myself there. The cave was just the right size — a little larger than Padmasambhava's over at Chiu, and even divided by a low wall of smooth stones into two sections. A pit full of ashes, sheepskins, scraps of paper and dried waterweed made up a bed, and the area of about three square feet between wall and door contained a small hearth, with a few shelves and recesses set into the stone above it. Roof and walls throughout were burnished ebony with a history of yak dung fires, and a red rose on a paper plate was grafted to the inner rock. A stone lintel stepped into the yard through the small doorway of mud and wooden beams. The yard, protected by its dry stone wall, was a pocket in the cliff's steep face, about three by eight feet and heaped at one end with dried yak dung. I swept the inside of the place with a bundle of feathers and tried to feel at home. I had anticipated immediate serenity, composed of the accumulated energies of all who had in the past lived and meditated there, but it just felt strange at first, rough and dark and prickly, and I was rather edgy about what animal life might be contained in the bedding.

But anyway — the water pounded at the edge of night, and one faint star in the violet sky was the first of a fleet of clear brilliance by midnight.

Inside the cave, the darkness grew on me insidiously. Caves are the last undisturbed receptacles of the contemplations and realisations left by the ascetics of old; the Chinese blasted apart every religious building in Tibet, broke every roof under which established rituals had sanctified the air within, but they were obliged to leave the caves.

I only stayed three days, and the knowledge that when I left I'd be leaving Kailash was sad and clear enough, like the new clarity that came with the colder, crisper weather. The thyme and sage and the starry blue medicinal flowers that grew at the base of the cliff wilted with the nightly frosts, and the first colours of dying vegetation were astonishingly bright. The new light penetrated every angle of the huge panorama — sitting on the narrow step of the gateway I overlooked the expansive blues of the lake, that began directly below and swept away to the clear-cut folds of the Gurla Mandhata. Now it was free of cloud, streaked with navy blue shadows, the hooks of the swastika plain to see.

At night I slept very soundly and comfortably and completely undisturbed; all day I kept burning a slow fire that heated beans, soya skin, asparagus soup and spices to a glorious last gastronomic bonanza. The wind powered the blue-grey smoke and blurred the immediate difference between rock and water. Spiders' webs and prayer flags caught on a few smooth green stones carved with the eternal mantra at the cave's front. Here man and nature met in a silent dry blood-brotherhood, in which neither life nor formality is shed. The rock keeps the mantra, and through the quiet handshake flows a mutual recognition of the extensive forces of nature.

Most of my time was spent perched in the narrow gateway, gazing at the lake with an idle pen in my hand and a blank page on my knee. Snakes of contrasting blues seethed and dissipated rivers into the lake from all sides. The eastern valley, the way by which I had first approached Manasarovar, glowed dismal purple, and the waves of Manasarovar on the beach accumulated recollections of all the waves I'd ever seen, falling on beaches all over the world. One large difference between here and anywhere else was that you could stretch your eyes as wide as you liked, in any direction, and never see a hint of human pollution; here there were no plastic bags or power stations to be blanched out — here just a complete vision of unresisted beauty. The water, dense with power and colour, was also clear as the air and fine as ether. I bathed in it, washed clothes in it, drank it and stared at it for hours; when I closed my eyes, all I could see was the water. Its presence saturated everything. It was so clean and pure that it could not be anything but holy. Many rivers flow into it, and from its region seep out again four great river systems;

ceaselessly it moves, inwardly turning and evolving, outwardly reflecting every ray of sun and star and moonlight. This was the perfect mind. And the perfection was not just in these things of beauty, nor even in the whole that was greater than the sum of the parts, but also in the elusively intent spirit whereby all these parts were sensed.

Unimportant as it was to this vast world of apparent timelessness, of the consuming black hole of the tiny cave and the vast sweeps of clear mesmerising water, my visa would run out in a couple of days' time. Waking up one morning I watched a flake of insistent sunlight that turned to frail blue the rock at the cave's mouth. The day had come when I had to visualise the long dry road back to Lhasa. I'd lost my toothbrush down the cliff the night before, and never did find it. It was time to begin to integrate this month of Kailash darshan with the rest of my life; and so, in high hopes, of a new toothbrush if nothing else, I set off widder-shins about the corner of the lake, back to Chiu Gompa. Round the first headland of cliff-face I met a couple of Tibetans, their high colourful bundles of bedding topped with a big black kettle. In the next cove I threw off my clothes and had a last swim.

That was the finest bathe I ever had in the lake. The water was charged and bright with life, and mirror-drops flew towards every luminous horizon. I filled a jam jar with some of the water, to take back to wherever I ended up, as prashadan; I threw drops of it over my head before leaving the shore, wondering if the lake would continue to pervade and obsess me, even after the long road back had been traversed.

Bathing in Manasarovar, the lake of the mind, is supposed to cleanse one of all one's sins — well, that's a Hindu way of looking at it. And whichever way, it seemed as if it had some divine quality by which all sins are purged. Whether one accepts sin or not, what is it caused by but desire? Here the magic waters soothed away all the usual demands; having arrived safely at Kailash, I had, for the first time in my life, no desire to go anywhere. Not even Lhasa.

49 - Preparing to leave

THE SOUND OF THE WAVES of Manasarovar gave way to the bubbling creek of wrinkled silver stone, where the hot springs lay. Just as I was ready to look for a truck on the wide empty plain, one appeared. I hurried down to meet it, but by the time I arrived, the engine had conked out. Three men had their torsos immersed in the hot black pit of the engine. When I asked them where they were going, they looked at me blankly. Oh well, false alarm, I thought, ambling on.

On the brow of the first hill they passed me, the engine roaring healthily away, the men all waving and grinning from the cab. I tried to flag them down, but they drove right past me. Wretches, I thought. But then — well, it was just their Tibetan sense of humour. They stopped after twenty yards more, hauled my luggage onto the back, arranged a saddle carpet over some sacks for me to sit on, and gave me a lift all the way back to Darchen — for no charge. I had the whole back of the truck to myself, and lay passively in the sunshine, eating dried apricots and not worrying very much about all the hairs that were stuck to them. Manasarovar became sopped up by mounds of apricot-coloured hills, and Kailash drew near yet again, obscured by the foothills as the mess of Darchen came into sight.

Darchen was more than usually cosmopolitan that day. A great travelling city from the west had descended upon the river banks — two buses, a couple of jeeps, and a large green army-looking tent, which was surrounded by a whole suburbia of little coloured tents. Aha — it must be the lama with his seventy-odd disciples gathered from around the world. The lama was nowhere to be seen, but his following was omnipresent. Italians lurked by the kitchen with chopsticks, a Swede raced down from the mountain, and, in the shop, English people smoked cigarettes, talked Tibetan and converted the prices into pence. The cook was serving meat in high spirits at tripled prices, and the Indians lurked on the sidelines of the barrage of action. I found myself eating home-made milk sweets with one of the girls in her room. Her mother was there, her forehead almost wiped out by three horizontal stripes of sandalwood paste in deference to Shiva, stepping from one set of clothes to another. 'Does this suit me? You think the colour is not a little too bright?' ... 'Mummy, I think this frock looks very lovely on you' ... 'Daughter, I don't think so. It needs some stitching here ... let me try that....' A deputation of Tibetans arrived to distract her with bundles of silver daggers inlaid with coral and turquoise.

An Australian girl called Emily was looking for me with a message from Purnima and Thomas, to say they were stuck in Ali, with no hopes of a lift to Lhasa in the immediate future. This was hardly a spur to leaving Kailash — but the visa, the visa....

Emily was ready to leave the party, and wanted to walk back by the southern road. She thought it would be a good idea to give me her place in the bus back to Lhasa, and invited me to supper for negotiations. A New Zealander with terrible gastric problems coordinated the stirring of potatoes with the churning of his stomach, while from the other tents around came a squall of complaint, going from person to person over the rough twilight stones. Each would seize on it, add their cynical opinions and pass it petulantly on. Choosing their words carefully, my dinner hosts let me know something of what it was like to travel with 'seventy-two Dharmites, each with their own idea of how it should be done.'

Well, they hadn't had an easy journey. They had applied from their quarters of the world, and had paid $3,500 each in the expectation of a nice adventurous pilgrimage across Tibet under the tutelage of their lama, Namke Norbu. First they had tried from Lhasa, but the ferry at Lhatze was already out of work by the time they arrived; nothing daunted, they'd turned round, returned to Lhasa, returned to Golmud, roared across Turkestan to Kashgar, and, with the PSB hot on their tail, had arrived finally triumphant at Kailash after two months on the road. Now they were here it was of course time for at least half of them to be setting off back again in a couple of days — those planes, those jobs.... The squabbling that undermined the camp tonight was normal, they said — but hastened to point out that there had been some marvellous adaptations made: there were older people who'd never slept a night outside concrete, now adept at knocking their own tent pegs in when the ground was hard, and at pushing the bus when the ground was too soft. 'But look at that!' screamed the New Zealander, suddenly pointing to a girl squatting in a desperate posture down by the water. 'How many times do I have to tell them that you don't go and shit by the river?'

An officious-looking woman with big plastic clips in her hair appeared. Emily put the idea of my taking her place on the bus to her, and the woman really thought seriously before, businesslike but not unkindly, reeling off all the possible replies: there'd bound to be some antagonism from the group at my presence, as I hadn't paid — well, you know, they wouldn't give lifts to anyone on the way here, not even Tibetans; but I just might be able to travel back in one of the supply trucks, but she couldn't promise anything — ah, now, here's Brian. She'd just introduce me to Brian. He was the co-organiser of the trip, and had Been Here Before. So I politely waited while my food went cold before he finally acknowledged me.

'You can count on nothing from us!' he spat. 'Nobody will like having you on board the bus, you haven't paid, and it'll just cause more trouble. You got here alone and you can damned well make your own way back alone. I did it!' And off he stomped. At ten yards' distance he paused to add the final factor in his argument: 'And besides, it's illegal!'

'But I've paid for the place!' wailed Emily. 'I want her to have it!'

'I think he just means he doesn't want me along,' I interpreted. And he was right — I could make my own way back.

50 - Waiting for a lift

THE INDIANS left whooping in a truck for Manasarovar, the Dharmites left on their kora, and Darchen was suddenly very quiet and peaceful. The usual sound and sight of vehicles pounding plumes of dust from the road was non-existent. Nothing came and nothing left, nothing had to go and pull anything out of the river because nothing had gone to get stuck in it. I didn't mind. At night I took my tent down to the river an hour below the village, and here I could bathe in the burning cold water that rushed in tangles out of the western valley, and I could have the tent sited so as to always have a good view of Kailash. By day I sat in the sun, turning the pages of the big German book for the steady flow of Tibetans who happened to catch news of the event. The guest house people, usually so odd, were all there; and the cook, who you could never be sure of — he'd dropped his prices again — came to have a look, and the cook's wife, gentle as a lamb, came too; and all of them were spellbound by the big glossy pictures. Look! A picture of a lump of meat, drying on this very gate here.

Out of the peace came a sobbing. One older Indian woman had stayed behind in her room, for she was not strong enough to go round either Kailash or Manasarovar. She hadn't eaten rice for fifteen days, she wept. Dorje consoled her. He would take her up the hill tomorrow, to a place where she would have a fine view of Kailash. She was comforted, and cheerfully went off to take a nap.

Somehow I became part of this expedition up the hill. The woman's name was Pushpa, and she was a Jain from Gujurat state. When at home, she ran a centre where the disabled could learn skills with which to make a living. But now, after sixteen days of no rice, she could hardly walk, never mind up the hill. We did not go up the gorge, but a more westerly slope, up which Dorje happened to know lurked this fine view. Pushpa was weak, but determined to have darshan of the holy mountain. In one hand she held Dorje's ski-stick, and Dorje pulled the other hand. My job was — she showed me just how to do it — to put my hands firmly on her hips, and to 'pooosh'. We had to stop for a substantial break every minute or two, and so in this way a few hours passed before we reached the spot Dorje had in mind. But the days were long. We had plenty of time, as Dorje pointed out. You see these foreigners, he said, they come here and they make an appointment, and if you're not there they come looking for you, and want to know where you've been, and then they get angry when you say you've been drinking tea with your friend and have quite forgotten the time. No. He'd been to school in India, he'd travelled in Nepal and China, he'd even gone so far as Shenzhen — but there was nowhere like his Tibet.

Eventually we pooshed Pushpa over the brow of the hill. The spot overlooked a view of both valleys, out of which rose very clear and undisturbed the great white face of Kailash. At the sight of it, the woman gave a cry, and fell on the ground. Tears poured down her face, and for ten minutes she heaved with an emotion which enabled her to say no more than: 'Bhagavan! Bhagavan!' She was looking at the face of God, and in this moment the prayer of her life's faith was answered. Now she had seen Kailash, and she would carry the darshan with her always.

We sat, the three of us with our three different ways, all looking at the same mountain with mutual wonder, adoration and respect. That Dorje had been born here, and that Pushpa had just seen it for the first time, made no difference. Difference was suspended, though there was plenty of variety of worship. Dorje did full-length prostrations, Pushpa brought out articles for a puja, and I sat and breathed. While Pushpa snapped staples off plastic bags full of nuts and incense and laid out shining steel bowls, Dorje went and collected brushwood. He carefully kindled a fire, which soon blazed up clouds of its own natural incense, and onto this Pushpa piled a whole box of sandalwood sticks from Mysore. Thick sweet smoke rolled up into the air. She laid out rice and nuts, flicked saffron, and began to read aloud in ecstatic Sanskrit from a small green book.

We had all taken our shoes off in deference to the natural temple of Kailash, and sat in cross-legged reverie. The devotional incense streamed through the air. I felt the energy lines radiating from the mountain, could feel their charge reaching beyond the circumference of the horizon and scooping up the whole earth in their subtle net. Bom bom, bom bom, bom bom.

Part Five

51 - The way back

IT WAS THE DAY my visa expired. I was idly cracking and throwing peanuts to some scruffy dogs in the sun, when the long silence was broken by the bitter roar of a jeep engine. I managed to persuade the two Chinese soldiers inside that I was small enough to squash into the back, and suddenly I was leaving Kailash. We stormed across the river and stopped to fill up with water. I leapt out to imprint a last view on my memory-reel. Having been at Kailash, what else was there in the world to work for? The impact was intensely sad, and I only prevented tears by hurling everything into the idea that it wasn't just a matter of location: time at Kailash is eternal, and the darshan of this month would last forever.

I watched Kailash disappear through the bleary distortions of the tiny rear window, and we were bumping swiftly over clear streams, through flowered expanses of turf alongside the northwesterly sweep of the Himalaya. I consoled myself by looking out for the mountain of Nanda Devi; perhaps I saw it. The Chinese soldiers would keep stopping the vehicle from time to time, to top up the radiators with clear water, or, if we were far from a stream, to rip the caps off 'Champing' (Chinese 'Champagne') bottles with their teeth, because the soft sweet pink fizz seemed to do the job equally well. A couple of times we stopped at army compounds, where I was treated very well with bowls of rice and vegetables, bread, and nacreous orange cups of jasmine tea. Then at about midnight we came to a rash of electric lights which were Ali.

While the nomads were preparing to sleep on the plains, with my own tent packed tightly in my rucksack, I walked through the concrete gate-posts into the Chinese hotel. The blue light of a television stung my eye from a corner room, and painted cranes flew across the big white foyer where Chinese youths played ping-pong. As I entered, everybody leapt into position — the receptionist into her box; the manager, eating an apple, into centre stage with a welcoming hand; the hot water ladies, jingling keys all over, to their cupboard. Becoming embroiled in a game of ping-pong, one of my friendly opponents asked me if I was the foreigner who had walked to Kang Rinpoche in twenty-seven days; the random figure I'd quoted to Dorje seemed to have caught on, but I said yes, to save bother. No-one seemed to have any idea where the twenty-seven started, but it ended at Kang Rinpoche and that was what mattered.

In a dormitory room to myself I had starched white cotton, flying red silk phoenixes on a bedspread and two thermoses of hot water. The smart clash of iron heels struck regularly up and down the corridor, and every time they passed my door they'd stop, and oriental eyes would peer in at me through the pane of glass; when I tried to exclude the voyeurs by making a curtain for the window, the whole door would open with a fine percussive sound, and I'd be obliged to do some kind of a show.

In the morning I was easily given a month's visa extension, and for eight days of that month I stayed right there in Ali. The ferry was still not able to do its job at Lhatze, so nothing was going to Lhasa. I didn't mind. Tall hills of deep dry brown lapped down from Turkestan, washing with them Moslems who squatted over bread ovens and piles of water-melons in the bazaar. I hung out there, where, as well as finding a new toothbrush with bristles as efficient as a steel wool scouring pad, I was able to eat green vegetables, bread and fruit to my heart's content. Outside the post office was a rousing mural depicting the new people of Liberated Tibet, lifting up shining faces and kathas to — the State? Ali is the capital of western Tibet, but the population seemed made up of imported Chinese and Moslems and the only Tibetans I saw there were living in tents on the outskirts.

There were a few other foreigners; one day I met a flamboyant Canadian climber on his way to Kailash, with two rucksacks full of mani stones and crampons and the impious intention of climbing the holy mountain; there were a few Japanese individuals, one of whom came cycling into town, down from Kashgar in nineteen days. Then there were the French, who had been here for a couple of weeks already; they could be seen every day locked deeper and deeper in conversation with the PSB over the impossibilities of a lift to Lhasa. They told me that 'hitch-hiking depends on your head'; seeing that they'd have first wind of anything going, I didn't bother even thinking about a lift. Alternating eating with sleeping with yoga, I was perfectly happy. Then one day the French vanished. There were various rumours about where and how they'd gone, but they'd gone. Perhaps I too should put my mind to departure.

I spent a few days sitting outside the town, and eventually something passed. It was a truck, piled with sacks and people. They stopped and said they were going to Saga. Half-way! Great! Climbing in, I was greeted by the smiling ripe-apple face of the Ani-la from Thugolho Gompa.

The truck went excessively slowly and the crew were easy-going enough; when we reached the top of a pass, the truck drove clockwise round the lha-tse of flags and stones twice while everyone exuberantly shouted: 'Tsho! Tsho! Tsho!' in gratitude and supplication for a safe journey. But on the second night they demanded money from Ani-la and I, and in the morning we awoke to find them gone. That afternoon we managed to fight for a place on a truck going as far as Gerze, but from the moment we arrived there that night, the world seemed to stop.

Gerze was composed of a few Chinese compounds surrounded by a heavy floating population of tents, set in the middle of a wide pink plain across which scampered dot-like horses. Far horizons presented bald and luminous hills over which peeked snowy mountains to the south, and the beautiful views seemed just to serve as a taunting back-up for the general air of humorous despair which characterised the place. Ani-la and I were among the luckier ones there — we only waited a week. That week in Gerze stands out as the longest week of my life. We took a room in a compound whose earth-daubed walls hosted vibrant white chalk murals of magnificent prancing horses, but after one night Ani-la moved into a tent with a family who had been waiting for two months. I stayed on in the room, and every day would optimistically pack up my bags and walk out to where the road pounded east. Only two vehicles ever passed me, and they were only going short distances; but I liked to sit there, reading a book whose pages flapped in the savage and interminable wind, talking to the various people who would come and pass the time of day with me. One day, out of desperation, I got drunk with a Khampa. The Khampa men are proud tall fighters; when there's no-one else to fight with, they fight with each other, but their great pride is in the role they took protecting the Dalai Lama on his flight out of Tibet in 1959. When we'd finished the five bottles of beer concealed in the pouch of his robe, he tried to arouse my sympathies if not my ardour by arguing that, as I had the fortune to have a mother and father (he'd seen the pictures), I owed it to him, who had neither, to go and spend the night with him, in that house over there ... he pointed to a dismal-looking speck on the plain and I staggered off, back to my friends at the camp.

There were a couple of faces at Gerze already known to me: there was the man with the pitted complexion who had carried my bag half-way up Dolma La, and there was the man with the lop-sided gait, the one who had been welcome at Diraphuk Gompa when I was not; now he was camping in a small white canvas tent supported by a pole with a cast iron trident on top. I became a regular visitor to two camps — the family with which Ani-la was staying, and the lama set. The latter was composed of a married couple in the maroon robes of the Nyingmapa sect, along with a young nun and a chain-smoking layman who always wore a towel about his head. I would spend hours with them, sitting by the fire, drinking tea, eating tsampa, listening to their chat and further exploring the delights of churra — the hard dry crumbly cheese with a strong and pungent edge which the Nepali at Manasarovar had introduced me to; mixed with tea, tsampa and sugar it resembled a sort of primitive cheese-cake, and could distract quite well for the moment from the serious task of Waiting.

The eternal mantra of Om mani padme hum became to a large extent replaced by repetition of the words: 'Mocha mindoo!' — No truck! — uttered in an infinite range of tones and all of them quite hopeless. The lama set had been waiting for three weeks; the married nun would roll about on sacks on the floor of their tent, droning: 'Ama mindoo, Apa mindoo, MOCHA mindoooooo!' — I have no mother, no father, and there's no-o-o-o TRUCK! Then she'd peep out of the folds of her grubby maroon at me, and explode with laughter. One day a truck did come, and everybody gathered about it, ravenous for a lift; but it was going to Kashgar. The younger nun leapt up and grinned triumphantly as she was borne away on a dusty cloud. After about five days I decided to simply start walking; it was my preferred pace anyway, and all this waiting was agonising. The family however forcefully prevented me from carrying out this plan; Ama-la, the mother, brandished a ladle of water, rolled her eyes all around and her head to one side, to vividly demonstrate that there was no water on that road. If I began to walk I would die of thirst. It sounded worse than drowning, so I stayed.

Under the vast platitude of waiting, trivialities assumed an intriguing importance. I, for example, became a major attraction; dozens of curious children, teenagers, fantastically-clad women, stray lamas and Khampas in fox fur hats were liable to walk into my room at any time of day or night; Ani-la and Ama-la could spend an hour at a time discussing the patterns on the vile nylon socks that were for sale in the compound yard. Then one day there was something else to talk about: I was returning from a walk out onto the plains, when Ani-la's voice summoned me from the midst of a crowd. 'Hey! Poo-mo!' This was the name by which she always addressed me, and means simply 'girl'. Going over, I gathered by the gravity of the people that Something Had Happened. With quiet importance, Ama-la assisted Ani-la to their fireside, and proceeded to unpeel the green canvas sneaker and filthy sock from her left foot. Blood poured, and everybody did whatever they could. A daughter ripped up a pair of trousers, bandaged up the foot and tied it up with string; Ama-la squeezed out the sock in a bowl of water which never ceased to emit a stream of gratifyingly blood-red black; I ran for a tube of antiseptic cream and someone asked Ani-la if it hurt. 'Yo-ray!' she exclaimed emphatically — it certainly did.

Unfortunate as it was for Ani-la, the incident was by way of an omen. The new moon put out a silver claw, and that night not one but two trucks rolled in, destined for Lhasa. The news spread like wildfire, and soon everyone was clamouring at the door of the drivers' room; good-humouredly, they undertook to carry everyone, including myself. That night there was a new spirit abroad; the sound of 'Mocha mindoo!' was replaced by a more than usually vigorous puja in the lamas' tents, and the air was saturated with elation. It was in a similar festive spirit that at five o'clock the following morning we all piled up onto the trucks and, cheering, drove out of Gerze under the bright stars.

That was a joyful journey. Each day we began at five, and nobody ever kept the drivers waiting. We'd rumble for about eight solid hours, past huge rocks whose swilling orange and white faces resembled maps of Mars more than any earthly scene, past salt lakes and sulphur springs, past snowy mountains, and stop for 'Cha dhoo!' by one of the brilliantly clear streams. Everybody would immediately leap out and, having emptied their bladders, set to building their fires. The expedition sub-divided into groups; the family for some unknown reason had stayed behind, so Ani-la and I always had 'Cha dhoo!' with the Nyingmapa couple and Towel-Head. Each group had their own means for fire — the drivers had huge cylindrical shaped gas-blasters, others had yak dung and the lama set had a sack of wood — and each group would have a fire raging in an astonishingly short time. Tea was prepared, offered to the four cardinal points, consumed with tsampa and churra — and the lama and his wife and Towel Head would be packed and sitting up on the trucks again, shouting at Ani-la and I to climb aboard quickly, even before the drivers had finished their tea.

Though I was officially part of the lama set, every group wanted to heap kindness upon my foreign head. Packets of biscuits and, most improbably, a bag of yellow coconut cakes, were forced upon me, and my cup, should I wander during the course of a meal, would be filled with tea heated on any of the fires. One of the drivers lent me a huge white sheepskin chuba, which served as a personal wind-proof tent by day and a mattress for Ani-la and myself by night. We would lie, completely warm and happy under the cold glimmer of the stars, and fall asleep to the sound of Towel Head's continually animated discourses on I know not what.

Down the centre of Tibet we rumbled, until one day we came to the point where the southern and northern roads join. I stood up and stared with gratitude at the blue sign into which I knew my name was scratched. Three sisters pulled me down again, and we bounced along the atrophied river-bed — the road I had travelled with Franca and our Chinese driver, before the full impact of the summer rains, was nearly all gone.

Travelling in this delightful, all-Tibetan company, it was for days as if the Chinese had never entered Tibet; even when we came to the ferry at Lhatze, nobody mentioned them, though the famous check-point was now imminent. But when, after hours of waiting, which we filled in very comfortably with an elongated 'Cha dhoo!' break, we finally crossed the Brahmaputra, I was not surprised when one of the drivers apologetically informed me that they could take me no further. I paid him my fifty kwai with all due respect, and hands waved and horns hooted till the trucks were blanked out by dust and a bend in the road.

Sad as I was to part from them, it was so good to be walking again that I walked for two days. It was harvest time, and a fine damp moved across the valley, bringing the scent of new-mown corn-stalks from the fields. The sound of high sweet singing poured from the throats of the people bending over heaps of shuffling gold harvest, and the last trees I'd seen on the way to Kailash were now, turning yellow and brown, the first ones I saw on the way back. From time to time I was invited to share thermoses of butter tea, and when night fell I was ushered quietly off the road by a girl who was mending the road; as if it were a natural extension of her duty, she swept me away to spend the night in her room where pictures of Chairman Mao and Padmasambhava rolled eyes at one another.

It was a new season and the start of a new cycle: Life After Kailash. A double rainbow arched over the flooded road to Lhasa, and I splashed through, full of hope.

52 - Return to Lhasa

Eventually I managed a ride with a Chinese army truck back to Shigatze, where they dropped me off outside the gates of the Tashilumpo. The monastery sang with bells and sutras from within that night as I hared off down the tree-lined road to eat vegetables. At the hotel I was greeted rapturously and, after some whispered negotiations, was again installed in the balcony bed under the sea-green wall. There was a note addressed to me and John on the notice-board, from Thomas and Purnima. They had taken the blue truck with the Tibetan drivers that the French had taken to Kailash and, they said in another note to the French, they couldn't understand why the French hadn't liked them, because they'd found them superb companions and had had a wonderful trip. Now they'd gone down to Nepal, Purnima to India, and perhaps they'd see us … I didn't see them, but I did see John there a couple of months later. He took Emily's place back on the bus with the Dharmites. Because the rivers would now be dried up, and with information I had given Dorje on its condition, they had been given permission to go back by the southern road: avoiding Brian, John sat back and enjoyed the views and the food. Apparently, the elusive Namke Norbu, the lama all the Dharmites had followed so tenaciously to Kailash, had been disappointed in their behaviour. Once at Kailash, he had slipped off on a horse with a few faithful Tibetan retainers to a secret place he had seen in his dreams, and there discovered a lost city. So rumour had it.

As for Emily — she had met the Canadian after his attempt at climbing Kailash had failed, and vented spleen and gall upon his hapless head for having dared to presume on the sacred summit; later she hitched back on the northern road. Franca meanwhile had made it up to Kashgar and had returned to India via Pakistan, and even the mystery as to which way the French had gone from Ali, and how, cleared itself up after a while; in desperation they'd stopped the driver of a jeep outside Ali, knocked him on the head and, leaving him unconscious, had jumped into his vehicle and driven it as fast as they could towards Lhasa. Hitch-hiking for them had turned out to depend on the driver's head. The police caught them at Lhatze, where they were imprisoned for two days before being released in the direction of Nepal — quicker than hitching via Gerze, at any rate.

Returning to the open gates of the Tashilumpo the next day, I heard the familiar sound of: 'Cha dhoo!' There on grass at the other side of the road, by a stream, the lama set had struck camp; they, like me, were not in the same hurry to return to Lhasa now that we were out of Gerze. There was a faint whiff of carnival about the return to civilisation: Ani-la had a new cardigan, the Nyingmapa couple had shaved heads, and Towel Head had a fresh towel. The three sisters had joined them, and were resplendent in new blouses of brilliant greens and purple. I had tea with them most days. They were days when apples were for sale everywhere, days flooded with clear autumn sunshine that illuminated the maroon robes about the fire with shades of transience. The bare silver birch trees and the elusive nature of the light reminded one how temporary it all was, and highlighted every moment. We were still on the way back from Kailash.

The food was good in Shigatze and I made new friends among the tourists, but I felt vague and drifty. On the walls of the Tashilumpo danced Demchog, the Tibetan interpretation of Shiva. Three angry red eyes popped from his dark blue face, red brains frothed from a skull-cup, held with delicate disdain between long fingernails arching from a red-palmed hand, whilst his feet were engaged in stamping out a vicious dance on an elephant-headed image of desire. Desire stretched out anguished limbs and endeavoured to eat a pink turnip, or perhaps it was a peach, but the pale withered flesh was pathetic and ineffectual under the wrathful feet of Demchog, protective deity of Kailash. Outside the gloomy halls there were deep red roses, delicate trumpeted gladioli and stunning orange marigolds, all blooming in the sunshine out of tin cans, and beyond the monastery wall it was still harvest-time. For over a week I floated from hotel to fireside to monastery, around the autumn woods, over the hills where wind horses blew, and only left when the hotel boss negotiated for me, of his own volition, a lift in a Landcruiser to Lhasa.

The journey to Kailash seemed to have taken the restlessness out of me; whereas before I'd been preoccupied with the process of getting to Kailash, now I had nothing else to devote my attention to but whatever was happening about me. The Lhasa scene about the Jokhang was superficially the same as travellers have described it for hundreds of years: prayer wheels swung, turquoise and coral nested in black braids glowed deeply against the high thin blue air, and the profiles they framed fascinated with their flat approach to beauty as stunningly as ever. Prayer-flags, incense and sutras unfolded everywhere, from tables to pole-tops, and the silent night-time dust, when the circuit was cleared of commerce, fluttered with the swish and the thud of full-length prostrations; the eternal mantra turned out from the heavy spins of the wheels and thickened the air with their swarming powers.

There was something in the air, and it was rather grim. At first it was noticeable only by evasions. October the first was a holiday — a Chinese holiday, not a Tibetan holiday, the Tibetan and Kashgari vendors in the market-place insisted. It was Liberation day, the liberation of the Chinese from imperialism, the day that Mao Tse Tung took Tiananmen Square and delivered from the steps of the Forbidden City of the emperors the incipient speech of Communist China.

Just after sunrise of October the first I was awakened by one of the hotel women, brandishing the can of hot water with which she filled my thermos. Instead of her usual lively smile was an urgency that I should look across at the Jokhang. Looking, I saw incense rising in billows across the sun. A strange quietness had fallen over Lhasa. Going out, the silence was confirmed in the absence of commerce, beggars, or people hassling you to buy their heirlooms and gew-gaws. Tibetans gathered in silent batches about the Barkhor and nobody circumambulated. Well — no Tibetan body circumambulated, that is. The Chinese army circumambulated alright — anti-clockwise, shoulder to shoulder in solid platoons, each one carrying a heavy stick. I stood and watched them do three koras, staring into the frightened young eyes that stared into mine each time they approached; but then I was accosted by a Chinese man in a suit and a policeman in high-ranking green who wanted to see my passport. 'Why,' I asked innocently, fishing vaguely about in my bag, 'are Chinese soldiers marching anti-clockwise around the Jokhang?'

'Let's see your passport, never mind.'

'Yes,' I said, getting it out, 'but why are Chinese soldiers marching anti-clockwise around the Jokhang?'

The uniformed one rolled his eyes skywards. 'I don't want to answer that question,' he answered with a disarming smile. They advised me to return to my hotel and take a rest — 'For your own safety,' they repeated twice.

I didn't return to the hotel, but roamed more surreptitiously than before. Of course, it had been a year ago that anti-Chinese riots had rocked Lhasa and put an end to the days of easy tourism in Tibet. This time the Chinese were determined to suppress protest before it began; a curfew had been imposed, and soldiers had been poured out of army trucks at nine o'clock the night before into the labyrinth of lanes that surround the Jokhang. Here they were, marching continually and insultingly anti-clockwise about the place where the faith of Tibet is

consolidated, the last symbol remaining to the Tibetan people in Tibet.
By the afternoon the soldiers' sticks had been replaced by fixed bayonets,
and by the evening every step that the soldiers took was accompanied by
a collective and threatening cry that seemed to come like a karate 'Kee-i!'
from the stomach. The Tibetans stood in silent groups while the sludge-
green river of the soldiers' legs surged past. The air was taut with unfired
bullets and unthrown stones, screamed that the Tibetans want nothing to
do with China, that they want the Chinese out. While the Chinese snarled
back: 'We are in control and we're too strong for your stones, so there.'

53 - Back to the world

NOTHING HAPPENED, then, but it was a few days before the soldiers
stopped marching and the numbness about the Jokhang relaxed
into devotions as usual. Yellow autumn leaves fell onto the wares of the
Chinese vendors who crept out and set up stalls on the avenues, for they
would not go near the Jokhang yet. Pilgrims again were free to dance or
prostrate around the temple, and the heart of Tibetan Buddhism was
heard to be beating soundly.

There were riots later in November, and again early in 1989. In April
the Tibetan flag was fixed for a day over the Jokhang, and shots were
fired, but when, on June fourth 1989, People's Liberation Army soldiers
shot down thousands of their own people, in the very Gateway to
Heavenly Peace where thirty-nine years earlier Mao Tse Tung had created
such wonderful visions, Tibetan news fell into obscurity again. Maybe a
positive aspect of the tragedy is that the world, now knowing what the
Chinese are capable of doing to their own people, may be more ready to
believe reports of Chinese atrocities in Tibet; another positive point may
be that one cannot fall into hatred of the Chinese race in general, for it
is obvious now that the government no longer represents the people.
Chinese pop music brays up from restaurants below the Potala betraying

yearnings and a recognition of loss that cuts through all political complexities. China has lost her own rich cultural heritage, but has failed to obliterate the heart of her neighbour. The Dalai Lama prays for the Chinese every day, despite everything, and the world is already beginning to take some notice. His Holiness was awarded the Nobel Peace Prize in 1989. Some subtle lotus still grows out of the muck and the slime of the deadlocked confusion.

But anyway, the tension was such that the PSB, who in Lhasa were no poppets, were issuing no visa extensions. It was time to leave Tibet. So I climbed onto a beaten up old bus one morning and took the road to Nepal. The bus lay under a curse; due to numerous break-downs we covered in four days what a Landcruiser had done in half a day. On the fourth day it flew off the side of the steep road down which we were descending, to land, by a miracle due perhaps to the 'Om mani padme hum's of the Khampas and the 'Hail Mary's of an American passenger, intact fifteen metres below. Its front wheels were jammed at mutually discordant angles deep into the bare earth, most of the windows were broken, and everybody cheered — first, because we were alive: the steering had gone, and, had it gone just a kilometre earlier, there would have been no nice flat hillside to land on; and secondly because the bus had died under its own curse, and would obviously never move again. It took a couple of days for a replacement bus to arrive, and several more days before that bus was fixed.

Mount Everest glowed pink and swung out of sight as the replacement bus drove off the Tibetan plateau and plunged down steep valleys of sheer rock faces topped with snow, down a fold in the tablecloth spread over the roof of the world. The bus took us to Nyalam and we walked about half the remaining forty kilometres to the border. The bleak and beautiful simplicity of Tibet now became dispersed into a million shapes and forms that needed appreciating; the hillsides roared with red and orange shrubs, and a few pine trees jutted horizontal limbs into the pale blue air which was just beginning to thicken with the loss in altitude. Streams that had sneaked through bare shingles of cold smooth grey, frozen white at the edges, were now crushed into a flashing turquoise river at the foot of the valley below. By the time we arrived at the border ten days after leaving Lhasa, I was nine days over my visa. But it didn't matter — the buck was passed among the officials at the border town until it had been sufficiently dispersed as to be not worth worrying about; I was stamped out of China and walking down a valley of grey landslides to the Friendship Bridge that joins Tibet to Nepal.

In the transition from the open plain to hotels, from Tibet to Nepal, from Nepal to the rest of the world, the clarity of Kailash has become forgotten in the distractions. Kailash recedes to an imaginary point of inaccessibility, to a place beyond time, space and causation as hard to obtain as the elusive samadhi of meditation. The remoteness of Kailash embodies Hindu ideals of detachment, and samadhi to them is the place of no return. Tibetan Buddhists, on the other hand, do not isolate the image, but bring it within the range of the (very purified) human heart. I turn over the paradox of Mahayana Buddhism: that, when one has advanced enough to recognise the emptiness of all things, including the grasping nature of the heart, and so qualified for entry into Nirvana — one must renounce this blissful state and plunge right back into the flames, in order to help save all sentient beings. By this time, much as I still admired the flourishes and enthusiasm of the Hindus, I tended to favour the Tibetan way of going about things. Tibetan Buddhism brings things down to earth a bit, lifts the earth to the regions of the gods a bit; earth and heaven combine their power, and things work. It didn't seem practical to just go to Kailash, space out, come back and think of it all as a dream.

Kailash is a magical place, but we can't be there all the time. Round the everyday shores of the usual mind prowl a pack of savage, ego-begotten mongrels which snap at one another's gaunt and hunger-haunted frames, rob moments or lifetimes of their divinity. Tibetan Buddhism asserts that everyday incidents are our teachers, and we have to convert the weapons of darkness into tools for changing the world about us. The physical presence of Kailash is powerful enough to still the wild beasts within — as long as one's there. But when one is no longer in the dharm, real as the mountain is, it is still no more than a cypher. Theoretically, we should be able to tune in at any time and any place, and pick up on the constant transformative powers, whether we've made a pilgrimage to the mountain or not. We could save the world if we wanted.

Maybe Kailash must remain banished to the realm of dreams and journeys of a lifetime. When one isn't a Bodhisattva, it's hard to remember that such a pure place as Kailash exists, anywhere. I'm glad I brought back a few stones to remind me.

Om mani padme hum.

Lamma Island, Hong Kong, sometime.

Glossary

T = Tibetan, S = Sanskrit, H = Hindi, M = Mandarin

ATP   Alien Travel Permit — needed for travel in restricted areas

ahimsa   non-violence H

ani-la   nun T

bodhisattva   someone who has achieved enlightenment but has renounced Nirvana until they have helped all other suffering beings achieve the same S

Bon   pre-Buddhist religion of Tibet T

Bon-pa   a person who practises Bon T

Bon-po   the collective noun referring to all practitioners of Bon T

Brahma   the creator within Hindu mythology S

Brahmin   the highest caste in Hindu society S

chakra   'wheel', the energy centres of the subtle body, eg. heart chakra, throat chakra S

Chenresig   Tibetan name for the Sanskrit Avalokitesvara, god of compassion; it is said that when he beheld the suffering of humans on earth he grew a thousand arms with which to comfort them. The Dalai Lama is the earthly reincarnation of Chenresig. T

choo chembow   'big water', meaning a high river T

chorten   a domed construction containing the remains of dead lamas T

chuba   long-sleeved Tibetan coat T

churra   hard dry crumbly cheese T

CITS   Chinese International Travel Service, a government institution

damaru   a ritual hand-drum S

darshan   the blessing incurred by being in the presence of a holy person or place S

Demchog   the wrathful, tantric interpretation of Shiva, god of destruction T

dharm   a holy place S

Dharma   the practice of Buddhism S

Dharmites   practitioners of the Dharma

Digungkargyu   a Tibetan sect of Buddhism who live and practice in caves T

FEC   Foreign Exchange Certificate, official money for tourists in China (abolished in 1994)

Ganesh   elephant-headed god of filial duty, son of Shiva and Parvati S

Ganga   the river Ganges *S*
Gelugpa   the so-called 'Yellow-Hats', the reformed sect of whom the
             Dalai Lama is the head *T*
geshe   a monk who has passed all the religious examinations to
             become what is usually translated as a 'doctor of divinity' *T*
gompa   monastery *T*
Inji   the generic name for Westerners in Tibet *T*
Jain   an Indian religion which stresses non-violence which some-
             times extends to extremes *S*
Kang Rinpoche   'Jewel of the Snows', Mount Kailash *T*
Kargyupa   Tibetan sect of Buddhism who live in caves *T*
karma   the universal law of cause and effect to which all who tread the
             wheel of cyclic existence are subject *S*
katha   white scarf offered in greeting, veneration and benediction *T*
Khampa   someone from the region of Kham in northeast Tibet *T*
kora   circumambulation of a holy place *T*
kwai   'sheet', colloquial for renminbi, q.v. *M*
lha-tse a pile of stones placed by pilgrims to mark the top of a pass or
             the first sighting of a holy place *T*
lingam   phallus, symbol of the male generative principle *S*
Mahayana   'the great vehicle', the Buddhism practised in Tibet and
             Japan, whereby it is possible to achieve enlightenment in one
             lifetime *S*
mandala   an image, either a drawing or a model, symbolising an ideal
             state of mind, used as a visual aid to meditation *S*
mani ribu   'precious pill', made of natural medicines such as herbs and
             parts, such as the fingernails, of high lamas *T*
Manjusri   the Bodhisattva of wisdom *S*
mantra   a prayer made up of sacred syllables whose repetition leads to
             equanimity *S*
Marpa   the tyrannical and exacting teacher of Milarepa, Tibet's great
             ascetic *T*
Matreiya   the founder-Buddha of the future *S*
Mendip   medicine *T*
Meru   a mythological holy mountain, precursor of Kailash *S*
Milarepa   Tibet's most beloved holy man, a poet and renunciate who
             lived in the twelfth century *T*
mocha   motor truck *T*
Nandi   Shiva's vehicle, a white bull *S*
Naropa   teacher of Marpa *T*

Nyingmapa   the old sect of Buddhism in Tibet *T*

Padmasambhava   the great magician, born in the Swat Valley, Pakistan, who was invited to Tibet in the eighth century AD in order to purge it of demons *S*

parikorama   circumambulation of a holy place *S*

Parvati   wife, or female counterpart, of Shiva *S*

prashadan   a gift from the gods, meaning anything imbued with divine qualities, such as food, flowers, stones etc. and given free to pilgrims *S*

PSB   Public Security Bureau, the police department responsible for dealing with foreigners

puja   ritual prayer and offering of incense and/or food to cleanse an atmosphere *H*

renminbi   'people's money', the common currency in the PRC *M*

Rinpoche   'precious one', an honorific title for reincarnated lamas *T*

rudrakshra   a brown seed, sacred to Shiva *S*

rungba kasa   conical lumps of brown sugar usually used as offerings at altars *T*

sadhana   religious practice *S*

sadhu   a Hindu holy man who has dropped out of conventional society to become a renunciate, living on what is offered though never begging. Often confused with the mysticism of smoking, sponging and bullshitting. *S*

Sakyamuni   the founder-Buddha of the present age *S*

samadhi   the state of non-attachment achieved by great meditation *S*

sanyasi   one who has reached a high level of practice *S*

sati   the Hindu practice, now outlawed, of a widow throwing herself onto her husband's funeral pyre and perishing with him *S*

shakti   the female function of any divine pair in Hindu-based mythology *S*

Shankar   another name for Shiva *S*

Shiva   god of destruction *S*

Shivalokha   Shiva's planet *S*

sutra   'string', set of aphorisms in Sanskrit literature *S*

Tantra   'weave', or 'web', high practices involving the organic manipulation and mastery of the forces that direct the rich weave of life *S*

tapas   austerities performed to gain spiritual advancement *S*

thangka   a religious painting *T*

therma 'hidden treasure', teachings which can take any form — from writing to statues, religious artifacts etc. — which were hidden long ago and which only manifest when the people are ready for them and the time is appropriate *T*

thorma devotional cake made of tsampa, butter and sugar *T*

thulku the reincarnation of any great holy person *T*

tok-cha objects made of a mysterious alloy known as 'sky metal', believed by the Tibetans to have fallen from the sky *T*

tsampa flour ground from roasted barley, the staple diet of Tibetans *T*

yab-yum 'father-mother', sexual union in meditation of the male and female principles *T*

yagadoo good *T*

yagamindoo bad *T*

About the author

WENDY TEASDILL was brought up in the English countryside along with two younger siblings by mathematical parents. Toys were expertly home made and holidays were always camping holidays, as far removed from the maddening crowd as possible. They brought her up to believe that the highest bliss is to lie in a flower-riddled summer meadow by running water under blue skies. Failing that, any snow or rainstorm was better than city streets.

She obtained a degree in English at Leeds University but, instead of settling into the English groove, immediately set off east, becoming one of the very last to travel overland through Afghanistan to India and Nepal. Back in England with the customary hepatitis obtained on such expeditions, she cured herself with yoga and studied to teach English as a Foreign Language. These two skills have sustained her ever since.

She has travelled throughout the Americas, around Europe and back to India many times. The study and practice of yoga increased, and she became a student of BKS Iyengar in India. She taught English from Mexico City to Tokyo to sustain herself, which required living in cities, but her free time would find her walking alone in the mountains, from the Andes to Andorra.

The great dream, however, was always to travel to Tibet, which must have the greatest mountain walking of all. For five years she was based in Hong Kong, where she taught English and yoga; this acted as a springboard for travels to China and, finally, Tibet.

Interest in Hinduism and Tibetan Buddhism, coupled with a love of walking in remote places, especially places of inherently natural power, led her to walk across western Tibet to Mount Kailash. It was a wild idea which paid off, due, she implicitly believes, to the grace of the mountain.

Wendy Teasdill is now married with two children, and based in England, where she is working on a pregnancy yoga book and writings based on her subsequent travels without children and with, in India, China and Tibet.

Other titles
from
Asia 2000

Non-fiction

Cantonese Culture	*Shirley Ingram & Rebecca Ng*
Concise World Atlas	*Maps International*
Egg Woman's Daughter	*Mary Chan*
Getting Along With the Chinese	*Fred Schneiter*
Hong Kong Pathfinder	*Martin Williams*
Red Chips — the globalisation of China's enterprises*	*Charles de Trenck*
The Rise and Decline of the Asian Century*	*Christopher Lingle*

Fiction

Cheung Chau Dog Fanciers' Society	*Alan B Pierce*
Chinese Walls	*Xu Xi (Sussy Chakó)*
Daughters of Hui	*Xu Xi (Sussy Chakó)*
Getting to Lamma	*Jan Alexander*
Hong Kong Rose	*Xu Xi (Sussy Chakó)*
Riding a Tiger	*Robert Abel*
Temutma	*Rebecca Bradley & John Sloan*

Poetry

Woman to Woman and other poems	*Agnes Lam*
New Ends, Old Beginnings	*Louise Ho*

Photo Books

Beijing Spring	*Peter & David Turnley*
USSR: The Collapse of an Empire	*Liu Heung Shing*

Distributed in the United States by
University of Washington Press, PO Box 50096, Seattle, WA 98145
and in Canada by University of British Columbia Press
6344 Memorial Road, Vancouver, BC V6T 1Z2

All other titles, please contact Asia 2000 Ltd
1101 Seabird House, 22–28 Wyndham St, Central, Hong Kong
tel (852) 2530 1409; fax (852) 2526 1107
email sales@asia2000.com.hk; http://www.asia2000.com.hk/